D0891476

THE POETRY OF JOHN CLARE

Also by Mark Storey

CLARE : THE CRITICAL HERITAGE (*editor*)

THE
POETRY
OF
JOHN CLARE

A Critical Introduction

MARK STOREY

Macmillan

First published 1974 by
THE MACMILLAN PRESS LTD
London and Basingstoke
Associated companies in New York
Dublin Melbourne Johannesburg and Madras

SBN 333 15760 5

Printed in Great Britain by
NORTHUMBERLAND PRESS LIMITED
Gateshead

Contents

Preface

This book is intended to serve as an introduction to Clare's poetry. My own interest in Clare was aroused when I was an undergraduate, too many years ago; it has been sustained and enhanced by the enthusiasm of students with whom I have talked about Clare. In many ways, this book is for them, a very inadequate response to their requests for some sort of critical help with the poetry. Clearly, in a book of this scope, many things have had to be by-passed, many points left undeveloped: I have not tried to be comprehensive. There are three main lines of approach: I have tried to show, firstly, both in general and in particular, the special interest and appeal and variety of Clare's poetry; secondly, some of the ways in which his poetry seems to work; thirdly, the development of his poetry, the coherence of his work as a whole, from the early efforts to the achievements of maturity. I have discussed details of biography only where these illuminate the poetry, and have for the most part taken such details for granted. No attempt has been made to present a rounded picture of Clare the man, in all his diversity (for that is, primarily, the province of biography), but rather to see the man in terms of his poetry, which is, after all, what he asked of posterity. A new edition of *John Clare: A Life*, by J. W. and Anne Tibble (1972), strengthened me in my resolve not to repeat facts readily available elsewhere.

When I had nearly completed the typescript of this study, John Barrell's book, *The Idea of Landscape and the Sense of Place, 1730–1840: An Approach to the Poetry of John Clare* (Cambridge, 1972), was published. Dr Barrell has examined in great detail Clare's descriptive processes as they differ from the tradition represented by Thomson's *Seasons*. This is a stimulating book in many respects, in particular for its demonstration of the subtleties of Clare's technique especially as exemplified in the sonnets. This present study differs in emphasis from Dr Barrell's: whereas he is interested especially in the idea of place, of the localness that so distinguishes Clare's verse in his middle period, before the move in 1832 to Northborough, I am concerned here with the more general question of Clare's development as a poet, descriptive and otherwise. I have chosen to take *The Shepherd's Calendar* as the focal point for an examination of Clare's mature descriptive technique.

The development of a poet such as Clare is of particular interest, for he faces peculiar problems, related to his own hesitancy and lack of confidence in his abilities (it is not yet possible entirely to discount his origins). To study this development, from the earliest gropings and imitations to the later poetry of vision, has seemed especially important in the case of a poet who is so often viewed in rather superficial terms (as if all his poetry were of the same kind and level of achievement). In order to understand the nature of his achievement (which is such that the usual evasive appellation 'minor poet' misses the point), Clare's early struggles are extremely relevant, as he attempts to translate his unique vision into poetry: for it is only with these difficulties in mind that we can appreciate the triumph of his mature work.

The early poetry is understandably humble. But Clare's humility becomes one of his greatest strengths, as he applies it to the writing of poetry about the beloved countryside of his youth: he transcends the limitations of an established genre, and makes of an enfeebled tradition something entirely personal and strong. But *The Shepherd's Calendar* and the sonnets were not the culmination of his work, merely important stages in the growth of a mind essentially visionary. Part of Clare's unique quality derives from this rooting of his vision in the actual; just as his descriptive poetry is seldom merely aesthetic or decorative, so his poems of yearning and dream depend upon a precise awareness of what it is that is lost.

If much of this study is concerned with Clare as a poet of nature, it is because that was the role which he chose for himself; but to speak disparagingly of him as a 'mere nature poet' hardly does him justice. The descriptive accuracy is linked not only to an increasing feel for the words and movement of poetry, but also to a growing realisation of his unique position, as the representative of a way of life that is disappearing. At the same time he sees the essential importance of love and innocence, and these two aspects of the past become related, so that a personal loss is elevated and universalised. From these two concerns, much of Clare's best poetry grows. As the past, and the scenes of youth, assume increasing significance for Clare, so poetry itself, with all its connotations of nature, love and joy, becomes the embodiment of a vision of eternity which embraces past, present, and future.

It is that development which I have wanted to chart in this study. I have for the most part concentrated on Clare and his work, rather than try to place him in a more general context of, say, romanticism or the poetic climate of the first half of the nineteenth century: if that is a valid exercise, I have left it for others to perform. Similarly, while I hope my debts to (and disagreements with) others' work on Clare are clear enough, I have not engaged in shadow-boxing with earlier critics, entertaining though that might have been: anybody interested can always turn to the volume on Clare in the *Critical Heritage* series. It might seem odd that in a study of Clare and his work I appear to have shirked the business of 'placing' Clare. This is a problem that has exercised people's minds for a long time, and I think and hope that it will continue to do so: no atmosphere would be healthy in which it could be settled once and for all who was major and who minor (as if that solved everything anyway). As I have already suggested, 'minor' in Clare's case misses the point entirely: that, after all, is what the bulk of this book is about. However mistakenly, I have not seen it as my task to 'place' Clare in any magisterial, definitive way; I have resisted the temptation to toss grand epithets about, or even to add a separate conclusion in which Clare's poetic achievement could be mapped out in summarised form, and an appropriate number of marks awarded. So far as putting Clare in the context of his contemporaries is concerned, I should have said that he did not have the stature of Wordsworth, Coleridge, Byron, Keats or Shelley. But in saying that I would want to add that that is not necessarily an adverse reflection on Clare, who has his own very special, unique achievements: Geoffrey Grigson has applied the word 'momentous' to Clare's poetry, and Donald Davie has spoken of it in terms of 'one kind of great poetry, sane, robust and astringent'. The underlying premise of this book is that such claims are not wild and irresponsible: I should not have written it if I had not thought Clare to be, at his best, a very good poet indeed, important and valuable, a poet we should cherish. He has still to receive the attention he deserves.

Acknowledgements

The author and publishers wish to thank the copyright-holders (named in brackets) who have kindly given permission for the use of extracts from the following:

The Later Poems of John Clare, ed. Eric Robinson and Geoffrey Summerfield (Manchester University Press)
John Clare, *The Shepherd's Calendar* (© Oxford University Press 1964)
Selected Poems and Prose of John Clare, chosen and ed. Eric Robinson and Geoffrey Summerfield (© Eric Robinson 1967 and reprinted by permission of Curtis Brown Ltd)

The publishers have made every effort to trace the copyright-holders but if they have inadvertently overlooked any, they will be pleased to make the necessary arrangements at the first opportunity.

Textual Note

There is no edition of Clare's poetry that is both complete and reliable. In a critical work of this sort, where the quotations need to be full and frequent, compromise is inevitable. Wherever possible, I have followed the readings of the *Selected Poems and Prose* (1967) and *The Later Poems of John Clare* (1964), both edited by Eric Robinson and Geoffrey Summerfield. For *The Shepherd's Calendar* I have used the same editors' text of 1964. For some asylum poems I have followed *Poems of John Clare's Madness*, edited by Geoffrey Grigson (1949). Otherwise, unless the notes indicate another source, the text used is that of *The Poems of John Clare*, edited in two volumes by J. W. Tibble in 1935. Whatever text I have used in any particular instance, I have tried to give in the notes references to whatever versions occur in the other volumes I have mentioned.

In the notes the following abbreviations have been used:

Eg.	British Museum MS. Egerton 2245-50.
NMS.	Northampton MS., in the John Clare Collection of Northampton Public Library.
PMS.	Peterborough MS., in Peterborough Museum.
LP	*The Later Poems of John Clare*, ed. Eric Robinson and Geoffrey Summerfield, Manchester, 1964.
Letters	*The Letters of John Clare*, ed. J. W. and Anne Tibble, 1951.
Life	J. W. and Anne Tibble, *John Clare: A Life*, revised edition, 1972.

Life and Poetry	J. W. and Anne Tibble, *John Clare: His Life and Poetry*, 1956
Poems	*The Poems of John Clare*, ed. J. W. Tibble, 1935.
Poems of Madness	*Poems of John Clare's Madness*, ed. Geoffrey Grigson, 1949.
Prose	*The Prose of John Clare*, ed. J. W. and Anne Tibble, 1951.
Selected Poems	*John Clare, Selected Poems and Prose*, ed. Eric Robinson and Geoffrey Summerfield, 1967.
Sketches	*Sketches in the Life of John Clare, written by Himself*, ed. Edmund Blunden, 1931.
SC	*The Shepherd's Calendar*, ed. Eric Robinson and Geoffrey Summerfield, 1964.

John Clare:
The Man and the Poet

The bare outlines of Clare's life have become familiar. Born the son of a thresher on 13 July 1793, in the Northamptonshire village of Helpstone, he passed through a variety of jobs in his youth: thresher, horseboy, ploughboy, gardener, limeburner. Because of family poverty, he left school when he was twelve, but went to the evening school at nearby Glinton in order to satisfy his growing appetite for learning. He began to write verses for his own amusement, too shy to tell his parents what he was up to; but in 1818, by the time he was twenty-five, he was seriously contemplating the publication of some of his poems. Spotted by a local bookseller, Edward Drury (cousin to the London publisher John Taylor), he was given the encouragement and the financial assistance he needed; Drury persuaded his cousin that here was a man worth taking under his wing. Whisked to fame by his first volume, *Poems Descriptive of Rural Life and Scenery*, in 1820, Clare was fostered and fêted by the London *literati* as the Northamptonshire Peasant Poet, wined and dined by John Taylor; but his second and subsequent collections of poetry did not have the same success, as the public acclaim faded into neglect. He had quarrels with his publisher, until they eventually fell out; he grew increasingly morose and difficult to live with, so much so that his wife Patty could not stand his odd behaviour any longer, and in 1837 he was taken off to Dr Matthew Allen's asylum in Epping Forest. He escaped from here in 1841, trudging the long journey home to find his childhood sweetheart, Mary Joyce, no longer there; six months later he was incarcerated in the Northampton General Lunatic asylum, from where there was no escape. For twenty-three years Clare rotted away, the act of writing his chief torment and consolation; his freedom to go into the town was eventually curtailed, as his unpredictability increased. When he died on 20 May 1864, no one in the outside world could really care less (to most people he was already dead); even when his body was taken back to his native village, Helpstone, there was nobody to receive it.

In its essentials Clare's life was one of unmitigated tragedy, and it is inevitable that we have it in mind when reading the poetry: it is understandable that the details have perpetuated themselves at the poetry's expense. We can see well enough what appealed to the writers of the women's magazines (and not only the women's) towards the end of the nineteenth century, when they churned out their potted biographies, adorned with elegant portraits. For here was the archetypal genius, the inspired untutored poet and the raving lunatic, rolled conveniently into one.

It would be dishonest and unrealistic to suggest that the poetry can altogether be separated from the life, that the biography is of no relevance. Like most nineteenth-century poets Clare reflects his life in his work, and his poetry, intensely personal, is a direct response to the anguish of living (though there is an intimacy here rarely found in the work of other poets of the period, a privacy that certainly removes his poetry from the realms inhabited by, say, Wordsworth or Keats: there is no real affinity, for example, between Clare's concern with himself, and Wordsworth's, whose egotistical strain is made valid and justified by the sublimity). Because any final division between life and work is ultimately factitious, it is essential, in order to come to some understanding of Clare's poetry – what it is trying to achieve and the quality of the achievement – to know something of the nature of the man.

The frequent characterisation of Clare as *the* Peasant Poet is instructive. The appeal, for the nineteenth-century reading public, of the young peasant in his role as poet was oddly great. There had been a vogue for such figures, partly as an exemplification of spontaneous genius, and soon practically anyone who could hold a pen was busy scribbling a few lines which some publisher was prepared to take on, probably against his better judgment, but backed by an impressive list of sub-

scribers. Stephen Duck, the thresher poet of the previous
century, had quite a lot to answer for; but his poem 'The
Thresher's Labour' (1730), an account of a thresher's life on the
farm, was at least tolerable, its chief interest lying in the
attention to detail, to life as it was for him, rather than the
usual pastoral trillings. Duck was wooed by the court, and,
ending up smothered by patronage, he turned to pathetically
formal odes. His subsequent ordination did not prevent the
onset of insanity, which led to his death by drowning in 1756.
At the beginning of the nineteenth century, Robert Bloomfield,
a Suffolk shoemaker and author of *The Farmer's Boy* (1800),
suffered a rather similar, but less glamorous fate, dying in
1823 in poverty and neglect. Burns often provided a warrant
and an excuse for this phenomenon, but he had the advantage
of being a real poet. As for Clare, nobody knew at first how
much of a poet he really was, so he was sucked into the spiral,
to join Ann Yearsley ('Lactilla'), the Bristol milk-woman poet of
the eighteenth century, and the nonentities celebrated rather
lugubriously by Robert Southey in his *Lives and Works of the
Uneducated Poets* (1831).[1]

Not surprisingly, Clare's poetry, and his attitude to himself
as a poet, was at first deeply affected by the conflicting stand
taken by the literary establishment on the peasant-poet issue :
acutely conscious of his origins, he was extremely uneasy about
his particular place in society. Just as the audience for peasant
poetry had to make allowances and adjustments, so the poets
themselves, inevitably sensitive, had to make their own adjustments. They were, after all, outsiders, most of them non-
starters. In Clare's case, for all the superficial *camaraderie*,
there was a yawning gulf between him and his patrons or
patronisers – even the Stamford bookseller Edward Drury, who
wrote to his London cousin John Taylor telling him something
about his latest literary find : 'He is low in stature – long
visage – light hair – coarse features – ungaitly – awkward – is
a fiddler – loves ale – likes the *girls* – somewhat idle – hates
work.'[2] Not a flattering description. Drury took a particularly
equivocal attitude to Clare (as he himself was not part of the
literary establishment, but a provincial appendage), anxious
to foster his talent, but anxious also to bolster his own repu-
tation; he was as appalled by Clare's ambition as by his drunken-

ness and ruderies. Small wonder that this rather diminutive countryman should show awkwardness and gaucheness in his presence, let alone in more distinguished company. When the weight of one part at least of the London literary and social establishment was brought to bear on the promotional antics for the 1820 volume of verse, Clare's sense of insecurity merely increased. Naturally delighted that he was going to appear in print, he was fully aware – as were many of his supporters and admirers, as well as his detractors – of the inherent dangers. Four editions of 1,000 copies each (and the fourth edition was all but sold out) would not ensure stability, financial or emotional: the precedents were not conducive to optimism. In any case social and moral pressures (and therefore literary) were applied with even greater rigour.

Not everyone who read *Poems Descriptive of Rural Life and Scenery* recognised the latent talent. But a discerning reader could have grasped (and some did) something of the self-doubts beneath the surface. Clare's facility (he is in many respects his own worst enemy) admittedly masks much of the real strength of feeling, but both 'Helpstone', the opening poem of the volume, and 'The Village Minstrel', which opened the next collection the following year, are marked above all by an intense concern over his own position as a poet in a rural community. Clare's sense of ambition, so regretted by Drury, had been aroused long before Drury came along: from an early age he had believed he was made for something other than day-labouring, job-gardening, or lime-burning. He was also made to realise that he was somehow different from the other boys in the village; neighbours talked; too clever by half, he was bound to come to no good, they said. Here he was reading books (and an odd assortment they were too), even writing when nobody was looking, and, sure sign of incipient madness, talking to himself. It is scarcely to be wondered at that in much of his early verse we find a struggle between his own desire to get on in the world, to achieve recognition, and his doom-laden sense of inferiority, his awareness of the obstacles in the way.

In his *Autobiography* (1826) Clare recorded how he 'always had that feeling of ambition about me that wishes to gain notice or to rise above my fellows my ambition then was to be a good writer'.[3] The effects of this are described in 'The Village

Minstrel' (its original title was, significantly, and more bluntly, 'The Peasant Boy'),[4] as he cautiously reaches out for something beyond Helpstone:

> Though, far from what the learned's toils requite,
> He unambitious looks at no renown,
> Yet little hopes break his oblivious night,
> To cheer the bosom of a luckless clown ...
>
> Ambitious prospects fired his little soul,
> And fancy soared and sung, 'bove poverty's control.[5]

But there is nobody there to listen to his song: 'there's few to notice him, or hear his simple tale.' The anomaly is emphasised:

> Folks much may wonder how the thing may be,
> That Lubin's taste should seek refined joys,
> And court th' enchanting smiles of poesy;
> Bred in a village full of strife and noise ...[6]

'The Village Minstrel' is transparently autobiographical, retrospective yet at the same time reflecting the anxieties, the tentative self-justifications, of someone about to have his first book of poems published (in its original form, the poem dates from 1819). Earlier poems are even more revealing in their self-consciousness, none more so than 'Helpstone', started in 1809 when Clare was sixteen but not finished until some time after 1813.[7] *A Rustic's Pastime*, an invaluable manuscript volume containing many of the early poems, testifies to the difficulty Clare had with this poem. It took a lot of knocking into shape, and in the end some of the knocking was done by Drury and Taylor, who saw the implications of the over-personalised tone: apart from anything else the good Admiral Lord Radstock, an important and influential figure who had taken an interest in Clare, would be (was) none too pleased with any attack on wealth and the ruling classes.[8] The poem begins (and these lines take time to settle down in the notebooks) with a nod towards Goldsmith:

> Hail humble Helpstone! where thy vallies spread,
> And thy mean village lifts its lowly head,
> Unknown to grandeur, and unknown to fame,
> No minstrel boasting to advance thy name.[9]

But the tone of affection quickly turns to irritation and scorn :

> Unletter'd spot! unheard in poet's song,
> Where bustling labour drives the hours along,
> Where dawning genius never met the day,
> Where useless ignorance slumbers life away,
> Unknown nor heeded, where low genius tries
> Above the vulgar and the vain to rise.

The extent of Clare's bitterness may be seen in six further lines, not included in the printed text :

> Whose low opinions rising thoughts subdue
> Whose railing envy damps each humble view
> Oh where can friendships cheering smiles abode
> To guide young wanderers on a doubtful road
> The trembling hand to lead, the steps to guide
> And each vain wish (as reason proves) to chide[10]

There are other instances in the poem of Clare's hammering at this point : a lengthy simile on birds in winter was cut because the lines were considered 'evidently unfit for the public eye'.[11] According to Drury, Clare sanctioned this removal; but what is important is that in its original state the poem was a much more personal, even vituperative, effort than that which the public was allowed to see. Clare had at any rate felt the need to continue the simile :

> Then flusht with hopes delusion's warmth supplies
> They spring & twit their visions as they rise
> Visions like mine that vanish as they fly
> In each keen blast that fills the higher sky
> Who find like me along their weary way
> Each prospect lessen and each hope decay[12]

The poem, even with the excisions, is a confused one, unfocused in its frustration. But if the third paragraph seems in its apparent acceptance of obscurity an echo of Bloomfield's invocation to Spring in *The Farmer's Boy*,[13] we might note that Clare's final resolve to return to Helpstone,

> And, as reward for all my troubles past,
> Find one hope true,—to die at home at last!

was followed, in the manuscript, by these lines of uncertainty:

> So when the traveller uncertain roams
> On lost roads leading every where but home
> Each vain desire that leaves his heart in pain
> Each fruitless hope to cherish it in vain
> Each hated track so slowly left behind
> Makes for the home which night desires to find
> And every wish that leaves the aching breast
> Flies to the spot where all its wishes rest[14]

There we have something of the paradox that imbues all Clare's work: the desire to get away from Helpstone, the realisation that that is where he belongs.[15]

Clare's apprehension about the future, about the reception he is going to get in the world of letters, is poignantly put in 'Narrative Verses', an ostensibly descriptive account, in a traditional genre, of a walk to Burghley Park (seat of the Marquis of Exeter). When he has climbed to the top of a hill, what he sees is not the usual set-piece:

> I wish'd and hop'd that future days
>   (For scenes prophetic fill'd my breast)
> Would grant to me a crown of bays
>   By singing maids and shepherds drest.

He continues on his way, unseeing,

> Save only when that destin'd place
>   As yet unknown, tho' long endear'd,
> Enrich'd with many a nameless grace,
>   Through fancy's flitting eye appear'd.[16]

The vision would be laughable if it were not so pathetic. But such moments constitute an important element in the early poems: the concern for his own position and prospects is closely related to the way he writes about the countryside, in that his place in society affects his place in the poetry.

Clare's understandably shaky self-confidence was buffeted, around the time of publication of his first two volumes, by the attitude adopted towards him by John Taylor, Edward Drury, Lord Radstock and the redoubtable Eliza Emmerson. Drury warned Taylor of Clare's liking for drink (Clare admitted the charge as readily as the one that he liked the girls),[17] and the general disquiet over this was not eased by Clare's rolling home after several pints to write a blurred letter to Taylor, who of course threw up his hands in horror. Lord Radstock wrote often but illegibly, telling Clare to remember his moral scruples; to drive home his point he sent down suitably edifying sermons in bound volumes, which Clare was instructed (by Mrs Emmerson) to inscribe 'A Gift from Lord Radstock'. Eliza Emmerson, a London woman married to an art dealer, and herself a versifier, took up Clare's cause with a vengeance, writing to him practically every week, until he went into the asylum. She obviously fancied Clare, and was fairly bold in a genteel way; she went so far as to tell Clare to assure his wife that there was no need to be jealous of their correspondence, and became impatient and cross when Clare couldn't be bothered to reply. The affection was not altogether returned, although Clare was always ready to confide in her, and to accept her gifts of clothes for his growing brood (he even named his second child after her). But Eliza Emmerson was at the head of those admonishing Clare for his irregularities and indiscretions, advising him to be grateful to everyone for what they had done for him. The two correspondents never saw eye to eye.[18]

The uncertainties and confusions engendered by Clare's initial anxiety, and then by his unlooked-for success, remained with him throughout his life. Whilst his circumstances placed him apart from the people in London, he was, for all his love of the alehouse and the country wenches, by nature a solitary figure, unusual, odd, unpredictable, relishing his own company and yet regretting his isolation. His sensitivity in itself made him a figure apart. In his marvellous sketches for an autobiography, he dwells on one particular childhood incident:

My indisposition, (for I cannot call it illness) originated in fainting fits, the cause of which, I always imagined, came from seeing − when I was younger − a man named Thomas Drake, after he had fell off a load of hay and broke his neck. The ghastly paleness of death struck such a terror on me that I could not forget it for years, and my dreams was constantly wanderings in churchyards, digging graves, seeing spirits in charnel houses, &c., &c.[19]

He goes on to describe the numbing fits he used to have. In 1821 he could afford to dismiss them fairly lightly. But such fits were symptomatic of the deeper malaise that increasingly ate at him. He suffered from a crippling autumnal melancholy that gradually extended from the beginning of the year to the end. What was moodiness or lethargy one day could the next be the utter despair of the blue devils: only Taylor's and Hessey's promptings persuaded him against suicide in 1825. This melancholy imbues much of his poetry, the desperate longing of a lost man for something to cling onto in a crumbling world. Clare finished his *Autobiography* in 1826 with this desolate observation: 'my friendship is worn out & my memorys are broken'. He was then thirty-three.[20]

Clare's life and his work were centred on the confusions wrought by change. Change took various forms: the enclosure of his native village, unexpected fame, neglect, marriage to the girl he had made pregnant, the loss of his childhood love, Mary Joyce, moving house in 1832 (only three miles, but too far for Clare), confinement in first one asylum then another.[21] Much of his poetry is a retrospective act of piety, a searching into the corners of memory, an attempt to create out of his losses a permanence denied him in the present. This certainly leads him to write a lot of mediocre, self-consolatory verse, nostalgic and winsome; but it is the source of his greatest strength, by virtue of the particularity and power of that act of memory. Through his poetry, Clare hopes to challenge the processes of change: the dying sunset, the transience of beauty, the tenuousness of love, the open landscape gradually plotted and parcelled, the fading of the past, his uncertain sense of his own identity.

At the centre of confusion is Clare himself, the solitary. Every important poem is a study of one aspect of isolation, of uniqueness sorrowful or exultant. *The Shepherd's Calendar* may be characterised as a full, detailed response to the communal life that Clare knew, and which he sensed was lost forever; but the sense of that loss comes through powerfully, so that against the social activity of the poem, its verve and abundance, we must set the recurring images of isolation. Man remains individual and alone. In the asylum it is this individuality, this awareness of self, with which Clare is primarily and understandably concerned.[22]

In his youth Clare faced two types of isolation: that thrust upon him by his particular circumstances and character (in which he used poetry as a consolation), and that of nature as experienced by the child. The retirement literature of the eighteenth century, so familiar to him from his reading, provided the literary context for such solitary communing, but we can see him remoulding the old forms and clichés as he struggles to find the personal significance behind them. In a number of early poems he is drawn to natural phenomena which suggest isolation and seclusion: he woos the violet as 'a lone dweller in the pathless shade', and wishes he could choose solitude himself, and avoid work.[23] The point of 'To an Insignificant Flower' is that it is 'Obscurely blooming in a lonely wild'.[24] Several songs, slight in themselves, are addressed to solitary figures. In 'Patty of the Vale' for example, Patty is distinguished by her seclusion, and this is part of her inherent attraction: isolation in the 'lonesome woods' makes her 'artless' and 'innocent'.[25] Conventional enough, yet for Clare a potent convention, as 'The Fate of Amy' makes clear. Amy, living in the wood, has no conception of the evils of the world that intrudes in the shape of the artful Edward:

> So artless, innocent, and young,
>   So ready to believe,
> A stranger to the world was she
>   And easy to deceive.[26]

And yet the implicit moral of the poem seems to be that we should seek the woodland solitudes, rather than that they are of no use in a cynical world. In 'Proposals for Building a Cottage' the seclusion advocated is comparable to that in 'Amy' and 'Patty': in this outline of his plans for a life of solitude in a cottage of his own choosing (suggested no doubt by Pomfret's 'Choice'), there is no mention of wife or family, but of the birds he is going to watch on the roof.[27] It is idyllic and unreal. Against this completely escapist attitude might be set the implications of 'Rustic Fishing', where, after a day's happiness in the open, night

> Drives home the sons of solitude and streams

And stops uncloy'd hope's ever-fresh'ning dreams.[28]

As they return home, the boys leave solitude behind and antici-
pate a beating from their parents. The town is opposed to the
country, repression against freedom.

As 'Rustic Fishing' suggests, solitude and the dream become
inseparable. The dream is of an idyll that cannot survive. 'The
Wild-Flower Nosegay' explores the connection. The context of
childhood is firmly established at the beginning of the poem, as
the poet frequents the shades and solitudes in his search for
different varieties of flower :

> In life's first years as on a mother's breast,
>   When Nature nurs'd me in her flowery pride,
> I cull'd her bounty, such as seemed best,
>   And made my garlands by some hedgerow side.
> With pleasing eagerness the mind reclaims
>   From black oblivion's shroud such artless scenes,
> And cons the calendar of childish names
>   With simple joy, when manhood intervenes.[29]

The importance of the search lies in its recreation of the past,
through the act of remembering it. The poem ends :

> 'Tis sweet to view, as in a favour'd book,
>   Life's rude beginning page long turn'd o'er;
> 'Tis nature's common feeling, back to look
>   On things that pleas'd us, when they are no more:
> Pausing on childish scenes a wish repeat,
>   Seeming more sweet to nature when we're men,
> As one, awaken'd from a vision sweet,
>   Wishes to sleep and dream it o'er agen.[30]

'The Wild-Flower Nosegay' contains all the constituents of the
dream of youth, urging an emphasis that increases in importance in the mid 1820s, when Clare is working on *The Shepherd's Calendar.*

One of the fullest expositions of Clare's ideas is to be found
in 'Solitude' (one of a number of poems based on the theoretical
implications of his attitude to poetry), a curious mixture of
literary influence and personal creed. The influence is partly
that of the minor poet Henry Kirke White, who is in turn
indebted to the tradition of secluded retirement : the Gothicism

about some of Clare's preferences makes this poem something
of a curiosity. Nevertheless, whereas in many of his poems on
this theme, the various elements tend not to cohere, here there
is a greater awareness of the complexity involved. The initial
point is not unusual: when alone he can see more clearly and
in the closeness of the observation he approaches a state of
visionary insight. But it is an insecure situation. Into the scene
blunders the 'plough's unfeeling share', which

> Lays full many a dwelling bare;
> Where the lark with russet breast
> 'Hind the big clod hides her nest,
> And the black snail's founder'd pace
> Finds from noon a hiding-place,
> Breaking off the scorching sun
> Where the matted twitches run.[31]

The mouse's nest is laid open and isolated by man's insen-
sitivity. That there is a hint of Clare's own deprivation here, his
own sense of uprootedness, is suggested by a significant return
to the image of the snail later in the poem.

> As snails, which in their painted shell
> So snugly once were wont to dwell,
> When in the schoolboy's care we view
> The pleasing toys of varied hue,
> By age or accident are flown,
> The shell left empty, tenant gone –
> So pass we from the world's affairs,
> And careless vanish from its cares;
> So leave, with silent, long farewell,
> Vain life – as left the snail his shell.[32]

Clare's life becomes, in effect, an attempt to return to the
shell, to rebuild the nest scattered by the plough.

One of the most poignant of Clare's accounts of the relation
between childhood and poetry, between the dream and reality,
occurs in this prose fragment:

> As we grow into life we leave our better life behind us like
> the image of a beauty seen in a looking glass happiness only
> dissemminates happiness while she is present & when she is
> gone we retain no impression of her enjoyments but a blank

of cold imaginings and real dissapointments – unless we
are determined to shape our conduct to her approval & then
she is ever with us not her picture but her perfection not in
shadow but reality – read this over again & profit[33]

This is the dilemma, and this is what Clare attempted, to
accommodate himself to the past, to relive it through memory,
to enter into a dream world where the past could continue as
the present. But it inevitably involved a cruel self-deception
which ultimately broke him. Clare faced the dilemma with
more honesty in another prose fragment:

> The spring of our life – our youth – is the midsummer of our
> happiness – our pleasures are then real & heart stirring –
> they are but associations afterwards – where we laughed in
> childhood at the reality of the enjoyment felt we only smile
> in manhood at the recollections of those enjoyments they
> are then but the reflections of past happiness & have no
> more to do with happiness in the reality than the image of
> a beautiful girl seen in a looking-glass has in comparison
> with the original – our minds only retain the resemblance
> the glass is as blank after her departure – we only feel the
> joy we possessed[34]

Poetry meant that original reality of childhood:

> There is nothing but poetry about the existence of childhood
> real simple soul-moving poetry laughter and joy of poetry &
> not its philosophy & there is nothing of poetry about man-
> hood but the reflection & the remembrance of what has
> been[35]

As Clare glances back in longing to the past, usually to the
Helpstone of his childhood, before enclosure came, it assumes
the features of Eden before the fall. Once again, his reading
assists: Milton, Thomson, Cowper and of course the Bible
(which contained, he thought, some of the best poetry in the
world)[36] provided reassuring precedents. The image of Eden
was a natural one: but for Clare it was, again, much more
than a simple literary trope. It was given added force by his
consciousness of deception. Just as he had lost the Helpstone he
knew, so he had lost his girlfriend, Mary Joyce. This was the

meaning of his Eden: in it he had caught a glimpse of the innocence of love and nature, the real love for which he hankered for the rest of his life, ideal because it never blossomed.

The biographical facts are slender. Mary was the daughter of a farmer, four years younger than himself, whom he met when he was about twelve. In spite of their extreme youth, there seems to have been genuine affection between them: Clare's heart

> woud turn chill when I touchd her hand & tremble & I fancyd her feelings were the same for as I gazd earnestly in her face a tear woud hang in her smiling eye & she woud turn to wipe it away her heart was as tender as a birds[37]

The girl's father apparently disapproved of the friendship, and the two were no longer allowed to see each other. It was a brief, undeveloped relationship which burgeoned in Clare's world of fantasy. As so often, his attitude was equivocal and contradictory:

> my passion coold with my reason & contented itself with another tho I felt a hopeful tenderness that I might one day renew the acquaintance & disclose the smotherd passion she was a beautiful girl & as the dream never awoke into reality her beauty was always fresh in my memory ...[38]

But another account says it was 'nothing else but love in idea' and that 'the first creation of my warm passions was lost in a perplexed multitude of names'.[39] Nonetheless the dream was sufficiently strong to sustain him even in the asylum: he could always love Mary (and what she stood for) in the idea, because she had always been out of his reach. The dream may have been shattered, but he could still cherish it.[40] The world (and, he thought, Mary) had deceived him, so he deceived himself. Mary became the symbol for his ideal love, for the lost past, for the innocence of youth. Paradise lay irrevocably (but that didn't prevent him calling for it) behind him:

> Ah what a paradise begins with life & what a wilderness the knowledge of the world discloses – Surely the Garden of Eden was nothing more than our first parents entrance upon life & the loss of it their knowledge of the world[41]

It is to this search for a lost world that much of his poetry is dedicated.[42]

Clare's life was self-contradictory. In *Child Harold*, a hybrid poem of near-madness, he acknowledges this:

> My life hath been one love – no blot it out
> My life hath been one chain of contradictions ...[43]

He was the countryman having to conform to the ways of polite society; the practical farmworker, living in a cottage of minute proportions, with his practical, down-to-earth wife Patty and his ever-increasing family, and yet yearning back all the time, away from that life, to the dream world of the past, to Mary; the poet of the observed and loved detail becoming, on that very basis, the poet of vision, creating hope from despair. The confusions and contradictions were sufficient in themselves to break his spirit : he had too many commitments, emotional and practical, too many calls on a nature only gradually able to assert its independence. Clamouring to be out of leading-strings, he was nonetheless glad of them : without Taylor, Hessey, Mrs Emmerson, he would have been lost. His unfortunate dealings with publishers, with the annuals and keepsakes, show how easily he came adrift in the sea of self-interest and literary unconcern; he might protest at his butchered poems and the fees that never materialised – but that didn't stop them being butchered or even get him his fees. In a life of paradoxes, the final one is that real independence of mind soared in the asylum, in the prison where he found freedom, where he was able to leave the concerns of the world behind altogether. And yet one of his last poems, so far as we know, is the most straightforward of pieces, based on direct and loving observation :

> Tis Spring warm glows the South
> Chaffinchs carry the moss in his mouth
> To filbert hedges all day long
> And charms the poet with his beautiful song
> The wind blows blea* oer the sedgey fen
> But warm the sun shines by the little wood
> Where the old Cow at her leisure chews her cud[44]

* Cold.

Approaches to Nature

I

In one of many vivid recollections in his *Autobiography* (1826), Clare recaptures the typical pleasures of a childhood Sunday :

> I often lingered a minute on the woodland stile to hear the woodpigeons clapping their wings among the dark oaks I hunted curious flowers in rapture & muttered thoughts in their praise I lovd the pasture with its rushes & thistles & sheep tracks I adored the wild marshy fen with its solitary hernshaw sweeing along in its mellancholy sky I wandered the heath in raptures among the rabbit burrows & golden blossomd furze ... I felt the beauty of these with eager delight the gadflys noonday hum the fainter murmur of the beefly 'spinning in the evening ray' the dragonflys in spangled coats darting like winged arrows down the thin stream the swallow darting through its one archd brig the shepherd hiding from the thunder shower in a hollow dotterel the wild geese skudding along & making all the letters of the alphabet as they flew the motley clouds the whispering wind that muttered to the leaves & summer grasses as it flitted among them like things at play I observd all this with the same raptures as I have done since but I knew nothing of poetry it was felt & not uttered[1]

This passage is characteristic in its careful attention to detail, its response to the multitudinous aspect of the scene that Clare knew, its combination of particularity and enthusiastic impressionism. There is nothing botanical about the writing, nothing quaintly squinny-eyed. As Clare absorbs the scene and the atmosphere, so the headlong syntax reflects the exuberant response, details artlessly crowding each other out. Although

Clare tells how he 'dropt down on the thymy molehill or mossy eminence to survey the summer landscape', he is worlds away from the picturesque irregularities and ruggedness advocated by William Gilpin, worlds away from the topographical set-piece.[2] What is particularly interesting about this passage is that last sentence, the bald statement that Clare knew nothing then of poetry : this is in fact an echo of a similar statement earlier on in the passage, and clearly one he means us to grasp.[3] That there is a uniquely responsive sensibility at play here (and elsewhere in the prose) cannot really be disputed : but the implications for Clare as a poet are important. In this chapter I shall be concerned with the question of how Clare begins to face this problem of turning what was felt, the things that 'made lasting impressions on my feelings', into what was uttered. It is by no means a simple or ready equation.

The problem of descriptive poetry had vexed the theoreticians, the critics and the poets of the previous century. To examine the debate in all its ramifications would lead us far from Clare, but a few points might be usefully made.[4]

In his lecture on 'Didactic and Descriptive Poetry' (first published in 1783), Hugh Blair was able to say that it was in descriptive poetry that 'the highest exertions of genius may be displayed'; it was 'the great test of a Poet's imagination, and always distinguishes an original from a second-rate genius'.[5] But ten years later the *Monthly Review*, prompted by Wordsworth's *Descriptive Sketches*, was protesting :

> More descriptive poetry ! Have we not enough ! Must eternal changes be rung on uplands and lowlands, and nodding forests, and brooding clouds, and cells, and dells, and dingles ? Yes; more, and yet more : so it is decreed.[6]

Towards the end of the eighteenth century, confusion in criticism and in practice was rife, and it is easier to sympathise with the *Monthly Review*'s despair (even if it did not appreciate Wordsworth's originality), than with Blair's rather complacent criteria, according to which the true poet gives a scene 'the colours of life and reality; he places it in such a light that a painter could copy after him'.[7] It was all very well (and all too frequent) for the poet-painter analogy to be invoked (*ut pictura poesis* was one of the most cherished critical phrases of the eighteenth century, echoing Horace),[8] but it rarely helped, when used in a general rather than a specific way, to suggest the distinctive quality of any particular poem. And that really was the problem, both for the poets and the critics: how was the scene, the reality of what was out there in front of the poet, to be transposed into poetry; what could the reader expect the poet to be doing, and how was he to respond? (The contempt for the genre voiced by the *Monthly Review* indicates not only a tiredness with the whole concept of descriptive verse, but also at least an awareness of the stylistic problems involved.)

Blair's elevation of the descriptive mode would have surprised the pre-Thomsonian generation. As John Aikin put it in his *Essay on the Plan and Character of the Poem [The Seasons]*, before Thomson it was thought that description

> could not legitimately constitute the whole, or even the principal part, of a capital piece. Something of a more solid nature was required as the groundwork of a poetical fabric; *pure description* was opposed to *sense*; and binding together the wild flowers which grew obvious to common sight and touch, was decreed a trifling and unprofitable amusement.[9]

(Pope had spoken of descriptive verse as a feast made up of sauces.)[10] Thomson's achievement in *The Seasons* (1726–30) (and there is no doubting his popularity and influence) had been to vindicate description as the central object of poetry: as Joseph Trapp observed in his sphynx-like fashion, 'Poetry consists much more in description than is generally imagined'.[11] But if *The Seasons* sanctioned descriptive poetry, it is quite clear that Aikin did not regard the poem as merely descriptive, a mere record of what the poet had seen. Although Aikin, in his *Essay on the Application of Natural History to Poetry* (1778), played some part in the theoretical move towards accuracy of detail in poetry, he went to some lengths, in his essay on *The Seasons*, to emphasise the element of 'beauty, grandeur and novelty' that 'agreeably impresses the imagination'.[12] Whilst this was an increasing emphasis in critical discussions of description in poetry, as a means of discrimination it was limited by its subjective vagueness: consequently critics tended to circle round the object rather than getting to grips with the surface texture of the poetry. In other words what could only be, ultimately, a stylistic problem was looked at in terms of a continuing debate between the differing claims of realism, detail, the poet–painter analogy, and the imagination. And this critical confusion was reflected in the poetry.

Thomson's poem set a fashion : ironically the situation arose in which just as Thomas Warton had pointed out despairingly that every poet since Theocritus, except Thomson, had imitated Theocritus rather than go to nature firsthand, so John Aikin declared, 'supineness and servile imitation have prevailed to a greater degree in the description of nature, than in any other part of poetry'.[13] It had become a 'mere phraseology', and the reader of poetry was 'wearied and disgusted with a perpetual repetition of the same images, clad in almost the same language'.[14] Aikin therefore set a premium on novelty which was to have far-reaching implications for the genre. Allied to his scorn for the lack of variety was his ridicule of descriptions that were 'faint, obscure and ill-characterised; the properties of the things were mistaken, and incongruous parts employed in the composition of the same picture'.[15] The purpose of his treatise was to redirect descriptive poetry onto the right lines : at the very least truth to nature could be observed and the poet

> who does not habituate himself to view the several objects of nature minutely, and in comparison with each other, must ever fail in giving his pictures the congruity and animation of real life.[16]

Truth to nature became an important criterion : although Wordsworth declared that between *Paradise Lost* and *The Seasons* nature poetry was devoid of anything fresh or original, and although John Taylor, in his Introduction to Clare's *Poems Descriptive* wanted to apply the remark to the period immediately before Clare,[17] there was a growing body of verse that reflected this tendency. Dyer, John Philips, Shenstone, Thomas Warton, Lady Winchilsea, Gay, Ramsay, Savage, Mallet, Langhorne, Akenside, Beattie, John Scott, James Grahame, Cowper, Bowles, Bloomfield – the list of poets working away at this vein is almost endless.[18] But even though Lessing's brilliant

Laokoon (1766) may, in some minds, have been thought to have discredited, once and for all, the *ut pictura poesis* theories (by demonstrating the impossibility of talking of one art in terms of another), the connection between poetry and painting was still the last resort (and sometimes the first) of critics trying to describe and prescribe the effects of description. In his celebrated *Three Essays on the Picturesque*, William Gilpin had characterised the task of the picturesque eye as to

> survey *nature*; not to *anatomize matter*. It throws its glance around in the broadcast stile. It comprehends an extensive tract at each sweep. It examines *parts*, but never descends to *particles*.[19]

Paramount was a respect for the general and the universal, rather than the particular: as Dr Johnson said in France, 'a blade of grass is always a blade of grass, whether in one country or another'.[20] (We should remember that the distinction between Johnson's attitude and that of, say, Clare, is made clear by what he went on to say: 'Men and women are my subjects of inquiry; let us see how these differ from those we have left behind.' For Johnson, as for Thomson, it was Man that really mattered.) Even John Aikin relied extensively on the painting analogy: the idea of the prospect kept details firmly in their place, and even put them in their place if necessary. Aikin's interest in truth was aesthetic, as can be seen from his suggestion that poetry and painting can do the same sort of thing: painting

> is at liberty to employ her pencil on what parts of nature she most delights in, and may exhibit the rural landskip, without encumbering herself with the mechanism of a plough, or the oeconomy of the husbandman.[21]

We may compare this (for its characteristic quality rather than for its discernment) with a general conclusion that Aikin draws:

> Thus does every scene of nature, foreign or domestic, afford objects from whence an accurate survey may derive new ideas of grandeur or beauty. Thus, where a careless eye only beholds an ordinary and indistinct landskip, one accustomed

to examine, compare, and discriminate will discern detached figures and groups, which, judiciously brought forwards, may be wrought into the most striking pictures.[22]

Aikin's defence of Cowper against charges of 'Dutchification', in *Letters to a Young Lady* (1804), was based entirely on this principle of picturesque selection and arrangement, and he applauded Dyer's *Grongar Hill* (1726) for its dwelling sensibly on generalities.[23] (William Gilpin, incidentally, was none too impressed by Dyer's prospect poem, complaining of its lack of wholeness, of the fact that there was 'nowhere a complete formed distance'.)[24] But what appeared to be aesthetic considerations could soon lead to matters of belief and sentiment. In his *Calendar of Nature*, an account of the various poetical possibilities of each month (one of a growing number of such miscellanies) Aikin wrote of August:

> This pleasing harvest-scene is beheld in its perfection only in the open-field countries, where the sight can take in at once an uninterrupted extent of land waving with corn, and a multitude of people engaged in the various parts of the labour. It is a prospect equally delightful to the eye and the heart, and which ought to inspire every sentiment of benevolence to our fellow creatures, and gratitude to our Creator.[25]

The tone of this suggests that Aikin has not moved far from Hugh Blair's insistence that the great charm of 'Pastoral Poetry arises from the view which it exhibits of tranquillity and happiness of a rural life' in which 'whatever is displeasing' must be hidden.[26]

The move towards some sort of literal accuracy, however qualified and blurred by preconceptions about the connection between poetry and painting, meant inevitably a move away from the escapes and artificialities of the pastoral. An interesting comment on this is the critical debate aroused by Crabbe's poetry. Crabbe was not entirely the revolutionary figure he has often been made out to be: as V. H. Lang has shown, he forms a link in a series of changes in the accepted pastoral tradition, stretching back to Gay's parody of Philips in *The Shepherd's Week*.[27] Even Ramsay in *The Gentle Shepherd* had acknowledged the unsatisfactoriness of the pastoral idiom, staled by custom and dulled by convention. Nonetheless, in spite of parodies and burlesques, innovation tended to be in terms of the pastoral, in that poets by and large were concerned simply with widening its terms of reference, rather than with examining the social implications. When John Scott (not at all a bad poet when it came to detail) wrote in his Preface to his *Amoebean Eclogues* (1768), touching on the usual point of desperate departure,

> much of the rural imagery which our century affords, has already been mentioned in poetry; but many obvious and pleasing appearances seem to have totally escaped notice – to describe these is the business of the following eclogues ...[28]

– when he wrote this, he was scarely aiming a blow at the false idealism of the pastoral. His apostrophe, in his poem on 'Amwell', to the 'Descriptive Muse' suggests well enough the familiar line he is taking:

> From all our rich varieties of view,
> What best may please, assist me to select,
> With art dispose, with energy describe,
> And its full image on the mind impress ...[29]

As the critic John Wilson ('Christopher North') saw, it was Burns, Wordsworth and Crabbe who were the first poets really to make the crucial connection between 'low-life', the detailed recording of *minutiae*, and 'the character and life of the People'.[30]

Crabbe's poetry finally raised the issue that lay behind much of the theoretical discussion of the eighteenth century: as the *Quarterly Review* put it, 'he wishes to discard everything like illusion from poetry. He is the poet of reality, of reality in low life.'[31] William Hazlitt echoed this:

> He chooses this subject only to take the charm out of it, and to dispel the illusion, the glory and the dream which had hovered over it in golden verse from Theocritus to Cowper.[32]

Not only was the pastoral myth shattered: the imaginative glow was apparently lacking as well. Wordsworth and Coleridge joined Hazlitt in the vituperative attack on Crabbe (at least he couldn't complain that no one was reading him).[33]

Hazlitt regarded the eighteenth-century interest in painting as one of the prime causes of the shift towards 'truth and fidelity' in 'imitations of nature', and succeeded in completely discrediting the painting analogy with his jibe: 'the adept in Dutch interiors, hovels, and pig-styes must find in Mr Crabbe a man after his own heart.'[34] But whereas in the eighteenth century the pictorial analogy had, at its best, served some stylistic purpose, in that poets were often trying to present a consciously ordered scene, for Hazlitt any such stylistic point was overruled: 'Painting gives the object itself; poetry what it implies.'[35] Although the aesthetic and philosophic basis of Hazlitt's strictures is dubious, such strictures are indicative of the development of the argument towards Coleridge's classic statement of the difference between nature, *natura naturata*, and the essence, *natura naturans*; so that Coleridge's formulation of the poetic power, whilst again resorting to the pictorial analogy, has completely altered the implications of that analogy: 'the power of poetry is, by a single word perhaps, to instil that energy into the mind, which compels the imagination to produce the picture.'[36] Wordsworth's criticism of Crabbe was conducted on similar lines: 'Crabbe's Pictures are mere matters of fact; with which the Muses have just about as much to do as they have with a collection of medical reports, or law cases.'[37] Although Wordsworth claimed that in *The Evening Walk* there was 'not an image in it which I have not observed', he was careful to point out that 'the country is idealized rather than described in any one of its local aspects';[38] and Hazlitt emphasised the importance of 'wholeness' in Wordsworth's descriptive verse, a wholeness similar to the unity Coleridge saw in a passage from *Paradise Lost* which he characterised as 'creation rather than painting'.[39]

If the argument, with 'wholeness' at its centre, might seem to have come full circle, the concept had changed between Thomson and Wordsworth. In *The Seasons* Thomson's concern with descriptive detail as such had been incidental: the drift of the poem was towards an expression of a particular vision, and one not merely personal or idiosyncratic at that. The completeness aimed at by Thomson was intimately related to a philosophy of the universe in which 'Man walked amid the glad creation', and any detail was there to further this concept of wholeness. The progression of the poem, its gradual unfolding in syntactical units large and small, became a determined reflection of that vision. For Wordsworth wholeness meant a complete, personal response to a landscape that was in effect a reflection, an embodiment, of the inner landscape of the mind. It is a radical shift.

II

Nature for Clare was a source of rapture that was wide-ranging and inspiriting, and at the same time well-defined and detailed. One of his initial concerns was accuracy: his curiosity led him into the passionate study of botany – the *Herbals* of Hill and Culpepper, the *Botany* of Lee, the works of Linnaeus (which puzzled him), Ray, Parkinson and Gerard. But he had a healthy distrust of the botanists' attitudes:

> for my part I love to look on nature with a poetic feeling which magnifys the pleasure I love to see the nightingale in its hazel retreat & the cuckoo hiding in its solitudes of oaken foliage & not to examine their carcasses in glass cases yet naturalists & botanists seem to have no taste for this practical feeling they merely make collections of dryd specimens classing them after Linnaeus into tribes & familys & there they delight to show them as a sort of ambitious fame with them 'a bird in the hand is worth two in the bush' well everyone to his hobby
>
> I have none of this curiosity about me tho I feel as happy as they can about finding a new species of field flower or butterflye which I have not seen before yet I have no desire further to dry the plant or torture the butterflye by sticking it on a cork board with a pin[40]

It is true that in 1824 he began a series of essays under the heading of 'A Natural History of Helpstone' which included topics as dry as 'The Sexual System of Plants', 'The Fungus Tribe', 'Mildew, Blight Etc';[41] but he was also contemplating (sparked off by Elizabeth Kent's *Flora Domestica* (1823)) a volume entitled 'A Garden of Wild Flowers', consisting of favourite quotations from prose and poetry.[42]

The scorn directed at over-zealous botanists was levelled also at sentimental and unobservant poets – a more serious charge, because poetry was the more important discipline:

> the poets indulgd in fancys but they did not wish that those matter of fact men the Naturalists shoud take them for facts upon their credit – What absurditys for a world that is said to get wiser & wiser every day[43]

Clare revolted against the pastoral, with its threadbare epithets and comforting generalities; in his recognition of what needed to be done he sensed his own vocation:

> everything else is reckond low & vulgar in fact they are too rustic for the fashionable or prevailing system of rhyme till some bold inovating genius rises with a real love for nature & then they will be considerd as great beautys which they really are[44]

In similar terms he denounced the folly of the city man who confused a thrush with a nightingale: 'such is the ignorance of Nature in large citys that are nothing less than overgrown prisons that shut out the world & all its beautys.'[45] Pope and Shenstone were dismissed as pastoralists: Clare's idea of the true pastoral was to consist of his own *Shepherd's Calendar*. As he put it, in connection with Shenstone, more was involved than 'Putting the Correct Language of the Gentleman into the Mouth of a Simple Shepherd or Vulgar Ploughman'.[46]

For Clare, what was important was a true recognition of the quality and dignity of the countryman's life. The people who came miles to see him in his cottage, in order to satisfy their curiosity as to what a 'labouring rustic' was really like, soon discovered that he was not the beautiful innocent genius Hilton's flatteringly false portrait had led them to expect.[47] In a letter to his Bristol friend, the artist E. V. Rippingille (14 May 1826), Clare warned him what to expect if he decided to accept his invitation to come to stay at Helpstone:

> ... to prevent dissapointments I will describe the spot & the sort of company & cheer you will meet with here with us – you know of our scenery our highest hills are mole-hills & our best rocks are the edges of stonepits yet we have a many

woods on one hand & a many nightingales but no Chloes or Phillises worth the mention we have brooks & wild bowers for Poets but no piping shepherds 'the walls of Jerusalem are desolate' of these pastoral beautys – the village itself is a 'dead letter' in life it is a large straggling place for a village but there is nothing in it of character the 'better sort' that imagine themselves gentry are dull money getting panders ignorant of the world & all that constitutes its glory genius & talent & merit are great words to them the men of greatest merit in their eye is those that have strength to do the most work & can keep from troubling the Parish the longest ... now if you think you can keep away the 'bluedevils' & the other humbugs of misery in these terribles & can drop your spirit into so low a mood as to venture to visit a brother poet not in a Pallace on Parnassus but in a Hut two storys high whose top windows you may reach with your walking stick & whose door you cannot enter without stooping whose chimney corner is open to the sky where the sut falls plentifully to remind me of storms & the storms pepper me so teazingly betimes as to make me wish for better shelter even in a hovel now if you can stoop your mind to these reallitys come & see me ... my Study is not thronged with the Muses but with the melodious mischief of 3 Childern & my Pastoral Mistress is on the eve of bringing another into the World to add to the band which is looked for every day I shall like you to come here about the beginning of August as the scenery is then in its greatest beauty the fields will be alive with harvest & the Rides through the Woods will be left to quiet & the lovers of Solitude as will the Heaths & all my favourite places ...[48]

Paradoxically Clare, who started off with the countryman's unblinkered vision of his own predicament, frequently referred his love of nature to his reading. Any poet who consulted nature was liable to win his heart – Aaron Hill, Charlotte Smith, Keats ('a child of nature warm & wild'),[49] Thomson, whom he admired *in spite of* the 'pompous cast' of the style.[50] He tended to oppose the country clown to the man of taste:

The rustic sings beneath the evening moon but it brings no associations he knows nothing about Milton's description of it 'Now comes still evening on & twilight grey hath in her sober livery all things clad' nor of Collins Ode to Evening

It was the cultivated man who recalled Wordsworth when he saw the celandine, Burns when he saw the daisy, Chatterton when he saw the kingcup 'brasted with the morning dew'; as he put it characteristically, 'to look on nature with a poetic eye magnifies the pleasure she herself being the very essence & soul of Poesy'.[51] Nature inspired poetry, but was also sanctioned by it. This had an important bearing on his own work, for he was very conscious of the established poetic tradition, of the long line of poets who went to nature for their images. This tradition provided him with reassurance, with a starting point. But in its context he needed to sort out his own particular path, if he was to become more than a mere imitator.

The title of Clare's first volume, *Poems Descriptive of Rural Life and Scenery*, is suggestively humble; but it is also deceptive in that it implies a directness that isn't always there. There are a number of modes at work in this volume, and it is helpful to note some of the major stylistic, technical preoccupations half-acknowledged by Clare.

Not surprisingly, perhaps, 'Dawnings of Genius' appealed to reviewers hungry for evidence of struggling genius, and they sentimentalised accordingly.[52] The point and interest of the poem lie not so much in the genius, as in the act of saying: Clare is at least honest about his uncertainty as to what he should be saying, and how he should be saying it. The opening lines state a doctrine that occurs in much of his work:

Genius! a pleasing rapture of the mind,
A kindling warmth to learning unconfin'd,
Glows in each breast, flutters in every vein,
From art's refinement to th'uncultur'd swain.
Hence is that warmth the lowly shepherd proves,
Pacing his native fields and willow groves;
Hence is that joy, when every scene unfolds,
Which taste endears and latest memory holds;
Hence is that sympathy his heart attends,
When bush and tree companions seem and friends;
Hence is that fondness from his soul sincere,
That makes his native place so doubly dear.

'The Village Minstrel' (1821) and even the bizarre *Don Juan* (1841) begin with similar statements of belief: the 'joy', 'sympathy' and 'fondness' associated with, and derived from, nature are as much the shepherd's as the scholar's. That is the meaning for him of 'genius'. Communion with nature is fundamental and spontaneous, the receiver rendered paradoxically inarticulate:

> Raptures the while his inward heart inflame,
> And joys delight him which he cannot name.

The poem, with all its obvious shortcomings, is a wrestling with this problem of inarticulacy. The dilemma of the would-be poet is economically stated: he cannot remain satisfied with the possession of a vaguely defined 'genius', with a rapture that is unexpressed. Fancy cannot sustain him, and she 'takes her flight'.

> Ideas picture pleasing views to mind,
> For which his language can no utterance find.

It is not that Clare has nothing to write about: there is too much, and he is too close to it all. It is worth remarking that Clare comes nearest to being objective, and successful, in those lines in which he manages to transmit the sense of joy to the verse itself, describing in concrete terms rather than merely stating:

> In those low paths which poverty surrounds,
> The rough, rude ploughman, off his fallow-grounds
> (That necessary tool of wealth and pride),
> While moil'd* and sweating by some pasture's side,
> Will often stoop inquisitive to trace
> The opening beauties of a daisy's face;
> Oft will he witness, with admiring eyes,
> The brook's sweet dimple o'er the pebbles rise;
> And often, bent as o'er some magic spell,
> He'll pause, and pick his shaped stone and shell.

Clare is torn in this poem between what he sees, and the effect this has on him. The curious thing is that he seems to be oblivious of his real strength – these lines, in the context of

* Worked hard.

the whole poem, are for him incidental, but they are clearly
the best part of it. What obsesses Clare is that he cannot get
beyond this sort of observation, there is nothing to give it
cohesion. It is gone before he has had time to register its
impact:

> So while the present please, the past decay,
> And in each other, losing, melt away.

This sense of confusion in the face of multiplicity – and,
just as important, in the face of change and decay – is explored
in some other poems. In 'A Sunset' the problem is brought
more sharply into focus, in that it is seen more specifically
in terms of a descriptive problem – how to counter the process of change in the natural scene. This is one of Clare's more
successful early poems.

> Ah, just as well as if but yesternight
>   I do remember on that self-same hill
> I dropt me down with exquisite delight;
>   The very hawthorn bush is standing still
> From whence I sought a twig of blooming may
>   And stuck it to my bosom when at rest.
> Oh, 'twas a lovely eve; the lambs at play
>   Scampt round and round the hill, and in the west
> The clouds of purple and of crimson dye
>   Were huddled up together in a heap,
> And o'er the scented wide world's edge did lie
>   Resting as quiet as if lulled to sleep.
> I gazed upon them with a wishing eye,
>   And longed but vainly for the painter's power
> To give existence to the mingling dye
>   And snatch a beauty from an evening hour.
> But soft and soft it lost itself in night,
>   And changed and changed in many a lumined track;
> I felt concerned to see it leave the sight
>   And hide its lovely face in blanking black.[53]

Again, this poem, clumsy but saved by the central lines, is
about descriptive poetry. As in 'Dawnings of Genius' Clare is
disturbed by the transience of what he observes: if only he
could eliminate the temporal quality and capture a precise

moment, a moment of stillness in which the suggestion of flux
could still be felt. The personal implications of this should not
be overlooked : a number of poems from this period concern
themselves with the fading of dreams, and 'A Sigh in a Playground', moving along the conventional lines of regret for the
passing of youth, concludes :

> So thou, dear spot, though doubtless but to me,
> Art sacred from the joys possess'd in thee,
> That rose, and shone, and set – a sun's sojourn;
> As quick in speed – alas, without return ![54]

Consumed as he is by such fears, Clare views the sunset in the
poem quoted above with especial misgivings. Because the
scene is constantly shifting, the frustration of the anxious poet
is allied to a sense of alienation in the face of nature's unconcern for him. The combination of these two factors is of some
importance in the development of his descriptive technique.

None of the poems I have mentioned is complex : each states
a problem without finding any way out of it. Nonetheless these
doubts that he voices help to explain the confused character
of much of his early poetry. Not only is he disturbed by his
inability to capture a particular scene, he is disturbed by the
effect such a scene has on him. He wants to respond totally,
to surrender to whatever mood is evoked, and the result is
inarticulacy. This emphasis on mood is clearly important to
him, but it is just as clearly debilitating, in that it takes him
away from what he can do well, the specific, towards the
beckoning allure of generalities that are beyond his reach. In
the same way he makes gestures towards the poet–painter
analogy which remain mere gestures, as, for example, in 'A
Scene' where, having invoked the idea of the prospect, he side-
steps its necessary syntactical implications and throws in the
towel rather desperately :

> All these, with hundreds more, far off and near,
> Approach my sight; and please to such excess,
> That language fails the pleasure to express.[55]

W. K. Wimsatt has demonstrated convincingly how the
emphasis on a personal response to nature is an increasing
tendency in Romantic poetry, and how Coleridge is disting-

uished from, say, Bowles, precisely because of his ability to find the right form for what is a new sensibility. The associative response of the typical eighteenth-century poet is radically altered by the unifying power of the imagination, whereby description and response become inseparable. As Coleridge put it in 1802 :

> The poet's heart and intellect should be *combined*, intimately combined and unified with the great appearances of nature, and not merely held in solution and loose mixture with them.[56]

In this climate Clare finds himself torn, seeming to want to respond to nature in terms of this developing sensibility, but with no notion of how this is to be done. The tradition established by Thomson was specifically designed for a specifically formulated response, grand and generalised, and yet that response was alien to Clare's way of thinking and writing. In all of the poems so far discussed it is the descriptive sections which stand out as offering a solution to this stylistic and expressive problem, but Clare seems unaware of the fact. At the same time his awareness of change is to provide him with a way into a solution. His descriptive poetry becomes, as he develops, an attempt to 'fix' nature, just as he had wanted to 'snatch a beauty from an evening hour'; and what is important is the acknowledgement that this is a personal as well as an aesthetic need. Clare is threatened by nature, by its tumultuous, ever-changing detail just as the landscape he knew as a child is threatened by enclosure. Consequently, in his best, most mature, poetry, we get not only a constant desire to place things in his poetry, by putting them there to make them permanent – there is also the awareness that permanence of any sort is impossible, that nature as he sees it consists of details that constantly shift, crowding each other out. The resulting conflict lends to his characteristic verse a tension which, whilst apparently similar to Thomson's well-directed efforts to keep nature in control, is something different, more wild and personal, more unpredictable.

The consequences of his initial confusion for his first volume of poetry are predictable: there is a lot of rather tremulous, ill-defined emotion spilling out, not knowing what to do with itself. Yet the interesting poems are those in which no mention of emotion as such is made, or those in which the more precise significance of the emotion is more sharply delineated. 'To Health' is an instance of Clare's unhealthy reliance on a tradition that has little to offer him :

> Thy voice I hear, thy form I see,
>   In silence, echo, stream or cloud;
> Now, that strong voice belongs to thee
>   Which woods and hills repeat so loud.
>
> The leaf, the flower, the spiry blade,
>   The hanging drops of pearly dew,
> The russet heath, the woodland shade,
>   All, all can bring thee in my view.
>
> With thee I seek the woodland shade
>   Beset in briery wilds among;
> With thee I tread the tufted glade,
>   Transported by the woodlark's song.[57]

There is nothing to distinguish this from the host of similar third-rate verses on this theme. If we expect concision and particularity from Clare, we don't get it here. The remorseless quatrains skate over the surface of the natural world, leaving her tastefully decorous and undefined, uninteresting because the poet shows no real interest himself. The stock nouns, collective and generalised, the stock adjectives, weak and comforting, are rolled out. Comforting is perhaps the point. So long as he can resort to such formulae, Clare feels relatively safe; he doesn't need to think out an attitude to nature, it is already supplied for him by the implications of an inherited vocabulary. It is clearly a dead end, even though it is one to which he repeatedly turns.

At the other extreme comes a poem such as 'The Harvest Morning' where comparison with a handling of a similar theme in Bloomfield's *Farmer's Boy* (1800) should help to suggest something of Clare's distinguishing features. Bloomfield is describing a field of wheat :

> Its dark-green hue, its sicklier tints all fail,
>   And rip'ning harvest rustles in the gale.

A glorious sight, if glory dwells below,
Where Heaven's munificence makes all the show.
O'er every field and golden prospect found,
That glads the ploughman's Sunday morning's round,
When on some eminence he takes his stand,
To judge the smiling produce of the land.
Here Vanity sinks back, her head to hide :
What is there here to flatter human pride?
The tow'ring fabric, or the dome's loud roar
And stedfast columns, may astonish more,
Where the charm'd gazer long delighted stays,
Yet trac'd but to the *architect* the praise;
Whilst here, the veriest clown that treads the sod,
Without one scruple gives the praise to GOD;
And twofold joys possess his raptur'd mind,
From gratitude and admiration join'd.[58]

Although the colours are effectively caught in the first line,
the pastoral myth is in effect bolstered, and the neatness of the
verse, its unruffled decorum, eradicates any impression of real
country life or real work. Stephen Duck, for all his awkwardness, got more life into his account of the harvest scene. Bloomfield's lines (fairly typical of the poem as a whole, competent
but undistinguished) are reminiscent of the attitude taken by
John Aikin (quoted above, p. 21). The ploughman consciously
takes up the standard prospect position, and the poet delivers
a sermon : what he actually sees is of minor importance, and
there is no attempt to do more than versify a common theme.

Against this we might set the opening of Clare's 'Harvest
Morning', in which preliminaries are avoided, as he throws
himself in with a series of visual and aural impressions.

Cocks wake the early morn with many a crow
Loud ticking village clock has counted four
The labouring rustic hears his restless foe
And weary bones and pains complaining sore
Hobbles to fetch his horses from the moor
While some are left to teem* the loaded corn
Which night unfinished left agen the door
And bird boy scaring sounds his hollow horn

* Pour out.

What busy bustling labouring scene[s] now
mark the harvest morn[59]

If this seems more vivid and alive than Bloomfield's account,
it is because of Clare's finer ear and more perceptive eye. We
experience the events as they affect the people involved, so
that the first two lines not only describe particular events, they
epitomise the ceaseless, weary round; they are not merely
picturesque notes, but an essential part of the scene. What can
be seen as artifice in Bloomfield, coy and distancing, is absent.
Of course it could be said that Beattie in *The Minstrel* (1771–4),
and Wordsworth in his *Evening Walk* (1793) achieve effects
much more poised and subtle, whilst still writing about what
they see: and it would be true. Here for example is Beattie,
in the same stanzaic form, exhibiting a greater sense of control,
more awareness of what he is doing:

> The cottage curs at early pilgrim bark;
> Crowned with her pail the tripping milkmaid sings;
> The whistling ploughman stalks afield; and, hark!
> Down the rough slope the ponderous waggon rings;
> Thro' rustling corn the hare astonished springs,
> Slow tolls the village clock the drowsy hour;
> The partridge bursts away on whirring wings;
> Deep mourns the turtle in sequester'd bower,
> And shrill lark carols clear from her aërial tower.[60]

It is not difficult to see why Wordsworth thought so highly
of Beattie: his own early essays at a descriptive poetry owe
much to *The Minstrel* in their careful combination of original,
alert observation and a reflective, generalised tone.[61] But, apart
from individual passages, Beattie is not really interested in
precision of observation. His complacency prevents him from
achieving, in the poem as a whole, much more than romantic
wishfulfilment. The comparison between Clare and Beattie in
this instance shows the support lent by the tradition, but also
the way in which Clare feels free to go his own way. For all its
artlessness, the opening stanza of 'Harvest Morning' is notable
especially for its lack of conventional controls: the attempt in
the last line to draw it together into a neat generalisation is

only a gesture. Unfortunately, Clare felt obliged to make such gestures, and the final stanza of the poem drops back onto the same comforting illusions which he seems, elsewhere, anxious to subvert. In spite of references to the pride of wealth, the sting has gone:

> O Rural life! what charms thy meanness hide;
> What sweet descriptions bards disdain to sing;
> What loves, what graces on thy plains abide:
> Oh, could I soar me on the Muse's wing,
> What rifled charms should my researches bring!
> Pleas'd would I wander where these charms reside;
> Of rural sports and beauties would I sing;
> Those beauties, Wealth, which you in vain deride,
> Beauties of richest bloom, superior to your pride.

In much of his early verse, Clare finds himself unable to choose between the two attitudes exemplified by this poem; if he sees the conflict, he is unprepared or unable to resolve it. The literary influence, with its only partial relevance to him, is undoubtedly to blame, to some extent. But at the same time, the stylistic conflict in 'Harvest Morning' points to a more personal conflict going on in Clare's mind, between his desire to get rid of all the nonsense of pastoral, and his own ardent delight in nature, in its beauty and abundance.

Something of Clare's uncertainty comes out in his attitude towards Bloomfield, whom he admired so much that he planned a biography of him.[62] He thought that 'Richard and Kate' was 'sufficient to establish his name as the English Theocritus & the first of Rural Bards in this country'.[63] This echoed what he said to Thomas Inskip, a Bedford watchmaker and a staunch friend, in 1824, when he wrote that 'in my opinion he is the most original poet of the age & the greatest pastoral poet England ever gave birth to'.[64] He even went so far as to class Burns and Bloomfield together, which certainly suggests a serious blurring of distinctions.[65] In talking of Bloomfield as an English Theocritus, Clare was taking a standard line: Bernard Barton acclaimed him as 'our own more chaste Theocritus' and Nathan Drake elaborated on this point:

Such indeed are the merits of this work, that, in true *pastoral* imagery and simplicity, I do not think any production can be put in competition with it since the days of Theocritus. To that charming rusticity which particularizes the Grecian are added the individuality, fidelity and boldness of description which render Thomson so interesting to the lovers of Nature.[66]

Although Bloomfield, wanting to herald the end of nonsense, had declared 'I was determined that what I said on Farming should be EXPERIMENTALLY true', he was obviously aware of the dangers, inherent in descriptive poetry, of being too particular.[67] For him, the answer was to regard nature as unchangeable, the same in Sussex as it was in Suffolk. As he wrote to his brother:

> I have read Gay's 'Trivia'; it descends to minute descriptions of London, more minute than mine do of the country; his minutiae must be more subject to change than mine, less dependent on nature.[68]

How much Clare seems to have absorbed of this attitude may be seen from his defence of 'The Village Minstrel' against charges of plagiarism: nature, he declared, was much the same at Helpstone as elsewhere.[69] But the whole drift of his poetry before 1832 was towards a particularity which denied any such premise.

If Clare and Bloomfield appear to face similar problems of choice and direction, we are never conscious of Bloomfield's being particularly bothered about the conflict. Clare's case is much more extreme. He cannot take the detached attitude of his hero: he is moved to amazement and wonder, rage and pity such as Bloomfield never knew. We seldom get in Bloomfield the sort of semi-hysterical outbursts that occur in Clare's early work: it is anger, distress, self-pity, confusion, untouched by art, or, if touched, tempered and softened unnecessarily. For example there is the frequent identification of himself with the down-trodden creatures of nature: we have seen how this affected 'Helpstone'. It was a short step from here to poems such as 'The Ant', 'The Primrose', 'To the Glowworm', 'The Robin', 'To the Butterfly'.[70] The common analogy between the seasons and the life of man found expression in 'A Reflection

in Autumn' or 'Falling Leaves'. In 'Ruins of Despair' Clare
appears to approach rather gingerly the sort of realism in
which Crabbe excelled, but the poem fails because of Clare's
inability to keep separate what he sees and what he feels. The
sensationalism works against any force the poem might have
had:

> Yon mouldering wall composed of naught but mud
> (Which has for ages in that manner stood)
> Is rightly styled the 'Ruins of Despair',
> For naught but wretchedness assembles there.
> All sons of grief and daughters of despair
> Within that hut: – but how can life live there?[71]

Admittedly, Clare provides suitably unromantic detail, but the
interesting point about the poem is the way he breaks off,
unable to continue:

> – Grief-searching muse, give o'er,
> On such a dismal scene essay no more;
> Stay thy too-curious search, forbear! forbear!
> No more describe the 'Ruins of Despair'!

This is too uncomfortably like Miss Mitford's reaction to the
workhouse, in her perambulation around the village.[72] When
we compare this poem with a more successful recreation of the
genre, the 'Elegy on the Ruins of Pickworth', the irony is that
here, lack of detail assists the poem's ends. Sorrow and rage
are more controlled, and have the support of a particular,
well-defined poetic ethos.[73] The debt to a literary tradition – in
this case suggested by a similar poem by John Cunningham,
has helped Clare to order his verse:[74]

> While vain extravagance, for one alone,
>   Claims half the land his grandeur to maintain,
> What thousands, not a rood to call their own,
>   Like me but labour for support in vain!

> Here we see luxury surfeit with excess;
>   There want, bewailing, beg from door to door,
> Still meeting sorrow where he meets success,
>   By lengthening life that liv'd in vain before.

Detail can be a positive disadvantage – disturbing and unsettl-
ing; for this reason Clare quite often does his best to avoid it.

   This brings us to the paradox of the early verse. Wanting
to get away from false postures, from literary clichés, Clare
frequently finds himself turning to well-tried modes for support. There is an air of experiment about much of the first
volume, a restlessness deriving from his uncertainty of direction, and from his own confused reactions to the world he
lives in and wants to write about. In the youthful poem 'Noon',
for example, it is significant that Clare, while apparently wanting to get away from the stilted quality of so many poems on
this theme, finds himself not only nodding towards the conventions ('Rural voices all are mute;/Tuneless lies the pipe and
flute'), but actually quoting a line from John Cunningham :

> And no longer in the stream,
> Watching lies the silver bream,
> Forcing from repeated springs,
> 'Verges in successive rings'.[75]

It is Cunningham who lies behind one of the best of these early
poems, 'Summer Morning' : in echoing him Clare manages to
produce a poem that has its own individuality.[76] The resemblance can be seen in the familiar quatrain, short staccato lines
containing brief images of events which are often balanced
within each stanza : Gray's influence is clear.[77] But Clare tends
to be more forthright :

> The cocks have now the morn foretold,
>   The sun again begins to peep;
> The shepherd, whistling to his fold,
>   Unpens and frees the captive sheep.
>
> O'er pathless plains, at early hours,
>   The sleepy rustic sloomy* goes;
> The dews, brush'd off from grass and flowers,
>   Bemoistening sop his harden'd shoes.[78]

The combination of literary convention and hopeful realism
can still jar :

* Slow, dreamy.

Again the bustling maiden seeks
  Her cleanly pail, and eager now,
Rivals the morn with rosy cheeks
  And hastens off to milk her cow;

While echo tells of Colin near,
  Blithe, whistling o'er the misty hills:
The powerful magic fills her ear,
  And through her beating bosom thrills.[79]

But there are several stanzas in which Clare avoids this trap,
where he is able to recreate an atmosphere with economy, and
where the range of reference contributes to, rather than
detracts from, the effect:

The misted brook, its edges reek;
  Sultry noon is drawing on;
The east has lost its ruddy streak,
  And morning sweets are almost gone.

In tortur'd haste, retreating cows
  Plunge headlong in the spangled flood,
Or sweeping by the oaken boughs
  Brushing trace the tangled wood.[80]

In this poem (and there are others like it) Clare realises that
detail can be accommodated in a poem, and still have its roots
in a reliable tradition. It is a discovery, hard-won, that is of
considerable importance in his development as a poet of the
natural world.

III

In his formative years Clare was in effect searching for a discipline that would be liberating rather than constricting: the
search extended to formal, as well as stylistic, properties. As
we should expect from a youthful experimenter, he was catholic in his choice of forms, but one to which he kept returning
was the sonnet. Half of the first two collections of poetry were
sonnets, and although many of these may have been regarded,
at least by Taylor, as useful padding, Clare used the sonnet
form so persistently throughout his life (even in the asylum)

that it is reasonable to suppose it answered some particular need.[81] As Mrs Emmerson reminded him, this was a 'Sonnet reading age':[82] but whereas the sonnets of even Coleridge, Shelley and Byron could not be considered their best or most characteristic work, those of Clare constitute a considerable part of his achievement. When others were floundering helplessly, Clare was, from 1824 onwards, achieving poems of great strength and idiosyncracy. Of course, sonnets in the legitimately accepted sense they were not; but to dismiss them apologetically as irregular, Bewick-like sketches, is to miss the point. Clare's sonnets are, by and large, no more irregular, unlegitimate, unPetrarchan or unMiltonic than most nineteenth-century sonnets. The prolonged debate over the validity of the strict Petrarchan form, followed by Milton and Wordsworth, showed how tenuous a hold such rules had on the minor poets: against Bowles's rigidity was the irregularity of someone like Charlotte Smith, and even proud manifestoes of adherence to the legitimate form by the popular Anna Seward only concealed what was happening beyond the Preface.[83] At a higher level Wordsworth stood out against the laxities of Leigh Hunt and the early Keats.[84] Clare's impatience with the rules was a symptom of his time.

Clare did not achieve real control and flexibility in the sonnet until about 1824. But in the feverish poetic activity of the early 1820s he was writing a large number of sonnets, sending them off for Taylor's approval, in an attempt to stave off the self-doubts that kept creeping in. Edward Drury sounded one of his misleading warning notes in the summer of 1820:

> Sonnets are beautiful, but every body can write a Sonnet, if they bestow labour and time, and have any idea of poetry – they may even produce sonnets of tolerable merit: but none but a real poet can produce a song like the Meeting & if you recal to mind the facts and circumstances that enabled you to write that you will write many as good on thousands of other subjects.[85]

But if Drury deterred Clare, Mrs Emmerson was transported with her customary delight: she told her protégé on 24 May 1820 that she was sure that 'you *excel*, in that class of composition, – & choice of subject'.[86] Later, in September, when she saw Clare's recent poems in manuscript, she commented especially on the quality of the sonnets, with their '*Simplicity and Sweetness*'.[87] Taylor, too, was quite interested in the sonnets. In a list of poems which he liked at first reading, several sonnets were included.[88]

Encouraged by this, rather than put off by Drury, Clare continued to compose his sonnets, and also to read those of other poets, in particular Reynolds and Keats. What he says of Reynolds might equally apply to himself: '2 or 3 of his sonnets I think fine in fact after what I had seen of his poetry this struck me he only wants a good subject short irregular Pieces is his fort I think ...'[89] A week or so later he was asking Hessey why they did not print any of Keats's sonnets, which Clare liked greatly.[90] Ten days after this he was pestering Hessey for his opinion on a sonnet he sent him;[91] in October he sent 'To the Ivy', since Taylor apparently liked the last sonnet he saw.[92] Taylor in his dilatory fashion acknowledged this on 12 December, and singled out of the poems received this sonnet. His comments show something of his attitude to Clare's methods of composition, and of his general response to his poetry. He does not want to go into too much detailed criticism :

> for I wish your own Mind & good Taste to lead you; it has prompted you to your best things, and will again; but I cannot help remarking the Sonnet to the Ivy in which you say 'Where thou in *Weak Defiance* strives with Time, & holds his weapons in a dread suspence' : this Figure is I think of the highest order of Poetry; and I would also observe the happy epithet of 'thy *green Darkness* overshadowing me.' But go on whenever you feel disposed, and *only then*, for at such Times your mind will urge you to compose Verses for its own Relief, and depend upon it I shall be pleased with what you do.[93]

Taylor was impressed when Clare showed his verbal dexterity: he also liked his attempts at depth of thought; but this only encouraged Clare to aim at a bombastic style beyond his grasp.

The sonnet form had been used often enough by minor poets with nothing to say : Clare's difficulty was that he was still not certain of what he wanted to be saying. Taylor encouraged him to tackle grand topics such as 'Anxiety' or 'Religion' or 'Time' (Clare sent the latter for comment, completely at sea as to its merits — 'wether it be poetry or fustian, inspiration or bombast common sense or nonsense your judgment will soon decide')[94] which were really beyond him. He felt confined, as when writing a poem in memory of Keats, and was not yet able to see that confinement had its advantages; as he realised in the case of the Keats poem, he would have said it better in an elegy.[95] But while Clare (and Taylor, too) vacillated over the virtues of individual sonnets, Chauncy Hare Townsend, a literary friend from Cambridge, pointed pertinently to their real quality:

> You excel particularly in that forcible conciseness, which presents the eye with a vivid picture, and the heart with a poetical feeling, in the short space of fourteen lines.[96]

This commendation had its relevance, as Clare hovered between the opposing claims the form seemed to make on him.

For his Prospectus to *Poems Descriptive* Clare chose the early sonnet 'The Setting Sun' as an example of his poetic powers.[97] This might seem an odd choice, but it reflects his desire to do the right and proper thing. In presenting himself in this fashion he showed the impeccable character of a religious believer, writing in an acceptably mediocre idiom. Furthermore the sonnet might be thought of as at least a respectable literary form. When *Poems Descriptive* were published, several of the reviewers quoted from the sonnets to excite public curiosity. The *Literary Chronicle*, in 1821, with reference to *The Village Minstrel*, said that the 'songs and sonnets are many of them very pretty, and some of them possess considerable merit'. No species of poetry was more common than the sonnet, yet Clare, they thought, succeeded here.[98] The *Eclectic Review* for 1822 was equally gratified by the quality of the sonnets.[99] The Reverend W. Allen acknowledged that the sonnet no longer required strict adherence to the rules; but once this was granted, Clare must be considered capable of writing some very good sonnets indeed.[100] We might not share the general enthusiasm for many of these poems; but we should not underestimate their value for Clare.

Many of the sonnets in *Poems Descriptive* brood on current morbidities: several of these early posturings seem to reflect

Clare's spiritual insecurity; but they do not contain much convincing poetry. There are, however, a few sonnets indicative of the type of poetry in which Clare would excel. In 'The Primrose', for example, there is none of the triteness and the laboured moralising that sucks up whatever life there is in most of these early sonnets, and there is a keenness of observation and a sense of occasion essential to this type of poem.[101] Clare manages to get his verse moving here: by contrast 'The Setting Sun' is tame and static. This sense of movement is important, for it becomes a recurrent feature of the later sonnets. Many of them are expressions of an exuberance and vitality almost unique to Clare, and the actual gait of the verse is always basic to the mood of the poem. The opening lines set the tone, the sense of *camaraderie* between the poet and nature:

> Welcome, pale Primrose! starting up between
> Dead matted leaves of ash and oak, that strew
> The every lawn, the wood, and spinney through,
> Mid creeping moss and ivy's darker green.

There is an intimacy not only between poet and nature, but within nature. Nature herself is pleased to see the flower, coming up between the dead leaves, the moss and the ivy. This inevitability of pleasure and delight occasioned by the approach of spring is conveyed in the expansive hope of the enjambements in this opening quatrain. It is stated explicitly in the next line, which counteracts the forward thrust of the verse up to this point with its reflective simplicity and wonder:

> How much thy presence beautifies the ground.

The primrose is the focal point of the poem; the schoolboy and the shepherd are both absorbed by it. The boy picks some of the flowers, gleefully, thoughtlessly, but without malice:

> And where thy fairy flowers in groups are found,
> The school-boy roams enchantedly along,
> Plucking the fairest with a rude delight.

The shepherd, more reticent, stops singing,

> To gaze a moment on the pleasing sight,
> O'er-joy'd to see the flowers that truly bring
> The welcome news of sweet returning spring.

As to the poem's peculiar and individual merits, it is visually precise; it is committed in that the sheer delight in spring is communicated throughout the verse itself, and in so far as the strength of the opening is maintained to the end of the poem. The other point to be made about this poem, connected with Clare's use of the verse structure, and his subtle variations of tempo within this basic structure, is the finality which he achieves in the closing couplet. Here it is linked syntactically with the previous two lines, so that there is no sudden jolt; and the image of the shepherd pausing to look at the flower is what the poem has worked towards, so that the rest of the sonnet is effectively contained in these last two lines. It is a poem of hope, reflected in the thrust of the flower through the leaves, in the pride of the primrose as it glows on the bank, in the enchantment of the boy, and in the humility of the shepherd. It looks forward to the carefully wrought sonnets of *The Rural Muse*, even if it does not attain their complete control and composure.

None of the other sonnets in *Poems Descriptive* matches 'The Primrose'. But *The Village Minstrel* contained a considerable number of sonnets of comparable merit. Clare is no longer so restricted by the influence of the melancholic sonneteers; he achieves a much cleaner style, even in those sonnets which merely express his own sorrows and pleasures in life. What had previously been little more than attitudinising becomes genuine statement of particular emotional reactions. There are some sonnets which persist in the expression of baleful gloom, and these are characteristically tiresome. 'On Death' for instance has little to commend it;[102] but such complete abandoment of hope and decorum is rare. Even in sonnets which bemoan the passing of time, Clare's verbal imagination usually saves the situation. In 'Autumn', after a laboured opening, there are four lines which, in their terseness and sad finality, characterise Clare's ability to use isolated instances illustratively, without pointing the comparison too obviously:

> The busy bee hath humm'd himself to rest;
>   Flowers dry to seed, that held the sweets of spring;
> Flown is the bird, and empty is the nest;
>   His broods are rear'd, no joys are left to sing.[103]

'The Last of April' carries this process a stage further.[104] In-

stead of using the poem as a vehicle for a rather trite moral,
Clare puts the burden of the poem's meaning onto the imagery: the emphasis is on April as much as on the sad lot of
humanity. After the Elizabethan-like image of the opening
statement, with the ambivalence of the dew captured across
the line-break:

> Old April wanes, and her last dewy morn
>   Her death-bed steeps in tears,

comes the arrival of May, putting April to rout. This juxtaposition of death and birth, past and present, is continued in the
lines on the primrose: Clare is careful to place any images of
growth in the past.

> The early primrose, peeping once so gay,
> Is now chok'd up with many a mounting weed,
>   And the poor violet we once admired
> Creeps in the grass unsought for – flowers succeed,
>   Gaudy and new, and more to be desired,
>   And of the old the schoolboy seemeth tired.

This lament for the past and the revered is put in a context
of what is new and gaudy. Things without the sanction of time
are worthless, yet they overthrow what is of real value: and
it is the primrose and violet that are of value – flowers that in
their time were symbols of hope and promise. Even if we are
disposed to regard the moral of the poem as unnecessarily
obvious and self-centred, the progression towards this moral is
carefully calculated. Clare places himself firmly on the side of
the primrose and the violet; but he also acknowledges that no
longer does he seek the violet. We are all as guilty as the
capricious schoolboy. Clare's honesty of attitude here ('we
once admired') raises the emotional tone of the whole sonnet.
This is a quality that we need to look for in his best work in
this genre. Already, here, his sense of melancholy is more
fully developed, his reaction to experience more intense and
precise, emotionally and stylistically.

The mood of delight in nature is contained in several of the
sonnets written between 1819 and 1821. In these poems, Clare
explores his attitude towards nature, and uses the sonnet form
to act out his drama between man and beast. This becomes a

serious preoccupation. However carelessly and cheerfully a poem may begin, there is often a twist in the tail. For Clare did not cherish any sentimental views about nature; it is often a harsh, cruel world. Thus the tension that is expected of the sonnet, the sense of antithesis, is in a way revitalised. It is not necessarily an antithesis between octave and sestet; Clare moves freely within his limits, refusing to be tied down. The movement of each sonnet tends to have its own peculiar individuality. 'The Wryneck's Nest' employs a grim humour :

> That summer bird its oft-repeated note
>   Chirps from the dotterel ash, and in the hole
> The green woodpecker made in years remote,
>   It makes its nest. When peeping idlers stroll
> In anxious plundering moods, they by and by
>   The wryneck's curious eggs, as white as snow,
> While squinting in the hollow tree, espy.
> The sitting bird looks up with jetty eye,
>   And waves her head in terror to and fro,
> Speckled and veined with various shades of brown;
> And then a hissing noise assails the clown.
>   Quickly, with hasty terror in his breast,
> From the tree's knotty trunk he sluthers* down,
>   And thinks the strange bird guards a serpent's nest.[105]

As in 'Home Pictures in May' where there is an astute reversal in the final couplet, so here the 'summer bird' of line one becomes in the last line the 'strange bird' that 'guards a serpent's nest'. Clare prepares himself for the end at the beginning. So, although the apparently innocuous bird is chirping its 'oft-repeated note', it makes its nest where the woodpecker once built. The phrase 'in years remote' lends an odd complexion to these lines, colouring the 'repeated note' and removing it to the world of a shadowy past. Clare's adroit use of rhyme comes out here : 'remote' haunts what has gone before, and consequently this very particular action of making her nest, domestic as it is, is effectively placed in a larger temporal context. The 'peeping idlers' who come to disturb the timeless ritual are made more insidious by the duplicity of approach; their unease is forcibly expressed as they stroll in 'anxious plundering

* Slides.

moods' but it is really only explained retrospectively in terms of the archetypal significance of the image. They are in fact aware of the sacrilege of their behaviour. This gives weight to 'anxious' as well as explaining the involved syntax that follows. In part it is a matter of visual and grammatical progression : the 'by and by' is carefully placed at the end of the line, but we have to wait two lines for the verb to appear. In between come the eggs 'as white as snow'; on this phrase is hinged the disparity between man and bird, between the present and the past, the actual and the ideal. Man can just squint in the hollow tree. By his placing of words Clare seems to want to avoid contaminating the bird's purity and her eggs by having the marauders gaze on them; he wants if possible to keep them separate. But man and bird are brought at last and inevitably face to face; we move from white to black as she looks up and waves her head in terror. The two worlds gaze at each other at this point of confrontation. The bird's terror, reasonable and positive, is contrasted with that of the clown, who slides down the trunk, thinking the bird 'guards a serpent's nest'. This emphasises the difference between the two, for the intruder has not gleaned anything from his prying, and the bird with her 'curious eggs' is stranger than ever. Clare laughs at his interpretation of the bird's angry hissing. But at the same time we are brought back to the prevailing tone of an archetypal image. What the boy foolishly credits the bird with harks back to the opening lines, with their flavour of remoteness and antiquity, and he places his own temerity and the bird's reaction in a wider context. This poem is an interesting example of a symbolic approach to action in itself extraordinarily simple. It is almost summed up in the last two lines, as the dialect word 'sluthers' places it on one level, while the snake image places it on another.[106]

The manner in which Clare has used the sonnet form in this poem shows how he strives to knit the sonnet together. He continues this process in several other sonnets, notably 'Home Pictures in May', which with its carefully unusual rhyme-scheme, aa bb cdcd ee fgfg, and its controlled use of the run-on line, is amongst Clare's boldest attempts to establish his descriptive technique.[107]

> The sunshine bathes in clouds of many hues
> And mornings feet are gemmed with early dews[108]

The sense of wantonness is continued throughout this part of the poem:

> Warm Daffodils about the garden beds
> Peep thro their pale slim leaves their golden heads
> Sweet earthly suns of spring[109]

The daffodils, thrusting themselves forward, are the counterparts of the sun, brought down to earth. Thus in the second couplet, the antithesis of the first begins to resolve itself. With the pun on 'son'/'sun' the gosling broods are introduced, who 'In coats of sunny green about the road/Waddle in ecstasy'. This incongruity, a favourite of Clare's, is neatly placed across the line-break, as the decorum epitomised in the solemnity of ritual of the first two lines is discarded and replaced by the extravagance of the farmyard. Even the old hen has 'rich moods', with her chicks

> Oft scuttling neath her wings to see the kite
> Hang wavering oer them in the springs blue light[110]

Again the placing of words is important, as the kite is left to hang into the next line. A note of menace creeps in, as we are made aware of nature's cruelty, and we are thrown back at the sky: the shifting perspective becomes part of the poem's meaning. Similarly with the innocence of the sparrow and robin:

> The sparrows round the new nests chirp with glee
> And sweet the Robin springs young luxury shares
> Tuteling* its song in feathery gooseberry tree
> While watching worms the gardeners spade unbares

This final couplet reveals the robin's glee to be partly malice, and the spring's luxury has a darker side, already hinted at in the hovering kite. The verb 'unbares' throws light on the prevailing wantonness of the poem, in more than an incidental way, providing an unpleasant contrast to the opening apparently careless antithesis. There the sun looked down on the

* Tootling.

earth, but here the robin looks hungrily down on the worm, just as the chicks had hidden in terror from the kite. Man is an actor in this ambiguous drama, symbolised by the bland cruelty of the gardener's spade.

Clare was astute enough to realise that this kind of drama was a vein he could mine with increasing confidence, as his individuality began to assert itself. As John Barrell has shown in great detail, this drama, this individuality, depends to a large extent on Clare's development of a syntax that enacts his sense of the uniqueness of what he sees and experiences. Whereas in his early poems there is no real sense – or at least no sustained sense – of the objects or events contained in the poem being there because they have to be, as part of the scene in front of his eyes (and the result is a curious mixture of traditional postures and first-hand observations), in these sonnets of the 1820s Clare is beginning to write about things that could not possibly be happening elsewhere than in the Helpstone he knows. This is what makes him so different from Thomson and Cowper. The paradox is that Thomson was one of the poets Clare most admired, and it is small wonder that in so much of his early verse Clare finds himself caught between the claims of that tradition, and the claims of his own strong sense of being part of Helpstone. By the time *The Shepherd's Calendar* was published in 1827 he had more or less solved the problem.

3

The Shepherd's Calendar

I

After the publication of his first two collections of poems, Clare's horizons were widened. There was the chance to consider and reflect on what he had so far achieved, and what direction his poetry might take. Several reviewers had commented on the apparent sameness of all his work, the lack of thinking in the poetry, the tendency to stop at observation. Much of the criticism was justified, and Taylor and Hessey were aware that something rather different had to be tried if Clare wasn't going to fade completely from the public eye. There were certainly positive achievements to point to, both in *Poems Descriptive of Rural Life and Scenery*, and in *The Village Minstrel*. In his use of the sonnet form, for example, Clare had shown that there was another way of responding to the essentially dramatic qualities of nature than that suggested by the tradition stemming from Thomson: but he could hardly write nothing but sonnets. In the long poem 'The Village Minstrel' that headed the 1821 collection Clare had, with some success, been able to place his response to the natural world in a wider context which embraced the whole village community. It was, in its own way, an audacious poem, in its implicit rejection of the ethos behind Beattie's *Minstrel*:[1] the reviewers had, some of them, asked for a long poem, but they would not have expected this panoramic view of country life, the combination of humour and compassion, love of seclusion and rage at the evils of enclosure. In writing this poem, Clare came to realise where his talents really lay, what his important preoccupations were: the poem has a substance and a firmness of purpose that hint at the strengths of his next long poem, *The Shepherd's Calendar*.

By distancing himself – the hero, Lubin, is an observed figure
and yet a reflection of the poet – Clare achieves a fullness of
response that is seldom mawkish. There is an infectious zest
about much of the writing, as opposed to the introspective con-
tortions of many of the early poems; and, at the same time, a
quiet reflective quality that seems to rub off from Lubin's own
character :

When summer came, how eager has he sped
Where silence reign'd, and the old crowned tree
Bent with its sheltering ivy o'er his head;
And summer-breezes, breathing placidly,
Encroach'd upon the stockdove's privacy,
Parting the leaves that screen'd her russet breast :
'Peace!' would he whisper, 'dread no thief in me',
And never rose to rob her careless rest;
Compassion's softness reign'd, and warm'd his gentle breast.

And he would trace the stagnant pond or lake,
Where flags sprang up or water-lilies smil'd,
And wipe the boughs aside of bush and brake,
And creep the woods with sweetest scenes beguil'd,
Tracking some channel in its journeys wild,
Where dripping blue-bells on the bank did weep :
Oh, what a lovely scene to nature's child,
Through roots and o'er dead leaves to see it creep,
Watching on some moss'd stump in contemplation deep.[2]

Against this might be set the insistence on the loss of pre-
enclosure innocence :

O greens, and fields, and trees, farewell! farewell!
His heart-wrung pains, his unavailing woes
No words can utter, and no tongue can tell,
When ploughs destroy'd the green, when groves of
    willows fell.

There once were springs, when daisies' silver studs
Like sheets of snow on every pasture spread;
There once were summers when the crow-flower buds
Like golden sunbeams brightest lustre shed;
And trees grew once that shelter'd Lubin's head;

> There once were brooks sweet whimpering down
>   the vale:
> The brook's no more – kingcup and daisy fled;
> Their last fall'n tree the naked moors bewail,
> And scarce a bush is left to tell the mournful tale.[3]

A few of Clare's earlier poems had touched on the theme of communal loss, but rarely with much success: however strong the passion, it seldom survived the translation into verse. The development in 'The Village Minstrel' towards a view of society outside himself is important in its anticipation of *The Shepherd's Calendar*. No longer is it simply a matter of a few lines that might irritate wealthy patrons: a complete poem is devoted to his own part of the world, its joys and sorrows. Out of his compassion the lament for enclosure springs naturally and with conviction.

In addition, Clare had demonstrated convincingly his lyrical tendencies, in a number of songs and ballads. Many of these are unpretentious, pleasing in their refusal to strain for effects:

> Winter's gone, the summer breezes
>   Breathe the shepherd's joys again,
> Village scene no longer pleases,
>   Pleasures meet upon the plain;
> Snows are fled that hung the bowers,
>   Buds to blossoms softly steal,
> Winter's rudeness melts in flowers:
>   Charmer, leave thy spinning wheel,
>   And tend the sheep with me.
>
> Careless here shall pleasures lull thee,
>   From domestic troubles free;
> Rushes for thy couch I'll pull thee,
>   In the shade thy seat shall be;
> All the flower-buds will I get
>   Spring's first sunbeams do unseal,
> Primrose, cowslip, violet;
>   Charmer, leave thy spinning wheel,
>   And tend the sheep with me.[4]

Such conventional invitations are often made more immediate by quick indications of a social context:

Mary, leave thy lowly cot
    When thy thickest jobs are done;
When thy friends will miss thee not,
    Mary, to the pastures run.
Where we met the other night
    'Neath the bush upon the plain,
Be it dark or be it light,
    Ye may guess we'll meet again.

Should ye go or should ye not,
    Never shilly-shally, dear.
Leave your work and leave your cot,
    Nothing need ye doubt or fear :
Fools may tell ye lies in spite,
    Calling me a roving swain;
Think what passed the other night –
    I'll be bound ye'll meet again.[5]

Clare can, in a short song, suggest the perturbations of love : the following is interesting for its carefully spaced use of telling imagery, the care in sharp contrast to Nelly's carelessness :

One gloomy eve I roam'd about
    'Neath Oxey's hazel bowers,
While timid hares were daring out,
    To crop the dewy flowers;
And soothing was the scene to me,
    Right placid was my soul,
My breast was calm as summer's sea
    When waves forget to roll.

But short was even's placid smile,
    My startled soul to charm,
When Nelly lightly skipt the stile,
    With milk-pail on her arm :
One careless look on me she flung,
    As bright as parting day;
And like a hawk from covert sprung,
    It pounc'd my peace away.[6]

Such songs look ahead to the full flowering of Clare's lyricism in the asylum. Other developments suggest how much *The*

Shepherd's Calendar represents the fulfilment of early promise.
In his first volume, he had offended many with his tales of
country life – 'Dolly's Mistake', for example, with its rough,
country humour, its rollicking disregard for literary decorum :

> Ere the sun o'er the hills, round and red, 'gan a-peeping,
>   To beckon the chaps to their ploughs,
> Too thinking and restless all night to be sleeping,
>   I brush'd off to milking my cows;
> To get my jobs forward, and eager preparing
>   To be off in time to the wake,
> When yielding so freely a kiss for a fairing,
>   I made a most shocking mistake.
>
> Young Ralph met me early, and off we were steering,
>   I cuddled me close to his side;
> The neighbours, while passing, my fondness kept jeering,
>   'Young Ralph's timely suited!' they cried.
> But he bid me mind not their evil pretensions,
>   'Fools mun',* says he, 'talk for talk's sake';
> And, kissing me, 'Doll, if you've any 'prehensions,
>   'Let me tell you, my wench, you mistake!'[7]

The mistake is finally made. The final two stanzas catch with
economy the inevitable family tribulations, the wavering of the
culprit when marriage is mentioned, the constant nagging of
the mother :

> In vain do I beg him to wed and have done wi't,
>   So fair as he promis'd we should;
> We cou'dn't do worse than as how we've begun wi't,
>   Let matters turn out as they would :
> But he's always a-talking 'bout wedding expenses,
>   And the wages he's gotten to take;
> Too plain can I see through his evil pretences,
>   Too late I find out the mistake.
>
> Oh, what mun I do with my mother reprovin',
>   Since she will do nothing but chide?
> For when old transgressors have been in the oven,
>   They know where the young ones may hide.

---

* Must.

In vain I seek pity with plaints and despairings,
    Always ding'd on the nose with the wake:
Young maidens! be cautious who give you your fairings;
    You see what attends a mistake.

A poem like this shows how readily and with what panache
Clare can throw off his awkward 'literary' pose. The manuscript notebooks are full of such narrative pieces, not all of
them equally successful, but several evincing the same lightness
of touch, the same awareness of characters in particular situations. (We can understand Clare's determination to write a
novel.)[8] This capacity for narrative comes out also in much
more stylised poems, in which Clare's affinities with the
eighteenth century emerge very strongly and convincingly. In
'Rural Evening', for example, the vignette with which the poem
closes looks ahead to his later achievements in the tales
intended for *The Shepherd's Calendar*:

> Now at the parish cottage wall'd with dirt,
> Where all the cumber-grounds* of life resort,
> From the low door that bows two props between,
> Some feeble tottering dame surveys the scene;
> By them reminded of the long-lost day
> When she herself was young, and went to play;
> And, turning to the painful scenes again,
> The mournful changes she has met since then,
> Her aching heart, the contrast moves so keen,
> E'en sighs a wish that life had never been.
> Still vainly sinning, while she strives to pray,
> Half-smother'd discontent pursues its way
> In whispering Providence, how blest she'd been,
> In Life's last troubles she'd escap'd unseen;
> If, ere want sneak'd for grudg'd support from pride,
> She had but shar'd of childhood's joys, and died.
> And as to talk some passing neighbours stand,
> And shove their box within her tottering hand,
> She turns from echoes of her former years,
> And nips the portion of her snuff with tears.[9]

We could not mistake this for Crabbe, nor for any eighteenth-

* Dregs.

century writer; but we can see how much Clare owes to that tradition. When he came to write his later narrative tales, he was in a position to combine the rural directness of 'Dolly's Mistake' with the more controlled movement of the couplet as seen in this passage.

In his first two collections of poetry, then, Clare had not only been exploring for himself ways of writing about the country-side : he had also demonstrated that he was able to master a number of different forms and styles. He was not narrowly digging in one small plot. Nonetheless, he needed time to con-solidate his position, to show that he could advance beyond the style of *The Village Minstrel*. He did not allow the waning public interest to keep him from this task.

Spurred on by various projects, Clare continued to write furiously, and plans were soon afoot for a new volume. This was an extremely active period of his life, during which most of his prose was written, and much of his best poetry, even though not all of it by any means was published. A large amount was left simmering, for inclusion, after revision and correction, in the later volume, *The Rural Muse*. The activity of these years is almost entirely literary, in the sense that every-thing was directed towards writing. There were visits to London, which Clare recorded in vivid detail in his *Auto-biography*; these visits no doubt encouraged his writing habits, for he came across most of the important literary figures of the day at Taylor's dinners, among them Lamb, Hazlitt, Coleridge and De Quincey.[10] Apart from his writing, the most important aspect of these years is the increasing illness and melancholy from which Clare suffered. The 'blue devils' attacked him with greater frequency as the years wore on : he became acutely anxious about himself, thought he was on the verge of death, and even contemplated suicide.[11] Yet, in spite of disclaimers to the contrary, these recurrent bouts of severe depression, which affected him physically as well as mentally, did not prevent him from writing, except for brief spells. All in all, though this was an extremely fruitful period, poetically, his poetry must always be seen in the context of his illness. His brooding morbid melancholy explains certain aspects of his poetry, certain attitudes to which he repeatedly returns. It also makes the volume that finally emerged a remarkable achievement: in what ways will become clear as we chart the growth of *The Shepherd's Calendar*.

The Village Minstrel (1821) contained a selection of Clare's poems based on village life. The original scheme of *Ways in a Village* (or *Week in a Village*) had been put aside for a variety of reasons. But neither Clare nor his publishers forgot the purpose behind such a scheme. Taylor had outlined his plan to Clare at the beginning of 1820:

> My advice then was, that you should divide the Week's Employments into the 7 Days, selecting such for each as might more particularly apply to that Day, which is the Case with some of the Occupations; – that the remaining which might be pursued in any Day should be allotted so as to fill up the Time; – that the Sports, & Amusements should in like manner be apportioned out into the 7 Days; – and that one little appropriate Story should be involved in each Day's Description. – A different Metre might sometimes be introduced; for instance in the Tale, if it were supposed to be related by one of the Characters of the Piece; or otherwise the various Days might be marked by a varied Measure, but this would be as you thought best & found most agreeable to you. –[12]

No sooner was 'The Village Minstrel' out of his hands than Clare wrote to Taylor on 17 February 1821, 'next winter I mean to start a long poem as some sort of Continuation of the Peasant Boy if it succeeds'.[13]

Clare himself sensed the increasing power of his poetry: writing to Taylor about the epithet 'pretty' attached to his first book by a Dr Noehden, an assistant at the British Museum whom Clare met in April 1821, he acknowledged the book's weaknesses:

> this first book is our plaything I consider it nothing more now – the muse is there in the bud in the next she will be in the blossom If I mistake not – & these will alter the note a little – a smile shoud dimple to say them pretty – but admiration shall redden the cheek with pronouncing they are good – & if not in the next – if we are left as I hope we

> shall to wind up the story : in the last admiration shall let
> fall her muscles into reverence ... the blossoms shall give
> way to the crimson berries which shall shine in every leaf
> as bright & as lasting as the vanity of a crackd-braind
> aspiring hopfull thankless son of the muses coud ever wish
> for —[14]

In reading this over Clare thought it 'very foolish stuff' but
nonetheless believed the sentiments behind the flowery language which he allowed himself on such occasions. He was
certainly right about the improvement of *The Village
Minstrel* over *Poems Descriptive*, and the poems he wrote after
the second collection also look forward rather than back-
wards.

The variety of poetic activity of these years calls for some
comment. At the height of his achievement comes the *Calendar*
itself. But other aspects are almost as valuable. The experimen-
tation with the sonnet form is extremely important, as I have
tried to show; it complements the achievement of the *Calendar*.
In other directions too Clare branches out : his underlying
melancholy finds an outlet in poems on life, death, and
eternity;[15] he begins to imitate other poets, especially the
Elizabethans;[16] he collects genuine ballads, which he then uses
for his own purposes;[17] he writes love songs of a much more
sustained power and musicality than ever before; he writes
poems like 'The Dream' and 'The Nightmare' which have their
relevance to his own emotional predicament in these years,
and also look ahead to the visionary poems of the 1830s and
1840s.[18] All these activities overlap. The descriptive discipline
acquired in the sonnets is applied to the *Calendar*; the sense of
loss and melancholy, nourished in the songs and ballads, contributes to the emotional force of the *Calendar*; the social
concern of the *Calendar* is reflected in the poems of nostalgia.
As he experiments with Elizabethan rhythms and cadences,
as he works among the deep simplicities of the traditional
ballad, his own verse becomes more taut, more malleable
to his needs. By the time the *Calendar* is published he
is moving towards a language of rich sonority, as exemplified
in 'Autumn' (printed in *The Rural Muse*), which uses the metre
of Collins's 'Ode to Evening'.[19] All this variety is bound to have

its effect on the poem that occupied his thoughts on and off throughout this period.

Clare was telling Taylor on 6 September 1821 that he was scribbling 'agen vehemently'. Apart from some village tales, he was busy with 'Wanderings in June', a piece later included in *The Shepherd's Calendar*.[20] But Clare was unhappy about the sort of tale he might write, so Taylor advised him:

> I cannot recollect any Story of Interest connected with my early Days, except such as appeared in Books, or Ballads, and were the common Property of all the County; but if I can learn or think of any Tale that seems likely to suit you I will communicate it. The worst of it is most of Such Tales turn upon Suicide after Seduction, and so they resemble your Cross Roads.[21]

But Taylor's own suggestions of 'The Gentle Shepherd – A Dramatic Piece', as the necessary long poem for the new volume, augurs ill.[22]

During these months, Clare sent up pieces for the *London Magazine*; some were accepted, but several turned down, often because of length.[23] But by February or March 1822 he was contemplating a long poem with considerable optimism: 'if my next attempt is not a masterpiece in its way its failing shall not be indifference or neglect.'[24] Taylor and Hessey both approved of a poem based on a month by month account of the year;[25] but although beginning with 'A May Mornings Walk' as a specimen, Clare felt 'Farewell to the Muses' would be a more appropriate title.[26] In his melancholy, he turned back to his childhood, and a possible continuation of 'The Village Minstrel'.[27] But he continued to mull over the idea of a long poem, and told H. F. Cary, the translator of Dante, that he was working on a new volume entitled 'Summer Walks'.[28] Other things, however, occupied him: on 4 January 1823 he sent Hessey a specimen of *The Parish*, which he had just finished.[29]

The Parish is an interesting poem, ambitious and lengthy; it is satirical, consisting as Clare says, 'of a string of characters farmers of the New & Old School a village politician & Steward a Justice of the peace &c &c ...'[30] It is related stylistically, and by its content, to some of the Village Tales that he had written or was soon to write. Clare's voice of social protest is heard most strongly here. Some account of the poem is necessary, if we are to see the connection between it and the *Calendar*. It has its merits, as even Mrs Emmerson (who declares on 3 February 1823, 'I almost hate the name of Satire ...')[31] allows of *The Parish* : it is 'Powerfully written & you have contrived to admirably blend feeling with severity'.[32] Clare had always preferred to write about real people in real situations; but on 6 January 1821 he had said to Taylor that he must 'avoid satire as much as possible'.[33] It is true that satire is not really his *forte* : apart from imitations of Burns and Crabbe and occasional early poems, such as 'Lubin Clout's Satirical Soliloquy on the Times', 'On the Death of a Quack', his lines on the Reverend Mr Twopenny, or 'The Bards & Their Doxeys', in which he pokes fun at the London literary circle,[34] there is little that is satirical about Clare, before *The Parish*, or after, with the exception of *Don Juan*. But here his grounding in Pope and Dryden has some effect. Apparently a rambling work, without any real unity, *The Parish* is sustained by Clare's driving sense of outrage.

It is the first really long poem that he wrote. There had, in earlier days, been some lengthy narrative poems, but none (not even his favourite 'Death of Dobbin')[35] had been informed by such rage and hatred. Although the poem was never published in his lifetime (Taylor gave it little consideration, but Clare tried later to get it printed locally),[36] Clare himself held it in high regard. He told Taylor that it was 'the best thing in my own mind that I have ever written & I mean to take some pains in altering & making it better still if I can ...'[37] It is true that he tended to make extravagant claims for some of his own poems, but there was usually some deep-seated reason for these excesses of enthusiasm.

I have already mentioned the importance of the Enclosure Act, as applied to Helpstone in 1809, in so far as it furthered Clare's sense of alienation. Several of the poems I have discussed referred, directly or obliquely, to enclosure as the crucial event which cut Clare off from the scenes of his childhood : Helpstone was never the same again. As John Barrell has demonstrated with subtlety, Clare's attitude tended to be equivocal, in that when he mourned the past it was not always in terms of the pre-enclosure Helpstone.[38] Nonetheless the en-

closure clearly had a profound effect on him, and it in fact
provided him with another tradition which he could fall back
on : he was not the first to bewail enclosure. (It was not, after
all, a new phenomenon.) In 1583 Stubbes had expostulated at
the power which enclosure gave to the rich, at the expense of
the poor; and this was a fairly frequent complaint between then
and the eighteenth century, when enclosure was sanctioned by
the crown. Part of the reason for complaint was the unique
position and importance of the commons in village life, for it
was these that were swallowed up in the new legislation.
Thomas Bewick records the role they played in village life :

> On this common, – the poor man's heritage for ages past,
> where he kept a few sheep, or a Kyloe cow, perhaps a flock
> of geese, and mostly a stock of bee-hives, – it was with
> infinite pleasure that I long beheld the beautiful wild scenery
> which was there exhibited, and it is with the opposite feel-
> ings of regret that I now find all swept away.[39]

In the zeal for economic progress (there is no doubt that the
commons system could be wasteful), motives of self-interest
could be concealed behind the appeals to common sense. Cobbett raged against the large landowners, but somebody like
William Marshall really believed that the open field system was
primitive and barbaric, and an impediment to progress.[40] The
view was expressed that the peasants were getting out of hand,
and needed to be kept in check. Enclosure was the solution.
Such reasoning obviously found little favour with the poor,
who faced an increase in rent with little to show for it except
increased hardship. Hostility to enclosure led to disturbances
that required suppression by the troops, a foretaste of the more
violent riots of the 1830s.

The picture may not be as simple as the Hammonds, in their
classic *The Village Labourer*, suggest; but whatever the economic justification for enclosure (it varied from one agricultural
area to another), there can be little doubt about its generally
damaging effect on the poor, who faced a loss in common
grazing and firewood and often an increase in rent. The Board
of Agriculture's reports are sufficiently specific : one report in
particular, in 1816, is a tale of perpetual woe.[41] 'Extreme

distress', 'absolute ruin', 'never so wretched a state' – these are common phrases in a report which announces that of 273 letters on the state of the labouring poor, 101 stress particularly misery and hardship.

This distress of course was the result of many things. David Davies, analysing the problem in 1795, showed that it was high prices as much as anything that ruined the poor : all peasants agreed that it was this that was the cause of their undoubted distress, and he produced a list of accounts collected in 1787 to prove his point.[42] He noted that the enlargement of farms, with the parallel deprivation for the peasants, had increased the number of the dependent poor. George Dyer had made similar observations, and drew similar conclusions, in *The Complaints of the Poor People of England* : 'since inclosures have prevailed, the great farmers and land-holders swallow up the less and thence the small farmer becomes a labourer; and hence the deserted village.'[43] (The sympathisers always had Goldsmith's poem as a text.) High prices put the 'necessaries of life' out of the grasp of the poor, who were inevitably exploited by the rich. The price of labour had not risen at the same rate as the price of food. Dyer, Eden, and Davies were humanitarians, rather than economists, openly advocating an amelioration of the inarticulate poor's lot.[44] The irony was that enclosure had originated in the necessity to increase productivity, especially during the Napoleonic Wars; but the so-called improvement, as measured in capitalist terms, led to the gradual destruction of the old rural community.

It is in these terms, simply and passionately, that Clare sees the overthrow of the social order of the past, and, with it, the loss of the old honesty and integrity, as wealth became the yard-stick for success. The post-1815 agricultural slump was an indisputable fact : Cobbett recorded the effects in his *Rural Rides*.[45] The grim facts of enclosure are of importance for an understanding of the poem, and of Clare's reasons for rating it so highly : his sense of the community comes out here in a unique way. If *The Shepherd's Calendar* seems to be the more characteristic culmination of Clare's early years, *The Parish* is its complement; not only because of its comparable length, but because of its comparable seriousness and gravity. In these two poems Clare becomes the spokesman for his community : his private anguish is absorbed into the larger more reverberant despair of his fellow countrymen.

As with Crabbe's earlier poems, such as *The Parish Register*, or *The Borough* (obviously of interest in this connection, since Clare clearly learnt something from Crabbe, although despising his comfortable vantage point),[16] what unity there is, is of a loose sort, imposed rather by the moral vigour of the poet, than by any aesthetic demands. For this reason the effect must be seen as cumulative. If Clare does not approach the complexities of Crabbe's best poems, this is partly because his aims are simpler. His manuscript note on the poem is revealing:

> This poem was begun and finished under the pressure of heavy distress, with embittered feelings under a state of anxiety and oppression almost amounting to slavery, when the prosperity of one class was founded on the adversity and distress of the other. The haughty demand by the master to his labourer was 'Work for the little I choose to allow you and go to the parish for the rest – or starve'. To decline working under such 'advantages' was next to offending a magistrate, and no opportunity was lost in marking the insult by some unqualified oppression.[47]

The views expressed in *The Parish* are straightforward, readily understandable, and impassioned. But there is not the hysteria that occurs in the later satire, *Don Juan*. Clare knows what his targets are, and attacks mercilessly. He speaks as one of the poor, and consequently attacks their exploitation by the wealthy; in abhorring the hypocrisy of the present day and age, he looks back nostalgically to the past, to the Eden before enclosure. He has, then, various moral standards to uphold, and the Parish is always seen in the light of these. There are few subtleties: but to Clare this is no subtle matter. Hypocrisy, the triumph of wrong and evil, has to be shown for what it is. Clare uses a hammer, rather than a rapier. In a sense he is too consciously the angered and indignant poet, aiming at satire, but achieving something less. The opening lines, for example, although reminiscent of Crabbe's avowal in *The Village*, lack his decorum:

The Parish hind oppressions humble slave

Whose only hopes of freedom is the grave
The cant miscalled religion in the saint
And Justice mockd while listening wants complaint
The parish laws and parish queens and kings
Prides lowest classes of pretending things
The meanest dregs of tyrany and crime
I fearless sing let truth attend the ryhme
Tho nowadays truth grows a vile offence
And courage tells it at his own expence
If he but utter what himself has seen
He deals in satire and he wounds too keen

We can, however, admire the courage of this stance: from
it springs the directness of diction and image that is the poem's
hallmark.

Like Crabbe, Clare uses common expressions, turns of phrase,
homespun aphorisms, to reinforce his moral standpoint. This
can often be extremely effective, as in his exposure of Dandy
Flint.

Next on the parish list in paltry fame
Shines Dandy Flint Esqr whose dirty name
Has grown into a proverb for bad deeds
And he who reads it all thats filthy reads ...

A sot who spouts short morals o'er his gin
And when most drunk rails most against the sin
A dirty hog that on the puddles brink
Stirs up the mud and quarrels with the stink ...

His mask is but of lawn and every space
Lets in new light to show cants crimping* face
He apes the lamb and is a wolf in grain
And guilty darkness dares the light in vain ...
(lines 225–44)

Farmer Cheetum comes in for similar treatment: Clare's scorn
is unbridled, but he displays a wry humour in the last two
lines:

These show his kindness in their varied ways
And gild his rotting name with dirty praise

* Wrinkled.

Like as when brooks are dry the village sinks
Boast their full dingy tide that flows and stinks
That seems to boast when other streams are dry
'Neath summer suns how brave a dyke am I'
(lines 309–14)

The smug self-satisfaction of Cheetum, and his moral turpitude, are captured here in all their dirty squalor.

Clare is certainly explicit about the squalor of his material. Nothing is allowed to escape his 'plain homespun verse'. For someone like Headlong Rackett he shows no mercy: this profligate youth, who 'deals openly in sin', is characterised in all his debauchery. Common sense is enough to see through him. His hypocrisy is clear in everything he does: hunting and womanising are different aspects of the same sport. He even despises poachers, not able to see that he and they are on a par:

With this one difference darkness brings their prey
And he more brazen murders his by day   (lines 219–20)

Clare's awareness of moral depravity may be over-sensitive: he may be giving a grotesque parody of village life as it really was: it is hardly to be wondered at that he never found a publisher for his poem. It was all very well to conclude with the proverb, 'Where the cap fits theyll wear it as their own' or to appeal to the common sense that told him he was right to censure. The anger and the hatred, the contempt and disdain, were not concealed. Even if Clare does overstate his case, this does not diminish the impact of the poem. But it is odd to reflect that in 1831 Clare was to rise to the defence of the wealthy landowners, when several newspapers suggested he had been badly treated. For no one was as outspoken then as was Clare in *The Parish*.

The interest of *The Parish* is twofold. Historically it is of importance, as a *cri de coeur* from one of the underprivileged poor. Whether it is overstated is for the historian to decide. From the literary point of view, it is a not inconsiderable achievement for Clare. Mrs Emmerson was right to talk of the combination of passion and severity: the verse seldom loses its sparkle and vitality. Clare knows his targets, and drives home the attack with pungency. The poem makes talk of

Clare's unconcern for the peasant, and of his merely sentimental interest in the past, seem particularly inappropriate.

Whilst Hessey remained silent, Clare was still turning to the continuation of 'The Village Minstrel',[48] but also to a poem 'On Spring of a Serious Length'.[49] In July he was talking to Taylor about the dedication to the 'visionary Vol. which I wish to publish next winter'.[50] Taylor and Hessey conferred, and in August Taylor suggested 'The Shepherd's Calendar', a month by month account with a narrative poem for each section. Other poems could also be included.[51] Clare was jubilant,[52] but doubtful about the merits of the manuscripts which Taylor had not yet seen. What worried him was the narrative tales: 'I could soon daub pictures anew for the descriptions.'[53] By October Hessey had looked through many of the manuscripts (while Mrs Emmerson tried to bolster Clare's sagging morale, and advised him to leave the new poem for the time being).[54] Hessey's reservations are interesting :

> my knowledge of the author, & my former familiarity with such scenes & objects give a charm to the descriptions which is not felt by all (by the way I should relish them much more if you would bestow a little more pains on the writing, the mechanical operation of writing, I mean). The descriptions however are too general to excite much Interest – their wants a human interest – a Story or a more particular delineation of character, and this might easily be given from the experience you must have had of life as well as from your own power of Invention & Combination. The Shepherds Calendar should consist of delineations of the face of Nature, the operations of the husbandman, the amusements, festivals, superstitions, customs &c of the Country, and little stories introduced to illustrate these more accurately and to fix an Interest on them.[55]

He proceeded to give a sketch of the plan he had in mind. It is worth giving this in full, in view of the course the poem subsequently took.

> *One*		January – New Year's Day – Winter
> 			Sports – Skating &c

Memory of Love	February – Valentine's Day – a good subject for a Love Story
	March – First Approach of Spring
Three	April – The Poem of Spring already written, with the addition of some little Story
	May – The Day Dream
Jockey & Jenny	June – Haymaking – an abundant theme for Stories
Four	July – Sheep Shearing – the same
Five	August – Harvest beginning/Last of Summer
Six	September – Harvest Home – A Capital Subject – describe a real Scene
Seven	October – the last of Autumn – Field Sports – Story
Eight	November – Dismal feelings on the Approach of Winter – Pathetic Story
Nine	December – Frost, Snow, Christmas Gambols, Winter Sports – Miseries of the very poor – Story.

The annotations in the margin are Clare's tentative gropings, as he tries to accommodate himself to this scheme; as Hessey says,

These are merely hints – the greater Variety the better, and various metres to suit the tone of the several pieces ... the Day Dream is a good Specimen of what the thing might be ... the Statutes won't do – it is too coarse – you may be faithful in your pictures but you must not be too close in the resemblance of the coarseness of the clowns.

Further encouragement and hints were contained in Hessey's letter of 1 November. He suggested that Clare drew upon the months that remained as they actually occurred, 'and as for episodes & adventures & reflections they are "as plenty as blackberries"'. He hoped that Clare's work would be able to stand comparison with the several good works that were due to appear that season.[56] At this stage, then, there is no doubt that Hessey was optimistically expecting the *Calendar* to be ready to be published before too long. Hessey's optimism was ill-founded: Mrs Emmerson continued to dissuade Clare, in his disturbed state, from the project,[57] while Hessey encouraged, applauded, and advised: 'The distresses of some classes of the poor in Winter may be finely & pathetically delineated – what is more painful than abject poverty & disease in times of general Merriment such as Christmas –.'[58] Clare hardly needed to be reminded of this.

The next three years saw a continuing wrangle between Clare and his publishers. His hopes of early publication were for ever being dashed, and he was not greatly cheered by the news that Harry Stoe van Dyk, a minor versifier he had met in 1824, was to be the new editor. Taylor slowly went over the manuscripts, irritated by the illegibility (his transcribers were making so many mistakes that he was having to copy them himself), and not at all sure that the volume was going to be any good. Hessey sounded gloomy towards the end of 1824:

I am sorry to say they are by no means fit for the public eye at present, and they will require much more alteration than we or anyone but yourself can give to make them so. In each of the Poems now sent there are many beauties, but they have evidently been written in too much haste and without the fear of the Public before your eyes. The great fault of the whole of them is that they abound too much in mere description & are deficient in Sentiment and Feeling and human Interest. You have already described in admirable colouring the Morning & the Noon & the Evening, & the Summer & the Winter, & the Sheep & Cattle & Poultry & Pigs & Milking Maids & Foddering Boys – but the world will now expect something more than these – let them come in incidentally – let them occupy their places in the picture, but they must be subordinate to higher objects ... You may still be a descriptive poet if you please, but, when you des-cribe Nature to those who see but little of her or to those who live daily with her, shew her as she appears to the Poet & the Man of Mind. Your colouring and your Sketching are excellent, but your Landscapes want Life and human Feelings.[59]

Recriminations were exchanged, Taylor continued to cut and prune, whilst Mrs Emmerson rightly despaired of publication 'this season'.[60] Taylor realised that there was going to be too much, and suggested leaving the Tales for another volume; but Clare thought more highly of the Tales than of the descriptive sections.[61] If Clare was becoming impatient, so too was Taylor:

> to make Good Poems out of some of them is a greater Difficulty than I ever had to engage with in your former works, – while in others it is a Complete Impossibility.[62]

He had nothing good to say of 'July', apart from a brief description of noon:

> The rest is a descriptive Catalogue in *rhyming Prose* of all the Occupations of the Village People, scarcely one Feature of which has not been better pictured before by you.

Clare was rather surprised (and hurt) by this verdict; he nonetheless obediently produced an alternative version, much to Taylor's satisfaction.

By the time the book emerged in 1827, Clare had almost lost interest in it: he was making new friendships, embarking on new projects. The *Calendar* had become a source of acrimony. Nobody took much notice when it was published. As Taylor wrote, 'The Season has been a very bad one for new Books, & I am afraid the time has passed away in which Poetry will answer ...'[63]

II

The Shepherd's Calendar is Clare's first mature poem. It states, as he had never been able to state before, his response to the world of nature, a response both intensely physical and spiritual, for this world was also that of his imagination. The dreams of nature, and the joys of nature, were not for Clare an escape into an idyllic Arcadia peopled by nymphs and shepherds:

they depended for their validity on the realities of the world he knew as a member of the village community.

Clare's version of self-revelation, in an age which expected it, was an unusual one. He stubbornly persisted in the writing of the nature poetry already derided when Wordsworth had produced *An Evening Walk*. Seemingly anachronistic, in more ways than one (the literary ethos implied by Clare's poem, and the way of life he described, had both, people hoped, been left behind), Clare's poem celebrated the natural world, the countryside he knew, and the men who worked there, with a delight in their existence as things and people to be observed. His picture was more objective than anybody else's, in that he saw the countryside as it was, and he saw it for itself, and not for any comfort or joy it had to offer him; at least, this joy and this comfort were now an integral part of the vision, part of the descriptive process. Thomson and Cowper had presented coherent visions of nature, but their concern was seldom with nature for what it was: what mattered ultimately were the lessons to be drawn from it. Even though Thomson was said to have written the first poem in which description was the sole justification, his description was really subsidiary and incidental, and the same was true of Cowper.

The tradition to which *The Shepherd's Calendar* belongs was an extensive one. Long before Thomson's *Seasons* there had been attempts at this type of long seasonal poem, in a variety of forms. Any comprehensive list of such poems would inevitably include Gavin Douglas's translation of the *Aeneid* (1553); Spenser's *Shepheardes Calendar* (1579); Giles Fletcher's *Piscatorie Eclogs* (1633); Pope's *Pastorals* (1709); Gay's *Shepherd's Week* (1714); Ramsay's *Gentle Shepherd* (1725). In the course of the eighteenth century, with Thomson as the inspirational model, either stylistically or in terms of detail, practically any poet was liable to produce occasional pieces on various parts of the year (or times of day), or longer poems devoted to the year as a whole.[64] But the number of poems devoted to a month by month picture of the year is relatively small. Poets were generally content to limit themselves to the four seasons; in this way their model could be followed fairly closely and easily, even though each poet did his best to add some touches of original observation to the inherited stock. A few poets attempted portraits of individual months, but not many tried the whole gamut.

Joseph Wise included a poem 'The May', in his *Miscellany of Poems* (1775). There is no need to dwell on this, with its pentameter couplets, stilted diction, and its complacence. Florimel and Colinet people this landscape:

> Now smiles the MAY: the solar fulgence glows:
> The mildest breeze in gentle silence flows.
> The banks all painted; spicy blossoms spring:
> The sprightly Birds desport on quivering wing.[65]

The peasants are given a paternal pat on the head:

> O happy peasants, delving in the soil!
> Whose wealth is vigor, whose amusement toil ...
>
> (lines 33–4)

In this rural paradise, tender bosoms 'Know only peace and innocence and love'. More interesting is Hugh Mulligan's 'The Months, six tinted sketches', in his *Poems chiefly on Slavery and Oppression* (1788). The months in question are February, April, June, August, October, and December. The elegiac abab quatrain, in octosyllabics, is used throughout; each month runs to ten such stanzas. The effect of the poem is very similar to that of the innumerable short elegiac pieces on such themes that were so common. In these poems, description is given a free rein, as in John Cunningham, but gentility often destroys the attempts at realism. The technique is familiar: brief outlines, quickly sketched, with occasional priggish assertions of religious obligations to the poor and needy. The quaint appeal of this type of verse does not diminish its essentially ephemeral nature. There is too cosy a feeling of conventional posture and diction:

> Tho' Sol now runs his winter's round,
> And dark and low'ring are thy days,
> Yet snowdrops deck the dusky ground,
> And flaming crocus' meet his rays;
>
> And presage of returning spring,
> Behold the virgin primrose blows;

> Faintly the thrush begins to sing;
>   Its green the weeping willow shews.
>
> With skilful hand the pruner now
>   Arranges well his garden's pride;
> The yeoman anxious tends the plough,
>   And steers the sullen clods divide.
>
> ('February', lines 1–12)

April may show us Ralph and Dobbin, but it also shows Damon and Phillis. In October, instruction is sought from the falling leaf, whilst December proves the moral, '. . . thro' each revolving year,/The hand that guides them is divine'.

The influence of Cowper's *Task* was strong, in particular on James Hurdis, who in 1788 published his long and rambling *Village Curate*. Hurdis greatly admired Cowper, and there was a mutually admiring correspondence between the two poets.[66] Hurdis's poetry is a similar mixture of the sublime and the bathetic, but he cannot sustain the tone convincingly. He opens his poem with a very mannered glance over his shoulder at Milton and Thomson, Hayley and Cowper:

> Of Man's first disobedience, and the fruit
> Of that forbidden tree, whose mortal taste
> Brought death into the world, and all our woe,
> With loss of Eden – of the glorious year,
> In all her changes fair; of gentle Spring,
> Veil'd in a show'r of roses and perfumes,
> Refulgent Summer in the pride of youth,
> Mild Autumn with her wain and wheaten sheaf,
> Or sullen Winter, loud, and tyrannous,
> Let nobler poets sing.

After praise of Hayley and Cowper, he announces his theme:

> Be mine the task to sing the man how blest,
> The Village Curate. (lines 19–20)

An unpromising theme, no doubt, and hence the apologetics and the literary allusions that crowd thick and fast in these opening lines. The anxiety to prepare the reader for an account of a humble village parson only serves to bring out the incongruity. Whereas Cowper can write in this light-hearted fashion, and not seem laboured, pale imitations soon wear thin. Carried away by his tricks of style, Hurdis produces a poetic language that when not openly risible (as some of it is), must surely be detrimental to his cause. In this passage on June, for example, the defiance may seem courageous, but there are more subtle ways of doing it:

> Mark we now
> A thousand great effects that spring from toil,
> Unsung before. The martial pea observe,
> In square battalion rang'd, line after line
> Successive; the gay bean, her hindmost ranks
> Stript of their blossoms; the thick-scatter'd bed
> Of soporific lettuce; the green hill
> Cover'd with cucumbers. All these and more,
> As carrots, parsnips, onions, cabbages,
> Potatoes, turnips, radishes, my Muse
> Disdains not.[67]

It would be unfair to Hurdis if we did not acknowledge his virtues. In the first place he is trying to carry *The Task* a stage further. He wants to write about things that are, in themselves, humble and often unnoticed, and yet which he believes to be important. This may lead him to unduly lengthy passages of moralising, but it also leads him to look at nature with a keener eye than most of his predecessors. He shows concern for the people in his curacy, the 'toiling swain', the 'gamesome schoolboys' who play 'social cricket', the 'weary smith', the mower, the 'sturdy farmer'. The joys of harvesting are depicted, the village fair, the comfort indoors on a winter evening. But these, we have to admit, are all fairly stock properties of the genre: Hurdis does not really extend himself beyond the accepted range of descriptive poetry. His poem is little more than a string of poetic sketches, hung together with long and rather tedious passages of moribund moralising. Awkwardness inevitably results, for nothing is presented for what it is in itself. A storm provides a chance 'To see th'Almighty electrician come'; the farmer views his crops, and sees the 'rich bounty Providence has strew'd'. The sight of the poor at work prompts this:

> I love to see
> How hardly some their frugal morsel earn;
> It gives my own a zest, and serves to damp
> The longing appetite of discontent.

The busy, tireless smith is upheld against the lazy clerk. The
romantic, idyllic vision of the countryside persists.

Another type of romanticism appears briefly : Hurdis looks
back at his childhood, and half grasps the fact that it is gone
forever. But he subdues this nostalgia quickly, and squeezes
out of the situation a praise for freedom. Nonetheless there
are hints here of a theme that became increasingly common,
the loss of childhood joys.

> Ah! happy days
> That recollection loves, unstain'd with vice,
> Why were ye gone so soon? Did I not love
> To quit my desk and ramble in the field,
> To gather austere berries from the bush,
> Or search the coppice for the clust'ring nut?
> Did I not always with a shout applaud,
> That welcome voice the holiday announc'd?[68]

This was to be a theme of great importance to Clare, and here
lies an indication of Clare's interest as a poet in this tradition.
For the problem of the long descriptive poem was, briefly, this:
as description became more acceptable, and more detailed,
there was the danger of complete divorce from personal concerns. This may be seen in the aridity of the didactic poems of
these years. But in many poems of nature, the personal element,
as in the early Clare, had been too stark, too consciously self-
centred and eventually unfruitful for emotional development.
It was partly as a reaction against this that detailed observation was at a premium. But something had to fill the emotional
vacuum. Often social ideals or mere humanistic sympathy were
sufficient. Alternatively, the moral aspect was nurtured, or the
divine immanence of nature. Poets remained preachers. (Hurdis
is the prime example of the preacher trying to be the poet.)
One way of accommodating the personal was to regret the
loss of the past, and here the most powerful influence was
undoubtedly Goldsmith's *Deserted Village*. Various trends in
the melancholy poetry of the eighteenth century prompted

occasional backward-looking glances, however undistinguished most of such verse was.[69] The poignancy of the contrast between the present and the past, especially when the poet was in the actual scenes of the past, usually of youth, was too much to be missed. The Quaker poet, Bernard Barton, produced some very typical reflections on this theme, but he was certainly not alone in his nostalgia. When Clare became retrospective, then, he was working in a tradition sanctioned by Goldsmith, and approved by many contemporary versifiers.

The Village Curate was published anonymously. But when *The Favorite Village* (1800) was published, Hurdis was the Professor of Poetry at Oxford, and therefore proud to put his name on the title-page. It is in some ways a more assured work, larger, more detailed, apparently more carefully organised. Concentrating on the village rather than on the curate, there is naturally more scope for description. Hurdis looks beyond his vicarage garden. The *Retrospective Review* regarded the poem as a series of sketches:

> ... this peculiarity, while it unfits the poem from being read continuously, renders it an appropriate *lounge* for any eight or ten minutes which we may have to spare occasionally. We know no composition which contains a greater number of elegant detached *morceaux*, passages pleasing in themselves, and which may be separated from the main work without injury.[70]

This is obviously the chief defect of this type of poem: however much variety there is in the poem as a whole, it needs some unifying theme to keep it together. Once Thomson had been dismembered, and reduced to a series of genre-sketches, any attempt to construct a long poem on the seasons was bound to be little more than a string of such sketches. It is ultimately a charge that can be laid against all the lengthy descriptive poems of the century.

In *The Favorite Village*, Hurdis abandons any strict attempt at a portrayal month by month of the year. The poem is divided into four substantial books, and these correspond to the four seasons, beginning with summer, and ending with spring. The ever-popular Thomsonian plan is thus reverted to: there is no obligation to distinguish between the various months. This obviously has its advantages. Poets were on the whole wary of committing themselves to monthly descriptions: these were thought more suitable for the prose writers of the day. And there were plenty of these eager to turn out the calendars popularised by John Aikin.[71] Because of the wealth of such literature, poets did not feel the need to keep to a strict plan. However, within the accepted framework, Hurdis does provide several glimpses of country life. Some of these are fairly common: the village funeral, haymaking, evening, a thunderstorm, in Summer; the harvest gleaners, an evening at home, in Autumn; the winter walk, the rainbow, forest, thaw, boys skating, the pleasures of Christmas, the tentative approach of spring, in Winter; the flock, the lambs, the birds, the walk at noon, the mower, the bean-field in Summer. All these themes were the stock-in-trade of the descriptive poet. But there are other aspects which are not so commonly mentioned in poetry; he portrays the bull, dismally it may be granted; the sound of the drone, and the ridiculous hen leading out its young ones before time. Many of these themes reappear in Clare.

But Hurdis has become more complacent in his established middle age. What concerns him above all is pleasure, and he is determined to seek this out. His dedication refers to the poem as 'Descriptive of those rural satisfactions and amusements, to which, in the spirit of true taste, he has, for many years, given their due preference'. The opening lines of the poem are:

> Place of my birth, O fondly let me sing
> Thy *pleasures* multifarious, pass the sun
> Through what fair sign it will.

His sensibility is even capable of drinking '*pleasure* at the peasant's grave'; but he soon turns away from '*painful pleasure*'. Innumerable examples might be given of the conscious reiteration of this word '*Pleasure*', carefully and coyly italicised. In fact, the faults of the *Village Curate* are here magnified, and it would require special pleading to suggest that Hurdis has really improved in any way: he may lavish more attention on detail, and occasionally catch the Cowperian note of domesticity, but he seldom sustains this. His style shows all the old signs of constipation. Any vision that we might have

been disposed to grant Hurdis disappears beneath the clogging
verbiage.

The Scots poet James Grahame was less ambitious : his poems
are freer from pomposity and ludicrousness. They include a
long poem on the *Sabbath* (1804), a series of seasonal *Sabbath
Walks* (1806), the immensely detailed *Birds of Scotland* (1806),
and an earlier poem *The Rural Calendar* (1797). *The Sabbath
Walks* have the inestimable advantage of brevity; even with
the inevitable religious motivation, some poetry survives. There
is a sensitive use of language and rhythm, and a consequent
gain in credibility and vividness. This passage illustrates the
virtues and defects of his verse :

> Delightful is this loneliness; it calms
> My heart : pleasant the cool beneath these elms,
> That throw across the stream a moveless shade.
> Here nature in her midnoon whisper speaks :
> How peaceful every sound ! – the ring-dove's plaint,
> Moaned from the twilight centre of the grove,
> While every other woodland lay is mute,
> Save when the wren flits from her down-coved nest,
> And from the root-sprigs trills her ditty clear, –
> The grasshopper's oft-pausing chirp, – the buzz,
> Angrily shrill, of moss-entangled bee,
> That, soon as loosed, booms with full twang away, –
> The sudden rushing of the minnow shoal,
> Scared from the shallows by my passing tread.[72]

There is here a careful balance between the scene, and the
delight it causes the poet. The tendencies of these *Sabbath
Walks* are to be seen also in *The Rural Calendar*. Again brevity
contributes to the poem's effect : epithets are correspondingly
sharper and more energetic. Blank verse is used throughout the
poem, but with considerable freedom of rhythm. Grahame has
a feeling for the labourer, which is more than merely sentimental concern. Such sympathy was by no means uncommon
in the tradition of the shorter descriptive poem; but its presence in larger poems was usually awkward, and either overtly
related to didacticism, or special pleading of the case for the
poor. (This is another direction in which Clare's poem is important.) Grahame uses the stock sights and sounds to bring out

the contrast between poverty and wealth, as in 'January'. The
actual descriptions have some immediacy:

> The cottage hinds the glimmering lantern trim,
> And to the barn wade, sinking in the drift;
> The alternate flails bounce from the loosened sheaf.
>
> (lines 3–5)

'February' similarly plays on the contrast between the town
and the country: images of treachery occur, the fowler and the
thawing ice. These images serve an important purpose, in that
the treachery of fowler and ice are complementary to the treatment of the poor by the rich, and the ambiguity of the season.
Within the space of relatively few lines, Grahame catches
something of the complexity of this time of year. His tone is
carefully varied. The opening lines, for example, juxtapose
the fowler's snare, the struggling bird, and his solitary walks
in the glen. Desolation is imaged in the silence, the loss of
Eden, the deceit of the fowler, the contrast between the flurry-
ing snow set loose by the frantic birds, and the 'untrod snows'
in the glen.

> The treacherous fowler, in the drifted wreath,
> The snare conceals, and strews the husky lure,
> Tempting the famished fowls of heaven to light:
> They light; the captive strives in vain to fly,
> Scattering around, with fluttering wing, the snow.
> Amid the untrod snows, oft let me roam
> Far up the lonely glen, and mark its change;
> The frozen rill's hoarse murmur scarce is heard;
> The rocky cleft, the fairy bourne smoothed up,
> Repeat no more my solitary voice.
>
> ('February', lines 1–10)

There are delicately drawn pictures of country life, as for
instance the schoolboys coming out at lunch-time. But Grahame
also looks at the children who work in the factories, to further
the nefarious ends of Commerce. He does not mince his words:

> ... health, morals, all must yield
> To pamper the monopolising few,
> To make a wealthy, but a wretched state.

Blest be the generous band, that would restore
To honour due the long-neglected plough!
                              ('July', lines 48–52)

Grahame has profound respect for animal life:

To man, bird, beast, *man* is the deadliest foe.
'Tis he who wages universal war.
                              ('August', lines 13–14)

This was a favourite theme of Clare's, and Grahame is one of
the few poets before him to speak out so boldly in these terms.
It is because of this respect and compassion that he is able to
write some quite pungent verse, where most other poets merely
adopt postures. His language shows a feeling for sensation rare
in descriptive verse of the age. In a couple of lines he writes
more poetry than Hurdis was capable of in ten times as many:

Languid the morning beam slants o'er the lea;
The hoary grass, crisp, crackles 'neath the tread.
                              ('November', lines 1–2)

The husbandman slow plods from ridge to ridge,
Disheartened, and rebuilds his prostrate sheaves.
                              ('November', last two lines)

It seems relevant to stress the superiority of Grahame over
Hurdis, and indeed, most of the other descriptive writers, for
he anticipates in several ways the developments discernible
in Clare's *Shepherd's Calendar*. The precise nature of Grahame's
achievement, slight though it may be in absolute terms, may
be more closely charted if we compare his poems with one by
William Cole, entitled more prosaically *A Descriptive Review
of the Year 1799, comprised in twelve monthly Sections*. The
poem was included in a later collection of 1824, slightly enlarged and revised, and retitled *Rural Months: A Descriptive
Poem, in Twelve Cantos*. Cole is not a poet of Grahame's
calibre. He tells us that his poem issued out of a challenge,
between himself and a painter. Each would depict, in his own
medium, each month of the year, 'for the mutual Amusement
of both families'. He is accordingly diffident to start with,
regretting his inability to 'catch one spark of THOMSON'S

sacred fire'. The Thomsonian influence nonetheless asserts itself, even though Cole adopts the pentameter couplet as the
vehicle for his observations. A glance at the arguments for
each month shows the amount of didacticism which settles on
much of the poem, whilst the familiar aspects of country life
reappear : the frozen winter's day, seen with a cold aestheticism, the schoolboys, the timid hare, the hungry birds, the
domestic robin. Cole does not share Grahame's distrust of
Commerce and mankind. January concludes:

> The zephirous winds will soon their ships unmoor
> And Commerce's golden pinions spread once more.[73]

There is not the same sense of social outrage; nor the same
awareness of torment and deceit in the winter months. No
doubts hedge about the end of February, although some do
at the end of March, where the pictorial tradition reasserts
itself :

> Scarce sprouts the turnip with its yellow green,
> And empty rick-yards close the rigid scene.[74]

Cole works uneasily between the two traditions, as does Clare
in his early verse. But Clare would never write this sort of
thing, about the lamb, who

> Alternate at the half-filled udder plucks,
> And down the life-inspiring nectar sucks.[75]

Once again, the stylistic barrenness destroys the poem. There
is a brief reference to the loss of the past, and childhood. This
lament at the end of April is not entirely convincing, for Cole
does not really indicate how deep his feelings are, and how
much he is having to console himself. But the lament is there,
nevertheless, sticking out incongruously, and again suggestive
of the way the long descriptive poem could develop. The more
conventional, religious musings of December, at the end of the
review of the year, illustrates the other possible line of development, and the one usually followed. April ends with these
lines :

> Well can I picture too in mem'ry's eye
> Those days of rural innocence gone by!

When *my* big bosom at the noon-tide hour
Throb'd at the springing of a vernal flow'r;
When tiptoe by the hawthorn hedge I stray'd,
Or in wild gambols o'er the village play'd;
Blest retrospection! of my childish years
Still your wild flights maturer reason cheers;
But ah! to trace thy devious steps is vain,
Youth's spring, once blossom'd, never blows again.[76]

One poet who tries to continue the *Deserted Village* tradition is William Holloway, whose poem *The Peasant's Fate: a Rural Poem* was published in 1802. Holloway's manifesto, contained in his Preface, is uncompromising in its hostility to wealth and luxury. He is fully aware of the importance of childhood scenes and memories:

It has been justly observed, that an attachment to the place of our nativity, ... to the scenes of childhood and youth, ... is a branch of the *amor patriae*, congenial not only to the glowing bosom of the Poet, but to the heart of every worthy man: yet will local description fail of its attraction, unless happily connected with incident and sentiment.[77]

The Wordsworthian emphasis on childhood belonged to such a tradition, and of course revitalised it. Holloway resorts to a sense of social outrage:

The changes in rural life and manners, which have taken place in this country, in the course of a few years, furnish ample matter for reflection and regret.

He is concerned with the plight of the peasantry, forced out of their small farms, and either driven from the land altogether, or forced to become '*servants* on the spot where they had once been masters'. He scoffs at the pastoral falsities which have been exposed for what they were. Thomson, Goldsmith and Cowper have furthered this process, and Holloway declares: 'Rural poetry should speak the language of Nature; and Classic Criticism has, of late, learned to relax his rigid brow, at the native wild notes of the British muse.'[78] He quotes Nathan Drake in his support. The poem itself echoes Goldsmith, rather than Thomson or Cowper. Written in pentameter couplets, it seldom rises above the insipid conventions of the form. For a poem ostensibly inspired by moral and social outrage, this will scarcely do:

> Let fond attachment dwell on pleasures past,
> By absence weaken'd, nor by time effac'd:
> But, while I mark the changes that appear
> In country manners, O, forgive the tear! (i, 9–12)

Nonetheless, behind the verbal imprecision lies some interesting comment on a way of life that has disappeared. The elegiac quality of the poem is worth noticing. Holloway portrays youthful pastimes and occupations; he is at pains to introduce tales of the countryside, such as that of the Suicide, or of Simon and the Ghost (a story characteristically told by his grandmother). This type of village tale became a common feature of rural poetry. Thomson had introduced narrative episodes into *The Seasons*, and these were sometimes followed with considerable fidelity by his imitators. As the pastoral as such became defunct, it was natural for rural folklore to be accommodated within the longer descriptive poem. The tales were usually of suicides (Cowper's Crazy Kate set the fashion), or of lovers. Because this became a tradition in itself, especially in local verse, we should not under-emphasise the approach to realism that is indicated. Historical and mythological tales are replaced by tales of genuine occurrences, or particular pieces of village gossip. Clare carries this process a stage further, in two directions. He incorporates in the months themselves long accounts of stories told to children on winter evenings; and he devotes whole poems to individual tales. Holloway, in mourning a way of life, anticipates Clare in several respects. He is, at the same time, echoing the tradition exemplified most recently by Bloomfield; Crabbe too, lurks behind some of his lines. There is a greater concreteness in the particulars of the poem, as though Holloway were writing about the people he knows. He gives their names, and thus announces that he is not writing in general terms. His poem embraces a wide variety of rural occupations. In the following passage, the general resemblance to some of Clare's descriptions of a similar type of scene is observable. But the neatness of the couplets is not what we find in Clare, and certainly not in *The Shepherd's Calendar*.

Her spouse, meanwhile, supports with equal glee,
The ceaseless round of honest husbandry;
Various the labours various seasons claim,
The process diff'rent, but the toil the same.
In winter, thro' the dark and drizzling day,
The flail and plough, by turns, his hand obey:
When fields are hid in snow, or sunk in mire,
The hedge, the ditch, his constant aid require;
Or new-fall'n lambs, a weak and trembling breed,
The hurdled cot and hourly nurture need.
When, like a blushing bride, the rosy morn,
First smil'd on floating fields of bending corn,
With poppies stain'd, or gold, or azure flow'rs,
Oppress'd with weight of night-refreshing show'rs,
Forth strode the mower, with his clouted shoes,
And, from the breathing clover, dash'd the dews,
While, where he treads, afar behind, is seen,
Along the lawn, a trace of darker green,
By which the later swains, with quicken'd pace
Pursue his progress, and his footsteps trace ...

                                    (ii, 335–54)

But, for all its occasional felicities, the poem is a curious mixture of jingoism and sentimentality, propped up with traditional personifications. Holloway does not go much beyond Goldsmith, and certainly does not approach him as a poet. It is significant that most of the other poems in the book are tales of rural life, in blank verse or elegiac quatrains.

In the eighteenth century, the two most important poems of description were Thomson's *Seasons* and Cowper's *Task*. Cowper perfects a particular type of discursive, descriptive poem, didactic, moralistic, conversational, fixed to actual observation, but also essentially civilised and civilising. *The Task* is a crystallisation of the genre. It was unlikely that any imitators would add to the tradition, after Cowper. The failure of Hurdis is a case in point. Those who did not follow Thomson or Cowper, followed, stylistically, either Goldsmith or Beattie, or simply churned out the poeticisms culled from the Popean or Miltonic heritage. Odes and elegies abounded. These poems were either attempts at plain description, or attempts to cap-

ture the essence of particular times of the year. But few descriptions were content to stay simply that; the Thomsonian
influence was too strong. Although we might point to many
poems of the countryside in illustration of the precept adopted
by William Holloway, in which compassion for the poor and
interest in village customs is paramount, seldom are these
poems worth much more than a cursory glance.

It is when we have in mind the weight of this dying tradition, that we can profitably turn to Clare's *Shepherd's Calendar*,
and see the revolution he is beginning, perhaps unconsciously,
to effect. Gone are the echoes of style caught from Thomson
and Cowper; gone are the moralistic episodes, the illustrations
of Divine Immanence. Even poverty is not held up as a thing
to be looked at and pitied from a distance. The truth to nature
that so many of his predecessors talked vaguely about, is here
seen, not only in clarity and variety of detail, but in the
economy of the style, the energy and movement that had been
denied to them. Clare does not preach; nor, on the other hand,
does he simply regurgitate the vignettes and genre-sketches
that abound elsewhere. Clare achieves here, for the first time in
a long poem, a plangent tone of regret untinged by sentimentality, a poem on country life that is neither didactic nor
moralistic. For many, it was precisely the tone of moral reflection that appealed to them in his early work. In the context of
the literary tradition it is remarkable that Clare could write a
poem on country life so free from the trammels of current
expectations.

III

It is Clare's directness of language which most immediately
and noticeably marks him off from his predecessors. It would
be true to say that no other poet of the eighteenth or nineteenth
centuries wrote as Clare did: absorbing the influence of such
writers as Thomson and Milton, Pope and Cowper, Keats and
Collins, the numerous Elizabethan writers he admired, he
evolved a style that was completely individual, true to his own
needs and intentions. If we can appreciate the merits of this
style, in its broadest sense, we shall be able to see what it is

that makes Clare of particular interest, in what way he is distinguished from other writers in this apparently limited genre. We shall see also, perhaps, that the genre is less limited than it appeared.

At about the time of writing of *The Shepherd's Calendar* Clare began to speculate on what he had achieved so far; in several poems he explored his own development, one of the more important being the lengthy 'To the Rural Muse', which eventually headed the 1835 volume. Perhaps the most interesting theoretical point made is the basic simplicity of poetry; his boldest affirmation of it comes in this stanza, from a rough draft of the poem. It might stand as an epigraph to Clare's poetic creed:

Is poesy dwelling in a nice-culled sound,
Or soft smooth words that trifle on the ear
Unmeaning music? Is it to be found
In rhymes run mad, that paint to startled fear
Monsters that are not and that never were?
Is it in declamations frothing high,
Worked like machinery to its mad career?
No, poetry lives in its simplicity,
And speaks from its own heart, to which all hearts reply.[79]

This is a clumsy attempt to justify simplicity; the theory seems better than the practice. But that was the problem. It took Clare some time to appreciate the distinction between flatness, and the real strength of a simple style.

The difficulties of achieving this ideal simplicity were recognised, at least in part, by Drury, and also by Taylor. Drury, in speaking of Crabbe, says that the point is that his 'tales, poetry, and versification, are so simple that ... everybody could not help saying to themselves "Oh, I could do such *easy* things as these" – till they tried, and found out their difficulty'.[80] But he was surely wide of the mark when he recommended Clare's poem 'The Meeting' for its simplicity. Taylor's advice was much sounder, if harder to put into practice:

If he has a Soul of native Fancies, Let him study to express what it dictates in that Language it will bring with it; then he will write like himself & no one else: if he has not that

innate Poesy he may write clever Poems like many others
who are called Poets, but he will have no just claim to the
Title.[81]

Taylor and Hessey, and Mrs Emmerson, frequently suggested
that the early poets (meaning the Elizabethans, but also Chau-
cer) provided the best models for a simple style. When Clare
began to write imitations of these older poets, trying to fob
them off onto local newspapers as lost originals, they tended
to encourage him, and Taylor was almost as anxious as Clare
that these pieces should be collected and published in a separate
volume (but nothing came of this plan).[82] At about the same
time, Clare's interest in ballad collecting (as opposed to the
cruder broadsides) reached its peak; these ballads had a profound effect on his writing, not entirely beneficial, as was suggested above. But the main purpose served by these imitations
and these collected ballads was a still greater emphasis on
clarity and unambiguity of statement, and a greater intensity
behind the apparent simplicity. Such were the qualities of the
ballad at its best, and as seen in several of the ballads in Clare's
versions. 'A Faithless Shepherd', for instance, epitomises these
qualities :

> I wish, I wish, but all in vain,
> I wish I was a maid again.
> A maid again I cannot be,
> Oh, when will green grass cover me?
>
> I wish my babe had ne'er been born,
> I've made its pillow on a thorn,
> I wish my sorrows all away,
> My soul with God, my body clay.[83]

But Clare was never altogether sure of himself, and this hesita-
tion produced some very odd poems. He was especially vulner-
able in his love poems, which readily descended into false
pathos and banality. The descriptive verse was at least tied
to reality, to actual circumstances, and this was a precaution
against too obvious or contrived a simplicity. Furthermore, it
soon becomes clear from his descriptive writing that Clare
was influenced as much by the example of Milton's octosyllabics, by Herrick and the Elizabethans, as by the ballads and

folksongs he collected. There is a clear affinity between Clare and *L'Allegro*; but also between Clare and, say, the *Pastorals* of William Browne.[84] Clare's partiality for Browne is readily understandable, for both men were writing in the same tradition. Although moving in a world of fancy, Browne did write with an eye on the countryside, and he was able to break through elaborate falsehoods and state unaffectedly what he saw :

> The Muse's friend (grey-eyed Aurora) yet
> Held all the meadows in a cooling sweat,
> The milk-white gossamers not upwards snow'd,
> Nor was the sharp and useful-steering goad
> Laid on the strong-neck'd ox; no gentle bud
> The sun had dried; the cattle chew'd the cud
> Low levell'd on the grass; no fly's quick sting
> Enforc'd the stonehorse in a furious ring
> To tear the passive earth, nor lash his tail
> About his buttocks broad; the slimy snail
> Might on the wainscot, by his many mazes,
> Winding meanders and self-knitting traces,
> Be follow'd where he stuck, his glittering slime
> Not yet wip'd off. It was so early time,
> The careful smith had in his sooty forge
> Kindled no coal; nor did his hammers urge
> His neighbour's patience : owls abroad did fly
> And day as then might plead his infancy.
>
> (Book ii, Song 2)

We have seen in an earlier chapter some of Clare's attempts at descriptive verse, and his increasing command of the medium. This involved a more comprehensive view of what he saw, a less simplistic manner of saying. This trend continues in *The Shepherd's Calendar*. We might be disposed to say of the style here that it is simple; but to say this is only to begin to understand what Clare is doing with language; it is not simple in the way that the Wordsworth of the *Lyrical Ballads* is simple, nor in the way that the songs are simple, nor in the way that Mrs Emmerson thought the beginning of *The Village Minstrel* was simple. Just what this style involves has been the chief problem bedevilling criticism of Clare. *The Shepherd's Calendar* is in many ways a test case for Clare's poetry, for the range and scope of his achievement. For if his descriptive poetry is to be vindicated, it is in this work that we must seek that vindication.

Something of the complexity of the problem may be seen in this quotation from 'March', one of the best of the sections in the *Calendar*. Clare is describing the varied weather at the beginning of the month, the ambiguities of the season :

> Yet winter seems half weary of its toil
> And round the ploughman on the elting soil
> Will thread a minutes sunshine wild and warm
> Thro the raggd places of the swimming storm[85]

Part of the effect here depends upon the presence of the plough-man in the scene; Clare is not simply stating dispassionately what he sees; he gives a countryman's view of March, both in his own role as a countryman, and, more importantly, in his awareness of the effect of the seasons on the countryman. Not only is he the spokesman for the ploughman, he imbues his description with the ploughman's presence, right at the heart of the scene. But the full force of the passage depends upon more than this. Firstly there is the personification of winter, and the relationship between winter and toil. The toil of the ploughman is set against the toil of winter, for Clare is des-cribing the capricious weather, the storm and floods. Winter is depicted ironically in terms of its effect on the peasant : the peasant himself is, we might readily imagine, half weary of his toil, but also of winter, and of the difficulty of work in winter. But winter itself is tired of its efforts, ready to allow the spring to have its say. The curious result of this devious ap-proach to the onset of warmer weather is that it actually seems a struggle : spring is seen in terms of the weariness of winter. The rhythmical and syntactical effect (in the first two lines of this passage) is one of weariness. Beyond this, there is a colloquial force in the 'half weary' that has the effect of emphasising the weariness, and this colloquial precision by understatement is an important aspect of Clare's art. The per-sonification of winter is clearly related to the diction, just as the ploughman is placed in a context of Northamptonshire dialect, with 'elting' derived from 'elting moulds', meaning the soft ridges of freshly ploughed land.[86] With this one word Clare catches the particular position of the man, and the distinctive nature of the soil. By stating this in dialect terms, and not condescendingly because this is the word he needs, he puts the ploughman into a closer relationship with the soil he ploughs. The second half of the quotation is equally distinctive, its character deriving from the continuation of the homely, complicated personification, the notion of threading a minute's sunshine through the storm's 'raggd places'. The domestic image is elevated by the epithets 'wild and warm', thrown onto the end of the line, and the only mention of actual warmth. The image loses its rustic flavour and becomes an almost rhapsodic touch, for there is an exuberance here even in the patchy metaphor, just as conversely there was in the first two lines a weariness where the emphasis would be expected to be on the hope of awakening spring. (The syntax is important : here it is worth observing the one active verb, so tenuous, yet so strong and suggestive, the burden placed on the epithets, in themselves vigorous and participial, more apparently active than normal adjectives; the antithetical structure of the two couplets, with parallel syntactical units of main clause, adverbial phrase, main clause, adverbial phrase, but with the sense joining the last three lines into one unit, one co-ordinate main clause, explaining the first line, recreating in its movement the sinuous, magical ray of warm sunlight.)

Obviously the whole poem is not conducted on this level of intensity, nor should we expect it to be; this type of moment achieves its impact because it is isolated and spaced, part of a larger context. To appreciate the full force of this passage, we have to have in mind the architectural structure to which it contributes. The poem is not a string of impressions, nor a collection of sketches to be enjoyed at random. Although this passage is characteristic of what might be called the heightened moments of the poem, there is clearly nothing of the purple passage about this; Clare is not being self-indulgent. It is merely that he concentrates his effects, drawing his various strands more tightly together at such points. These moments act as points of reference, the reverberating crucial moments by which the rest of the poem asks to be read and judged. The principles that operate here may be seen throughout the poem, in differing degrees.

Another effective instance of the use of such moments of reverberation occurs in 'March', where Clare plays on the theme of expectation and delay. The portrait of the sturnels seems wryly to reject any suggestion of hope:

> Soon as the morning opes its brightning eye
> Large clouds of sturnels* blacken thro the sky
> From oizer holts about the rushy fen
> And reedshaw borders by the river Nen
> And wild geese regiments now agen repair
> To the wet bosom of broad marshes there
> In marching coloms and attention all
> Listning and following their ringleaders call[87]

As the shepherd boy beguiles his loneliness with daydreams, the movement of the verse hints at the desperate nature of his self-deception:

> his eye percieves
> Sun threads struck out wi momentery smiles
> Wi fancy thoughts his lonliness beguiles
> Thinking the struggling winter hourly bye
> As down the edges of the distant sky
> The hailstorm sweeps –

After the hallowed memory of boyhood, when he had likened the geese in the sky to letters of the alphabet, comes a startling image of the crane, alone in his flight. Ironically, it flies to unfrozen dykes, the signs of the end of winter. But for the crane life is one long winter, and the brief suggestion of spring is a sardonic comment on the frozen vista. The dreams of summer, the wild hopes of the rest of nature, are denied:

> While far above the solitary crane
> Swings lonly to unfrozen dykes again
> Cranking† a jarring mellancholy cry
> Thro the wild journey of the cheerless sky

One of the immediately noticeable elements in the passage quoted earlier is the presence of the ploughman at the centre of the scene. This may not seem an intimate part of the stylistic

---

* Starlings.
† Singing dolefully.

effect, but a reading of the poem as a whole makes it clear
that it is precisely because of these figures, so closely related to
the action of the poem, that there is a unique tone of practicality, a feeling for the countryside expressed in the movement of the verse. The spirit of communal life is to be seen on
every page, the activity of people in the countryside: the old
landscape-topographical tradition is left behind.

There are several ways in which Clare constantly keeps
these country people before our eyes. Most importantly, he
describes things as they seem to such people, rather than
merely to him. This emphasis on the relationship between man
and nature is constant. 'March' is particularly rich in such
points of detail: for example, we are shown the 'stooping
ditcher' as he drains the water off the land, the old woman
bringing in the watercress, the ploughman singing, and unclog-
ging the ploughs, the sower, the driving boy, all within the
space of relatively few lines.[88] All these portraits have an
immediacy which it is impossible to separate from the mode
of presentation. In the portrait of the ditcher, no attempt is
made to describe him in any obvious way: his actions are
eloquent;

> The stooping ditcher in the water stands
> Letting the furrowd lakes from off the lands
> Or splashing cleans the pasture brooks of mud
> Where many a wild weed freshens into bud

The power of the qualifying word, illustrated here, may be seen
in the account of the old woman, as she 'gladly drags to land'
the watercress, 'Wi reaching long rake in her tottering hand'.
Never afraid to say too little rather than too much, Clare lends
his portrait no more than the necessary touch of liveliness.
More dramatic is his description of the ploughman, with its
dependence on dialect words:

> The ploughman mawls* along the doughy sloughs
> And often stop their songs to clean their ploughs
> From teazing twitch that in the spongy soil
> Clings round the colter terryfying toil

---

* Drags along wearily.

The weary effort and the toil 'through claggy and moist land'
(as A. E. Baker puts it) are felt throughout this passage:[89] in
the homely application of 'doughy' to the muddy ground,
echoed later by the 'spongy soil', the bother of the twitch
caught in the colter, and the annoying interruption of song on
account of this. The sower is equally vivid, depending again on
the vigour of the verbs and adjectives, on the hard consonants,
but not on any easy alliteration, which Clare eschews:

> The sower striding oer his dirty way
> Sinks anckle deep in pudgy* sloughs and clay

Clare's version of the scene has a much greater immediacy
than we find in Thomson:

> White through the neighbouring fields the sower stalks
> With measured steps, and liberal throws the grain
> Into the faithful bosom of the ground:
> The harrow follows harsh, and shuts the scene.[90]

Less part of a distinctive philosophical attitude to the world,
Clare's version is far more closely anchored to the experience
of the sower. The relation between his actions and the growing
seed is stated in his own terms, the detail not super-rogatory
but functional, explaining the meaning of the present by reference to the vividly realised future:

> And oer his heavy hopper stoutly leans
> Strewing wi swinging arms the pattering beans
> Which soon as aprils milder weather gleams
> Will shoot up green between the furroed seams

The portrait of the driving boy that concludes this section
before Clare turns his attention to the birds, furthers the
impression of stoical endurance of dirt and mud. Criticism that
refers to Clare as a poet with mud on his boots may seem
merely sentimental; but without doubt it is the awareness of
mud, 'clinging' and 'spongy', that brings this whole section so
much to life.

> The driving boy glad when his steps can trace
> The swelling edding as a resting place
> Slings from his clotted shoes the dirt around

* Full of puddles.

> And feign would rest him on the solid ground
> And sings when he can meet the parting green
> Of rushy balks* that bend the lands between

Just how carefully associated are Clare's descriptions with their contexts might be seen if we compare this with another account of the driving boy, in 'May'. Here what contributes to the dominant tone of the portrait is the element of sheer fantasy and beauty, the infectious gaiety, nonetheless rooted in concrete, physical action:

> The driving boy beside his team
> Will oer the may month beauty dream
> And cock his hat and turn his eye
> On flower and tree and deepning skye
> And oft bursts loud in fits of song
> And whistles as he reels along
> Crack[ing] his whip in starts of joy
> A happy dirty driving boy[91]

The difference in tone here is partly attributable to the more sprightly movement of the octosyllabics, and the consequently more noticeable jerkiness of the syntax, as epithets are pruned to the minimum, and effects gauged more mutedly. But if the second passage is consistent in its tone of carefree happiness in summer, with just the right balance between detail (cocking his hat, reeling along, the crack of his whip, his essential dirtiness, in itself a constituent element in his happiness) and emotional response (his vacant dreaming 'oer the may month beauty', which is, in actual terms of what he sees, 'flower, tree and sky' – and note the effect of 'deepning' here – his loud fits of song, his starts of joy), the first passage is equally true to itself, with the telling epithets 'swelling' and 'clotted', and verbs 'slings' and 'sings' relating the physical condition of the landscape to his own participation in the scene, his relief when he meets the 'rushy balks' ('sings' echoing 'slings' and suggesting both correspondence and contrast). There is less fantasy here, more practicality, but this is precisely the point Clare wishes to make.

In this series of portraits of farmworkers in March their actions reflect the countryside, its present muddy turmoil, and

* Unploughed strips.

the hope of spring, the 'wild weed' that 'freshens into bud', the 'seed' that will 'shoot up green between the furroed seams', the 'parting green of rushy balks'. This interaction between the various parts is one of the chief strengths of the poem. But it was not fully appreciated by Taylor, nor has it been by more recent critics. It is, above all, the vigour of his descriptions, his recreation of a way of life neither idealised nor sensationally realistic, but essentially loving, that exalts his poem.

Clare's vision is vindicated because of his closeness to its source. This has an important bearing on the style. On the one hand there are the potent images, the metaphors for the dream of nature; on the other hand, there is the diction of the poem, so often practical and colloquial. Without doubt, one of the ways in which Clare recreates the landscape from the country-man's point of view is his use of the Northamptonshire dialect.

In general, Clare's dialect words, or 'provincialisms', were accepted by the early reviewers, partly because Taylor had made them acceptable with his usual suavity in his Introduction to *Poems Descriptive of Rural Life and Scenery*.[92] He pointed out Clare's

> inability to find those words which can fully declare his meaning. From the want of a due supply of these, and from his ignorance of grammar, he seems to labour under great disadvantages. On the other hand, his want forces him to an extraordinary exertion of his native powers, in order to supply the deficiency. He employs the language under his command with great effect, in those unusual and unpre-cedented combinations of words which must be made, even by the learned, when they attempt to describe perfectly something which they have never seen or heard expressed before.[93]

It was in this light that Taylor apparently welcomed Clare's provincialisms, and he added the further excuse that they were part of the English language, however old, and there was good precedent for such practice in the great poets. But Taylor sounds more convinced here than he really was: his doubts are very apparent during the compilation of *The Village Minstrel*.

On 23 January 1821 he complained about the 'unpoetical' language of 'Woodcroft Castle', which formed part of the

original 'Peasant Boy'. It was too 'common-place': 'you tell the
Tale too much in the Words in which a prose Narrator would
tell it.' It was not far from this to complain about the presence
of provincialisms. Taylor is unequivocal:

> We have but few Provincialisms in the poem, & I should be
> glad if we could get rid of one that is left *Himsen*; but if it
> cannot be easily done never mind. Real English Country
> Words are different in my Mind & should be judged differ-
> ently from those which are only peculiar to a district, &
> perhaps *himsen* & *shanny* are of the latter Class. – Shanny
> is not used beyond the Trent, tho' Himsen is common enough
> I know.[94]

Taylor's distinction was feasible, but of little relevance to
Clare. It is the Northamptonshire flavour of his dialect words
which is important to him, something distinctive and particu-
larised. But that Clare's intention was expressiveness, rather
than any desire to introduce dialect for the sake of it, is clear
from his comments on a word that Taylor had chosen to
correct: 'you cross'd "gulsh'd" I think the word expressive
but doubt its a provincialism it means tearing or thrusting up
with great force take it or leave it as you please.'[95] Taylor felt
no obligation to take what he could leave, and *The Village
Minstrel* and *The Shepherd's Calendar* were denuded of some
of those words which had been used by Clare because they
were 'expressive'.

Taylor's tactics did not deter Clare: the *Calendar* was
sprinkled with dialect words, but on the whole more judiciously
chosen. Taylor found it necessary to warn Clare against affect-
ing too much the common vulgarity of country folk.[96] This
was a temptation in his country tales, where Clare adopted a
very easy, conversational, unpoetical style. Charles Lamb chided
Clare for his common language, and he must have been thinking of the narrative tales, as much as anything:

> Transplant Arcadia to Helpstone. The true rustic style, the
> Arcadian English, I think is to be found in Shenstone. Would
> his School-Mistress, the prettiest of poems, have been better,
> if he had used quite the Goody's own language?[97]

This was a valid point, made by Coleridge against Wordsworth's theory of diction.[98] But it does not mean that dialect words of the sort found in the *Calendar* should be avoided. For here 'expressiveness' is the point.

It seems very likely that Clare was encouraged in his use of the language of rustics by his reading of Ramsay and Burns. These two poets were profound influences on Clare's early verse. His *Rustic's Pastime* was headed by a quotation from Ramsay, and it included several imitations of these poets, both metrical and stylistic.[99] Their 'homespun' quality comes out in much of Clare's writing, especially his long pastoral tales in a rollicking metre that infest the manuscript notebooks;[100] it comes out in the deliberate imitations, such as 'Address to a Lark' and 'Familiar Epistle to a Friend'.[101] It was out of this habit that arose, gradually, his more discriminating use of dialect words, not to be homespun, but because they were poetical for him, part of his vision of the Northamptonshire countryside. As he said with his usual honesty to Hessey in October 1820, 'I think vulgar names to the flowers best as I know no others [if] it pleases twill add a fresh spark to my ryhming pride & start me off'.[102]

In 'January, A Cottage Evening' the portrait of the shepherd who has finished his day's work, and is enjoying his home comforts, is certainly enlivened and enriched in these two lines, with their clusters of resounding consonants:

> Or toasting sloe boughs sputtering ripe
> Or smoaking glad his puthering pipe . . .[103]

But even here, apart from the dialect words, and their parallelism of form, syntax and rhyme, the effect derives just as much from the image of the shepherd 'toasting sloe boughs', so that the rustic activity is reflected onto the participial adjectives. Clare achieves here a synthesis between his countryman's vision and his form of expression, so that even 'smoaking' lends its colouring to the whole (although it would be difficult to analyse the precise effect of this variant form, or any misspelling, except to say that many of Clare's spellings are phonetic, and thus indicate the way he thinks of his verse as sound, and related to the speaking voice). Use of dialect here is sparing, but effective.

One of the best examples is to be found at the end of 'February', where the harsh actuality is captured in the two final lines, each participle lending effect to the other :

> Thus nature of the spring will dream
> While south winds thaw but soon again
> Frost breaths upon the stiffening stream
> And numbs it into ice – the plain
> Soon wears its merry garb of white
> And icicles that fret at noon
> Will eke their icy tails at night
> Beneath the chilly stars and moon
>
> Nature soon sickens of her joys
> And all is sad and dumb again
> Save merry shouts of sliding boys
> About the frozen furrowd plain
> The foddering boy forgets his song
> And silent goes wi folded arms
> And croodling shepherds bend along
> Crouching to the whizzing storms[104]

There can be no doubt that the dialect 'croodling' (huddling) is an integral part of Clare's vision here, as in the previous stanza with 'fret' (thaw) and 'eke' (enlarge).

Mention has been made of some of the interesting uses of dialect in 'March'; others worth mentioning include the 'watery brood/Of swopping (pouncing) white birds', and the line, 'And where the stunt (steep) bank fronts the southern sky',[105] where internal rhyme strengthens the impact. The portrait of the crow and the daws receives a sharper delineation from its mixture of colloquialism, wondering half-simile, and evocative dialect word :

> While close behind em struts the nauntling* crow
> And daws whose heads seem powderd oer wi snow
> To seek the worms[106]

The beautifully modulated account of the solitary crane (see

---

* Holding himself erect.

above, p. 90) is characterised by the use of the verb 'cranking' (singing dolefully) in conjunction with 'a jarring mellancholy cry'. This is one of the high points of the poem, and it is certainly significant that Clare does not steer clear of a dialect word at this point, any more than he avoids a literary echo.[107]

IV

Dr Johnson complained of *The Seasons* that it lacked organic structure;[108] the *Retrospective Review* made the same charge against Hurdis. The problem inevitably faced Clare. In establishing his own version of the sonnet form, he had solved the problem in one direction, but in an extended poem a more comprehensive vision (and a form to encompass it) was called for. Something of Clare's achievement may be seen in 'January'.

'January' plays on the theme of hardship, and the struggle against the elements. Winter is a cruel time for the worker. He dreams of better times to come. But there is also the dream of the past, when all was innocence and ease in the Eden of childhood. This is the basic structure of the whole section, and it is continued with modifications into 'February' and 'March'.

The opening of 'A Winter's Day' is Clare at his best.

> Withering and keen the winter comes
> While comfort flyes to close shut rooms
> And sees the snow in feathers pass
> Winnowing by the window glass
> And unfelt tempests howl and beat
> Above his head in corner seat
> And musing oer the changing scene
> Farmers behind the tavern screen
> Sit – or wi elbow idly prest
> On hob reclines the corners guest[109]

The very directness of this contrasts markedly with the tradition that Clare invokes only to side-step: Thomson's complacency in the face of Winter's 'congenial horrors' has no place here, nor has Cowper's aestheticism. Neither of these poets, nor Bloomfield, had felt able to start so abruptly, with so little ceremony. Here for example is the opening of Thomson's 'Winter':

> See, Winter comes to rule the varied year,
> Sullen and sad, with all his rising train –
> Vapours, and clouds, and storms. Be these my theme;
> These, that exalt the soul to solemn thought,
> And heavenly musing. Welcome, kindred glooms!
> Congenial horrors, hail! With frequent foot,
> Pleased have I, in my cheerful morn of life,
> When nursed by careless solitude I lived
> And sung of Nature with unceasing joy,
> Pleased have I wandered through your rough domain;
> Trod the pure virgin-snows, myself as pure.

The vigour of the passage from 'January' resides partly in this opening shock, but it involves more than surprise : Clare makes it clear that he is concerned with the effect of winter on nature as a whole. The precision of effect underlines the seriousness of intention, as in line three where the force of the verb 'sees' reflects comfort and complacency, for 'feathers' indicates the vision of comfort : the snow appears featherlike to the comfortable observer safely protected in his close shut room, but, as the next line reminds us, the snow still winnows past the window. Similarly line five, with its combination of passive and active verbs, emphasises the farmer's immunity and the reality of the winter weather. Clare's other poems on winter affirm that this was for Clare a vivid reality. Warmth and comfort are desirable commodities. But in 'A Winter's Day' the contrast is not quite so simple. For, although on one level there is the obvious contrast between the two parts of January, 'A Winter's Day' and 'A Cottage Evening', on another level indoor comfort is itself something of a delusion. Whereas previously the dichotomy between poverty and comfort, cold and warmth, had been stated plainly and without ambiguity, here the connection between public and private aspects of winter is so carefully balanced that the bleakness of winter and isolation echoes the spiritual bleakness; in this situation comfort is self-deluding. As the farmer sits in the warmth, he muses 'oer the changing scene'. This is a reference to the changing weather outside, but also, as the succeeding lines suggest, to the political and social scene, and by implication, to the changing fortunes of mankind, symbolised in the upheaval of enclosure – which prompts and informs a large part of the poem's underlying moral indignation. The farmer is portrayed with a cool accuracy that catches his uneasy predicament; his faith in his almanack, his trust in better times to come, the sense of resignation without the final despair. He dreams over his troubles that are nearly ripe, about to be harvested. For winter has its own harvest, one of disaster, storms, and ruination, averted only by faith in hope and superstition, by optimism for the second, real harvest. For all his comfort in the inn, the farmer is ill at ease, relying on his own good luck to survive. It is a question of self-deception and trust. This human predicament, coming in the first few lines, is central to the structure of the poem. By his technique of suggestion Clare plays on the idea of storm as a reality, something to be seen from the comfort of an inn. But his inside comfort is illusory, as his use of the harvest-image indicates : the elemental cycle leads to hope, but also to self-deception. Furthermore, the farmer is a dreamer; much of this part of the poem centres around the complexities of the dream world, and its relation to reality. Ironically the farmer is 'dreaming oer troubles nearly ripe' : he is in a twilight world, ambiguously placed between hope and despair, reality and non-reality.

The cumulative effect of this opening verse paragraph depends upon the simultaneity of activity within and without :

> Yet not quite lost in profits way
> He'll turn to next years harvest day
> And winters leisure to regale
> Hopes better times and sips his ale
> While labour still pursues his way
> And braves the tempest as he may

This connection does more than emphasise the contrast; it serves to underline the effect of winter on humanity, the retreat from nature, the dreams of warmth and spring. The farmer suggests comfort as the thresher suggests labour, so that outdoor action offsets the somnolence inside : this outlines an interesting pattern in which comfort and warmth are linked with sloth and inaction, whilst labour and cold are linked with action and bustle. But cold also suggests the frozen heart.

The bitter world of fact is introduced with the almost cynical personification of labour. The generality is a prelude to the individual instance, the thresher, the foddering boy, the shepherd, just as comfort heralded the inmates of the inn. The impersonality of the last couplet quoted above, by its very nonchalance, reflects the attitude of the comfortable and comments upon it. The repetition of 'Tempest' (line five had 'unfelt tempests') serves a similar purpose. The description of the waking world as it sets to work is more than a pot-pourri of earlier vignettes. It emphasises the dreamlike quality of the scene, the isolation of the winter months. Clare describes what his characters actually do; in the darkness they cannot be seen, and Clare relies on sound, on the bellowing of the animals for their food.[110] The reluctance of winter is caught in the boy's movements, as is the recurrent nature of the episode. It is a remorseless cycle, day in, day out.

> And foddering boys sojourn again
> By ryhme hung hedge and frozen plain
> Shuffling thro the sinking snows
> Blowing his fingers as he goes
> To where the stock in bellowings hoarse
> Call for their meals in dreary close
> And print full many a hungry track
> Round circling hedge that guards the stack
> Wi higgling* tug he cuts the hay
> And bares the forkfull loads away
> And morn and evening daily throws
> The little heaps upon the snows

A few lines further on comes one of Clare's images of stark loneliness:

> While in the fields the lonly plough
> Enjoys its frozen sabbath now

The intentional irony of this is echoed in the next couplet:

> And horses too pass time away
> In leisures hungry holiday

* Searching.

The horses' leisure reflects the uneasy leisure of the farmers in the tavern, their dreams of food ('Rubbing and lunging round the yard/Dreaming no doubt of summer sward') resemble the farmers' dreams, and echo those of the owl, dreaming of day. Clare is also enjoying his own literary joke here. Thomson had referred in 'Spring' to the 'well-us'd plough' which 'lies in the furrow loosened from the frost'; Clare might also have had in mind Bloomfield's 'slumbering ploughs', for he seems to remember this in 'February' when he refers to the 'rested plough'.[111]

After some more telling detail, with bows of acknowledgement to Bloomfield and Thomson, comes the description of the boy at the pump. This masterly passage is what Taylor chose to omit. The noise of the pump is a symbol of hope, as is the splintering of the frozen waters, whilst the sleepy geese wait, sad and silent. The geese have their brief moment of delight, before the pond is again frozen. Clare is indebted to Bloomfield's description of Giles breaking the ice in 'Winter', but he goes far beyond Bloomfield's tentative approach to realism :

> At clanking pump his station takes
> Half hid in mist their breathing makes
> Or at the pond before the door
> Which every night leaves frozen oer
> Wi heavy beetle* splinters round
> The glossy ice wi jarring sound
> While huddling geese as half asleep
> Doth round the imprisond water creep
> Silent and sad to wait his aid
> And soon as ere a hole is made
> They din his ears wi pleasures cry
> And hiss at all that ventures nigh
> Splashing wi jealous joys & vain
> Their fill ere it be froze again[112]

With a change of mood, the scene is occupied by the play of children, but they too are defeated by the cold; the image of the cloud passing the sun is a sure indication of the hollowness of their mirth, of the fleeting nature of their pleasure.

* Mallet.

Or seeking bright glib* ice to play
To sailing slide the hours away
As smooth and quick as shadows run
When clouds in autumn pass the sun[113]

Again, we cannot but be aware of the literary heritage here,
with the resemblances to scenes from Hurdis, the glancing
allusions to Pope and Wordsworth. But the real interest lies in
the conflicting tone that operates here, with the inherent joy
of motion and activity offset by the static frozen lake and the
fear of the 'morehen', driven away from shelter. The enjoyment
of some depends upon the oppression of others; pleasure is
frantic and ephemeral, as the geese learn.

The description of the flight of the birds is a variation on a
well-tried theme. But coming after the relatively dainty Thomsonian account of the robin, its effect is startling;[114] the small
shred of comfort is soon dispelled by this dizzy view of the
birds as they fly aimlessly to and fro. The image of sleep, the
dream of winter, is invoked by implication, in the dreary
inevitability of the process, framed in the diurnal cycle, and
reiterated in the conventional attributes of morning and of
sun: the defunct descriptions underline the pointlessness, the
heavy weariness of the journey.

The clouds of starnels† dailey fly
Blackening thro the evening sky
To whittleseas reed wooded mere
And ozier holts by rivers near
And many a mingld swathy crowd,
Rook crow and jackdaw noising loud
Fly too and fro to dreary fen
Dull winters weary flight agen
Flopping on heavy wings away
As soon as morning wakens grey
And when the sun sets round and red
Returns to naked woods to bed[115]

There is a moment of hope after this, as pigeons and sheep
share a meal, and green turnip leaves come up through the
snow, and icicles begin to thaw; but again it is deceptive, for

* Slippery.
† Starlings.

once the sun disappears, the icicles return, and day hurries
to its close, overtaken by the swift night (running like the
children outside).[116] The day returns to sleep, whence it was
awakened at the start of the poem. Everyone heads for home.
The sense of relief is achieved with economy : it is the well-
deserved resolution of the winter's dreary day. But although
shelter is achieved here, we cannot forget the main body of
this section. The contrast between fireside warmth and winter
tempests, suggested at the end, is only one element in the
structure. This account of 'A Winters Day' is a vividly personal
vision of what this means in terms of hardship, of a personal
struggle against nature and against isolation. The victory is
only temporary. The sun soon creeps out of sight behind the
woods, going to his bed like the chilled birds, pale as they are
naked.

There are ebbs and flows, as there are differences of focus, as
for example the change from the robin to the starnels. The
plough is a symbol of waste, of a harvest yet to come, and yet
frustrated : it is a grim and desolate sabbath. (The point is
wryly made by Clare, in view of his intense concern for the
Sabbath as a time for freedom and hope.) The melancholy
journey of the birds is another image of this aimless lack of
purpose. Everyone is to some extent apt to dream : the harsh
reality is out of doors, and all inside is limited in its concept of
reality; the labourer returns when the day has shut his eyes,
and night begins to dream again. The battle is over for another
day, but that is all. Another winter's day begins tomorrow,
and the struggle will be resumed. Again the world will be
frozen, and the personality, the essential individuality of man,
will be numbed. It is no coincidence that Clare echoes Pope in
his final couplet. Pope had written 'How oft in pleasing tasks
we wear the day', and also 'Recall those nights that close thy
toilsome days'.[117] Clare concludes sadly and bitterly :

> Thus doth the winters dreary day
> From morn to evening wear away

The full significance of 'A Winters Day' emerges towards
the end of 'A Cottage Evening'. In many ways this second part
of 'January' is inferior to the first. It is more loosely con-
structed, and some of the descriptions border on the self-

indulgent. But as a depiction of an evening in the cottage, with the old dame telling spine-chilling stories of love and death, it is not only an extremely interesting piece of social comment, but also a well sustained piece of lively verse writing, capturing the sheer thrill of the children, their joy in being alive. It is clearly important that Clare succeed in this portrait of family life, since he is to finish this section with a lament that this is all past, that the ecstasy of childhood is over, and with it the power of poetry. He is using his description of the winter day as a comment on the passing of his childhood vision:

> O spirit of the days gone bye
> Sweet childhoods fearful extacy
> The witching spells of winter nights
> Where are they fled wi their delights ...
> Where are they gone the joys and fears
> The links the life of other years
> I thought they bound around my heart
> So close that we coud never part
> Till reason like a winters day
> Nipt childhoods visions all away
> Nor left behind one withering flower
> To cherish in a lonely hour[118]

Vision has been overthrown by stultifying reality: now he hears stories, but remains unmoved, no longer afraid. His responses are numbed, he is like the dreary inhabitants of earth on a winter's day, travelling the dull journey of the sky, but not climbing with hope and sense of adventure, like Jack and the Beanstalk. Romance is dead. Frozen with apathy, he cannot even enjoy the *frisson* of cold terror and dread. This statement of exposure to the real world helps to explain the apparently incongruous opening to the 'Cottage Evening', where there is a sense of warmth and mirth indoors, in contrast to the outside realities. There is still the emphasis on dream, but it is a dream of contentment, the dream of childhood, the warmth of personal expansiveness and social communion; everything is relaxed and open. It suggests the lost innocence and the faded vision, just as Adam and Eve on the painted screen are about to divest themselves and the world of innocence, and the clock booms out behind them, announcing the passing of time, the departure of childhood. The children laugh at their own faces in the gleaming polished pan lid on the wall; Clare looks at his own reflection, but no longer laughs. The shadows on the grass are a reality, the clouds are again across the sun, and it is a time of doubt, in which the only thing left to be trusted in is Moore's *Almanack*. The cyclic process is completed.

Clare's view of nature is not so pessimistic that he cannot enjoy the summer when it finally arrives: in the sections on May, June, July, August and September he celebrates the rich happinesses of the summer months, always with precision, always with clarity. In the opening sections of the poem, Clare had been able, to some extent, to rely on images of expectation and frustration for the needed emotional coherence. Once he has established that, he can draw on it in his portrayal of the summer, so that the dominant note throughout these months is one of release and fulfilment. At the same time, Clare rarely forgets that there are still shadows lurking. This passage from 'May' suggests the depths at which Clare's surface simplicity reverberates:

> While wood men still on spring intrudes
> And thins the shadow[s'] solitudes
> Wi sharpend axes felling down
> The oak trees budding into brown
> Where as they crash upon the ground
> A crowd of labourers gather round
> And mix among the shadows dark
> To rip the crackling staining bark
> From off the tree and lay when done
> The rolls in lares* to meet the sun
> Depriving yearly where they come
> The green wood pecker of its home
> That early in the spring began
> Far from the sight of troubling man
> And bord their round holes in each tree
> In fancys sweet security
> Till startld wi the woodmans noise
> It wakes from all its dreaming joys[119]

* Clearings.

In 'October' and 'November' the initial sombre note reasserts itself, as the images of isolation once again dominate the scene. In the closing lines of 'October' for instance, nature's dreams of beauty imbue the carefully modulated description of the gradually darkening countryside: the interesting point here is that the connection effected between this melancholy bleakness, so reminiscent of the opening dull dreariness, and the dreams of joy, is only explicable in terms of the inherent joy of the whole section, a joy that recognises its own sobriety:

> The starnel crowds that dim the muddy light
> The crows and jackdaws flapping home at night
> And puddock circling round its lazy flight
> Round the wild sweeing* wood in motion slow
> Before it perches on the oaks below
> And hugh† black beetles revelling alone
> In the dull evening with their heavy drone
> Buzzing from barn door straw and hovel sides
> Where fodderd cattle from the night abides
> These pictures linger thro the shortning day
> And cheer the lone bards mellancholy way
> And now and then a solitary boy
> Journeying and muttering oer his dreams of joy[120]

The conclusion of 'November' is equally memorable, with its invocation of the spirit of the community before the revelries of Christmas:

> At length the busy noise of toil is still
> And industry awhile her care forgoes
> When winter comes in earnest to fulfill
> Her yearly task at bleak novembers close
> And stops the plough and hides the field in snows
> When frost locks up the streams in chill delay
> And mellows on the hedge the purple sloes
> For little birds – then toil hath time for play
> And nought but threshers flails awake the dreary day[121]

What this underlines is Clare's fidelity to his subject: rather than impose a pattern on her, he lets one emerge. Take for

* Swaying.
† Huge.

example what happens in 'June', a section which illustrates something of the range of Clare's response to the summer months. The opening lines portray the month as a time of noise, bustle, activity, song, glory, colour, and wildness.

> Now summer is in flower and natures hum
> Is never silent round her sultry bloom
> Insects as small as dust are never done
> Wi' glittering dance and reeling in the sun
> And green wood fly and blossom haunting bee
> Are never weary of their melody
> Round field hedge now flowers in full glory twine
> Large bindweed bells wild hop and streakd woodbine
> That lift athirst their slender throated flowers
> Agape for dew falls and for honey showers
> These round each bush in sweet disorder run
> And spread their wild hues to the sultry sun[122]

In the glory and the flowering, there is also a painful thirst and striving. Summer's 'sultry bloom' is not merely picturesque. Clare works out a pattern of contrasts: he sets against such wildness the leisurely aestheticism of the spider; the swelling wheat is seen in opposition to the wild flowers of May and their 'gaudy show'; nests are left more protected but at the mercy of the schoolboy nonetheless. Clare's fullness of response in this passage is paralleled by his free use of the couplet, his varying of pace as suits the occasion, catching the unwearied melody of the bees and the wildness of the twining flowers. The poem flowers from the opening statement, explaining this bloom and hum in particular terms. When he turns to the people labouring in the fields, he has created the sense of a complexity of activity by which they are to be appreciated. A later progression of thought echoes the opening of this section. The thirsty flowers have their reflection in the thirsty plough-men. Again anguish brings out the best in Clare:

> The ploughman sweats along the fallow vales
> And down the suncrackt furrow slowly trails[123]

The community spirit is again invoked. Clare watches the old men as they remind themselves of past customs. The farmer

Recalls full many a thing by bards unsung
And pride forgot – that reignd when he was young[124]

Retreating into the past, he recalls the merrymaking, the huge
bowl, the large stone pitcher, the old songs they sang (in turn
stretching back to previous generations). But not all the old
customs are gone; the winter of pride has not blighted them
all. Proceeding to an account of such customs, with an
extended catalogue of flowers sought by the 'timid maid', and a
long description of the young man's advances, Clare cannot
avoid the reverberations of the past:

> And ale and songs and healths and merry ways
> Keeps up a shadow of old farmers days
> But the old beachen bowl that once supplyd
> Its feast of frumity is thrown aside[125]

At the year's climax Clare remembers the social distinctions
and the upheaval, just as Bloomfield did less powerfully in
The Farmer's Boy.[126] Taylor deleted the last four lines of the
poem as it appeared in Peterborough MS. A29 : in fact he was
fairly ruthless with his excisions in what was not a particularly
long section. The whole point of this section gains from these
lines, as nostalgia grows into social protest :

> All this is past – and soon may pass away
> The time torn remnant of the holiday
> As proud distinction makes a wider space
> Between the genteel and the vulgar race
> Then must they fade as pride oer custom showers
> Its blighting mildew on her feeble flowers[127]

But more than the vigour of protest is involved. This imagery of
decay (echoing the lines at the end of 'May') is in stark contrast to the opening of the poem. The mildew of pride is seen
as an actively insidious force, while the past is seen in all its
weakness and insecurity. It is all too easy for custom to fade.
But at the beginning, in the present, nature is an active force.
The implications of the contrast are, however, not contradictory : Clare can feel the vitality and joy of present nature.
At the same time, although not always looking over his
shoulder at the past, the joys of the present are to be viewed in

a wider context that includes the past, when nature bloomed in a different and more exalted world.

V

Clare had thought the Tales were better than the descriptive accounts of the months. Four were included in the 1827 volume: 'Sorrows of Love', 'Jockey and Jenny', 'The Rivals' and 'The Memory of Love'. In all of them Clare evinces an astonishing ease, relishing the country tales told by the fireside, forgoing obvious moralistic attitudes. The village chatterbox comes to the end of her story in 'Valentine Eve' (one of Clare's favourites, but not published in 1827):

> 'Hark thats the clock well I must up and roam
> My man no doubt sits waiting me at home
> Wholl scold and say by sitting here till nine
> That Im an old fool keeping Valentine
> So good night all' and hastening from her seat
> She sought her clogs and clocked adown the street
> The girls were glad twas done – and in her place
> The happy cat leapt up and cleaned her face
> While crickets that had been unheard so long
> Seemed as she stopt to start a merrier song[128]

This is characteristic in its handling of a conversational tone, and in the way Clare moves from that to a wry comment on it. But not all the tales are light entertainment-pieces. 'Jockey and Jenny; or The Progress of Love' ends with the two characters safely married; yet in these lines Clare hints at the darker side of love, as he himself has experienced it, and this sobriety reflects the tone of much of the *Calendar* itself, with its emphasis, especially in the winter months, on hopes unfulfilled:

> First Love, how sweet! ah, would it longer last:
> Though Time remembers it when felt and past,
> 'Tis but a shadow of a substance gone, –
> A setting sunbeam to a rising one.

> Love, as the plant called Sensitive, is such,
> Fair to the eye and with'ring to the touch;

Revealing cares that marriage vows await,
Which bring repentance that is brought too late.[129]

'The Sorrows of Love' is perhaps the most moving of these
Tales. Again the framing device puts the story in perspective,
showing how the teller is affected by what she has to tell.

To sober with sad truths the laughing mirth
Of rosy daughters round the cottage hearth,
And pass the winter's lengthen'd eve away,
A mother told the tale of Sally Grey.
'How time', she said, 'and pleasure vanish by!'
Then stopp'd to wipe the tear-drops from her eye;
'Time gains upon us distance unawares,
Stealing our joys and changing them to cares:
'Tis nine-and-thirty years ago', – the date
To prove, she look'd above her where she sat,
And pull'd the Bible down – that certain guide
When boys and girls were born, and old friends died –
That lay with penny stories nestling near,
And almanacks preserved for many a year;
Stopping her story till she found the place,
Pulling her glasses from their leathern case –
'Twas right: and from her cap, in sadden'd vein,
She took her knitting and went on again.[130]

Sally is the victim of a youth's idle affections, a 'clown, as
shifting as the summer wind' who 'saw a prison in a marriage-
vow'. The old woman knew Sally well:

'Poor girl! I felt in trouble for her end –
A next-door neighbour and an early friend:
Her father kept a cottage next to ours;
He was a gardener, and he dealt in flowers,
And Sally's bean would buy his flowers the while
With double prices – money and a smile,
And many a whisper of love's cheating powers,
Calling her fairest of her father's flowers.'

Everyone in the family likes the young man who pays his atten-
tions to Sally: her sisters romp and play with him, and he gives
them presents, promising them some wedding-cake when he

is married to Sally. The father gives up his seat in the corner
to his prospective son-in-law. But once he is secure in her
affections he begins to tease and taunt, enjoying her jealousy.
The old woman sees what is happening:

> 'Yet, when I caution'd her of love's distress,
> And bade her notice the wild fellow less,
> Saying she show'd her love too much by half,
> "Mary, you jest!" she said, and made a laugh.'

The parents, too, begin to appreciate the position, but cannot
see how distressed their daughter really is. As parents do, they
try to laugh it off:

> 'At length her parents, though with added fears,
> Saw through her heart-throbs and her secret tears;
> And when they found the only crime was love,
> They joked at times, and would at times reprove,
> Saying, if that were all the world possess'd
> For causing troubles, few would be distress'd.
> But all was vain! she put her best looks on
> When they were there, and grieved when they were gone.'

Questions are asked, and Sally has to put on a brave face, until
she can stand it no longer. As she lies in bed, the remorseful
lover comes to her, asking forgiveness. It is a poignant moment:

> 'I sat beside her bed:
> He asked her how she was, and hung his head:
> The tears burst from her eyes; she could not speak.'

Hope is revived, the wedding-day fixed. But it is too late.

> 'Upon that very morn that was to see
> The wedding sunshine and festivity,
> Death did so gently his cold fingers lay
> Upon her bosom, that she swoon'd away
> Without a groan; and but for us that wept
> About her bed, you might have thought she slept.'

When she has finished her story, the old woman says she would
like her children to read her the psalm that was sung at Sally's
grave. But she decides it would be too much, the sorrow too
great.

She ceas'd her tale, and snuff'd the candle wick,
Lifting it up from burning in the stick,
Then laid her knitting down, and shook her head,
And stoop'd to stir the fire and talk of bed.

The succinctness and pathos of this tale (characteristic of the others) are impressive, all the more so when placed beside the barely controlled hysteria of parts of *The Parish*. Clare's success in this form – granted he doesn't seem to me to achieve anything like the moral weight of Crabbe – suggests how perceptive Taylor and Hessey were to encourage him to write such tales. In the event the original plan of tales alternating with descriptive sections proved impracticable, and so the final form of the volume was not entirely satisfactory. In any case, the inherent weaknesses have to be admitted: the repetitions, which a final version might have ironed out; the thinness of 'April', which Clare acknowledged was poor by comparison with his longer section 'Spring', which was not included; the second version of 'July', cobbled up in a fortnight to please Taylor, had little of the verve of the first, and longer, version. But such faults and shortcomings are slight when set beside the evident accomplishment of the poem as a whole. Here was Clare's demonstration that he was much more than the curious wonder of 1820. Some of the critics had demanded proof of his ability to write something sustained and original and thoughtful. In 1827 they had their proof, but most chose to ignore it.

4

'This Visionary Theme':
The Rural Muse

I

Clare's final volume, edited by Taylor and the indefatigable Mrs Emmerson, was published in 1835.[1] *The Rural Muse*, hailed by Edmund Blunden as one of the richest and most melodious volumes of its kind – and decried by Ian Jack as an anticlimax after *The Shepherd's Calendar* – was something of a mixed bag.[2] It could have been a much better book, if Mrs Emmerson had not let her sentimentality influence so strongly her choice of poems from the wealth of manuscript material. Nonetheless there is considerable variety in the volume as it stands: it is almost as though Clare were exulting in a sense of freedom after the difficulties over *The Shepherd's Calendar*. There is certainly in many of these poems a confidence that seems to belie the personal agonies that afflicted Clare in the decade leading up to its publication.

Clare is catholic in his choice of subjects, but also in the way he approaches them. Apart from the straightforward descriptive pieces, there are many poems in which he explores his attitudes to the natural world. Linked to these are the poems about birds' nests (Edwin Paxton Hood, in the *Eclectic Review*, christened Clare 'the laureate of birds' nests', and talked about them 'beautified in this rich mystical halo of verse'),[3] exceptionally fine and chiselled poems in which Clare moves so freely within his own self-imposed limits that we are made aware of a new grasp, both technical and emotional. The connection between these poems and the sonnets becomes apparent, but these nest poems are grander, more consciously designed pieces, for all their seeming artlessness. There are, by

comparison, more formal pieces, with the sonorous reverberation of classical odes, Collins-like in their solemnity. These
again are really different from what he had done before. There
are one or two poems which sound the deeper, almost mystical
note that is common in the asylum period, but which lends
resonance to the poems of this period too. The songs and
ballads, although not a new departure – for they represent what
seemed to come most easily and frequently to Clare – are nonetheless interesting for their greater finish and poignancy. Finally there are a few agonisingly personal poems such as 'Decay',
written at a crucial point in his life, at the time of the move
from Helpstone to Northborough. It is to poems such as this
that we must turn for an understanding of Clare's personal
turmoil.

At the beginning of 1824, when he was embroiled in the
preparations for *The Shepherd's Calendar*, Clare announced
that he would not publish anything else for eight or ten years.
In the meantime he intended to write a hundred sonnets; significantly these were to be pictorial. As he wrote, they would be

> as a set of pictures on the scenes of objects that appear in
> the different seasons & as I shall do it soly for amusement I
> shall take up wi gentle & simple as they come whatever in
> my eye finds any interests not merely in the view for publi-
> cation but for attempts[4]

In other words the tendencies of the better of the earlier sonnets would be continued; there are consequently fewer sonnets
on such grandiose themes as Religion, Hope, or Anxiety. The
vast majority of these sonnets is basically descriptive, even
though there is a wider variety of approaches within this broad
category. There is a consistency of quality which claims our
admiration, so completely does Clare recapture atmospheres,
moments in time, the drudgery of labour, the joys and delights
of the seasons.[5] There is seldom the sort of *gaucherie*, the intrusion of his own personality, which marred so many of the
early sonnets. At the same time, the language is sharper and
more direct, as the redundancies and poeticisms disappear.

Clare, however, was not altogether happy with them; at
the end of 1828 he was contemplating a lengthy poem entitled

'The Pleasures of Spring', but both Taylor and his new friend, the poet George Darley warned him against it.[6] Darley demanded more action in his pictures of nature, and Taylor was afraid that Clare would repeat himself.[7] It was better to keep himself to shorter forms: Taylor seems to have had in mind the rather insipid songs that Clare wrote, but Clare's reply is instructive; what he says of the problem of repetition and action in poetry applies especially to his sonnets, and his reference to 'little things' could refer to sonnets as well as anything else:

> Your opinion of my intended Poem is in some instances correct for the same images must certainly occur of which I have written before yet if I could succeed others would be added that would do away the impression of repetition but action is what I want I am told & how action is to get into the pleasures of Spring I cannot tell
>
> I think many of the productions of the day that introduce action do it at the expense of nature for they are often like puppets pulled into motion by strings & there are so many plots semiplots & demiplots to make up a bookable matter for modern taste that its often a wonder how they can find readers to please at all – I still do as you say & go on with little things[8]

It was partly a desire to get away from such 'little things' that Clare had started his 'Pleasures of Spring'. But he continued with his descriptive sonnets, perhaps encouraged by the advice of H. F. Cary: 'What you most excel in is the description of such natural objects as you have yourself had the opportunity of observing and which none before you have noticed though everyone instantly recognises their truth.'[9] Darley was simply voicing the anticipated reaction of the public: he was only advocating the inner drama of which Clare was perfectly capable.

'Pleasures of Spring' remained unpublished during Clare's lifetime. Drama and action were perhaps easier to achieve within the shorter bounds of the sonnet. But he was still very conscious of the apparent smallness of his achievement; he felt about his own work as Dr Johnson did about Milton's sonnets. He wrote to Cary in 1832, after he had moved to

Northborough: 'I sit sometimes & wonder over the little noise I have made in the world untill I think I have written nothing as yet to deserve any praise at all ...'[10] He described how he was urged by ambition to write down more poetry, 'those little madrigals' that he 'Hum[s] & sing[s] inwardly' about his house and garden; he thinks they are good until a second reading, '& then the charm vanishes into the vanity that I shall do something better ere I die so in spite of myself I ryhme on & write nothing but little things at last –'.

In spite of these doubts, Clare continued to write sonnets. He was still tempted by the grandiose theme, but was able to achieve on occasions the effects that had earlier eluded him. The obsessions become more pronounced and more moving. 'Obscurity' is characteristic of these poems.

> Old tree, oblivion doth thy life condemn,
> Blank and recordless as that summer wind
> That fanned the first few leaves on thy young stem
> When thou wert one year's shoot: and who can find
> Their homes of rest or paths of wandering now?
> So seems thy history to a thinking mind,
> As now I gaze upon thy sheltering bough.
> Thou grew unnoticed up, to flourish now
> And leave thy past as nothing all behind,
> Where many years and doubtless centuries lie.
> That ewe beneath thy shadow, nay, that fly
> Just settled on a leaf, can know with time
> Almost as much of thy blank past as I;
> Thus blank oblivion reigns as earth's sublime.[11]

The complexity of this is much more impressive than the fretting over his own insignificance of five years previously. Here there is an awareness of time as an accumulation which cannot easily be swept aside, and in that awareness is a hint of his deepening, more introspective and meditative, approach to the natural world.

Clare's sense of freedom within the form, evinced by 'Obscurity' – he captures, in his increasing use of run-on lines especially, something of the breadth of the Miltonic sonneteers, without actually employing the Miltonic rhyme-scheme – is even more noticeable in the more overtly descriptive sonnets. He manages to infuse an inevitability into these pieces (even when the rhyme scheme has been reduced to a series of couplets), so that what might appear as the most transparent narrative sequence becomes a carefully modulated portrayal of an action momentarily frozen. 'Schoolboys in Winter', with its majestic ending, is one of his best sonnets:

> The schoolboys still their morning rambles take
> To neighbouring village school with playing speed,
> Loitering with pastime's leisure till they quake,
> Oft looking up the wild-geese droves to heed,
> Watching the letters which their journeys make;
> Or plucking haws on which the fieldfares feed,
> And hips, and sloes; and on each shallow lake
> Making glib slides, where they like shadows go
> Till some fresh pastimes in their minds awake.
> Then oft they start anew and hasty blow
> Their numbed and clumpsing* fingers till they glow;
> Then races with their shadows wildly run
> That stride huge giants o'er the shining snow
> In the pale splendour of the winter sun.[12]

The sonnets are used to explore the relationship between man and nature, continuing the preoccupation of *The Shephard's Calendar*. Clare realised that the sonnet, as he had developed it, was an ideal vehicle for a vision of nature that embraced the simultaneity of what he saw, the interconnectedness of everything outside himself. The form itself, through the syntax and the often complex rhyme-schemes, keeps in check the sort of abundance that is so characteristic of his prose accounts. This is true, for example, of 'Summer':

> The woodman's axe renews its hollow stroke,
>   And barkmen's noises in the woods awake,
> Ripping the stained bark from the fallen oak,
>   Where crumpled fox-fern and the branching brake
> Fade 'neath their crushing feet. The timid hare
>   Starts from its mossy root or sedgy seat,
> And listening foxes leave their startled lair
>   And to some blackthorn's spinney make retreat.

---

* Frozen.

Haymakers with their shouldered rakes sojourn
    To hedgy closes, and amid the wheat
The schoolboy runs, while pleasures thickly burn
    Around his heart, to crop corn-bottle flowers,
Scaring the partridge from its quiet bourn,
    That hides for shelter from the summer heat.[13]

A poem like this shows how far Clare has come from the immature ejaculations of the earlier sonnets, how he is now able to contain his emotions within his portrayal of action. There is no simplistic wondering here.

Clare's sense of personal tragedy can obtrude into even the happiest of poems. As so often, the final couplet effects the sudden change of mood. This is true of 'June', where the first twelve lines place the emphasis on the delights of nature: 'ecstasy' and 'rapture' are important words. The spiritual ecstasy is matched by the physical vigour, the 'breeze's wanton cry'. But the couplet negates all this; his heart does not agree with his eyes:

Yet mid this summer glee I cannot borrow
One joy, for sadness chills them all to sorrow.[14]

The cause of Clare's melancholy is frequently the realisation that joy is past. 'The Boys' Playground' concludes dolefully:

A passing bell scarce makes a deeper sigh,
    Than the remembrances of days gone by.[15]

'Field Flowers' relives some of the pleasures of flower hunting, when life was a 'partner too'. Clare asks pathetically, like the deceived child,

Why did he turn a foe and fill our path with cares?[16]

Occasionally it seems as though something can be salvaged, in spite of the fact that

... cares have claimed me many an evil day
And chilled the relish which I had for joy.

He still climbs the crab-tree, but as much for the 'old esteems' as for anything he might find at the top:

Till the heart stirring past as present seems

Save the bright sunshine of these fairy dreams.[17]

One or two sonnets explore this fading of the dream: in viewing beauty he sees its inherent brevity, and the common idea is revitalised because of Clare's personal involvement, his pathetic reliance on dream imagery:

> The fairy sunshine gently flickers through
>   Upon the grass and buttercups below;
> And in the foliage winds their sports renew,
>   Waving romantic shadows to and fro,
> That o'er the mind in sweet disorder flings
>   A flitting dream of beauty's fading things.[18]

Even an object as full of associations as Burthorp Oak will sooner or later die. Clare's inability to face the full measure of this tragedy may be seen in the faltering of the first line in this passage:

> And desolate fancies bid the eyes grow dim
> With feelings, that earth's grandeur should decay
> And all its olden memories pass away.[19]

Several of the descriptive sonnets are imbued with the sorrow deriving from this perception. It frequently retains a dignity for which Clare is remarkable. In 'Autumn', a lament for the passing of summer, he maintains a nice balance between the bustle of summer and the peace that is left.[20] Structurally, the poem consists of an opening announcement of the theme:

> Summer is gone and all the merry noise
> Of busy harvest in its labouring glee;

followed by an enumeration of the joys of summer, and a conclusion stressing the sadness of the passing. The central section is impressionistic, a wild mixture of sights and sounds, concise and clear descriptions that rattle along unchecked.

> The shouts of toil, the laughs of gleaning boys
> Sweeing* at dinner-hours on willow tree,
> The cracking whip, the scraps of homely song,
> Sung by the boys that drive the loaded wain,
> The noise of geese that haste and hiss along

* Swinging.

> For corn that litters in the narrow lane
> Torn from the waggon by the hedgerow trees,
> Tinkles of whetting scythes amid the grain,
> The bark of dogs stretched at their panting ease,
> Watching the stook where morning's dinner lay –

This catalogue is suddenly broken into by the two final lines:

> All these have passed, and silence at her ease
> Dreams autumn's melancholy life away.[21]

Clare has allowed himself only the slightest adjustment of tone, but to the maximum effect. There is a touch of irony in the image, for it recalls the dogs in summer 'stretched at their panting ease'. The languorous somnolence of autumn is caught to a nicety.

This melancholy is sometimes extended, as Clare reaches out for the expression of nature's strangeness; it lies behind the surprise that comes at the end of a later sonnet, 'The Heronry':

> And when the spring with joy the earth invests
> Each tree-top seems as bending down with nests;
> For there a troop of heronshaws* repair
> And yearly pile a stack of dwellings there,
> Crank† on the trees and on their branches stand
> And the whole scene seems changed to foreign land.[22]

Or behind the conclusion of 'Mouse's Nest':

> The young ones squeaked, and as I went away
> She found her nest again among the hay.
> The water o'er the pebbles scarce could run
> And broad old cesspools glittered in the sun.[23]

This is matched by the brilliance of 'November' in which, although no attempt is made to recreate syntactically the relationships between the various figures in the scene, Clare elevates, in his series of disjointed clauses, the November day to the status of myth:

> The shepherds almost wonder where they dwell,

* Herons.
† Sing dolefully.

And the old dog for his right journey stares:
The path leads somewhere, but they cannot tell,
And neighbour meets with neighbour unawares.
The maiden passes close beside her cow,
And wanders on, and thinks her far away;
The ploughman goes unseen behind his plough
And seems to lose his horses half the day.
The lazy mist creeps on in journey slow;
The maidens shout and wonder where they go;
So dull and dark are the November days.
The lazy mist high up the evening curled,
And now the morn quite hides in smoke and haze;
The place we occupy seems all the world.[24]

There is no other poet of the nineteenth century who could
achieve that.[25]

II

The greater range and flexibility I have mentioned in connection with Clare's development is exemplified in the so-called
birds' nests poems, where he advances beyond the mere lightness of touch that characterises so many of his poems (of this
period and earlier), such as 'Insects' or 'Pastoral Fancies'.[26]
Whereas he had often been content to spin a thin melodic
line, uncomplicated and unpretentious, he develops this technique, by a subtle change of tone, into something richer and
more reverberant. The nest poems are among Clare's most impressive achievements before 1832, representing the culmination of a style he had been gradually moving towards for
some time. They celebrate seclusion and isolation, with an intense awareness of the fullness and uniqueness of what he is
observing so closely. *The Shepherd's Calendar* had celebrated
a way of life and its passing; the nest poems show Clare trying
to understand the mystery of nature itself, in terms of the
solitude which for him suggested innocence and beauty. We
have, however, to avoid the rash equation made by the enthusiastic Mrs Emmerson, whereby Clare and bird become one.[27]
The achievement of the poems is precisely in Clare's ability to
understand and love, intimately and in wonder, to respect the

birds' essential singularity, and the separateness of their existence.

In the opening paragraph of 'The Nightingales Nest' Clare is trying to engage the reader's confidence; he is in control here, guiding us, directing, cajoling:

> Up this green woodland ride lets softly rove
> And list the nightingale – she dwelleth here
> Hush let the wood gate softly clap – for fear
> The noise may drive her from her home of love
> For here Ive heard her many a merry year
> At morn and eve nay all the live long day
> As though she lived on song[28]

This control is reflected in the movement of the syntax: what is apparently so easily informal is neatly contained by the rhythmical structure, and the seemingly careless rhymes remind us of these formal limitations, without making the verse in any way stiff or self-conscious. A sense of conspiracy, awe, hushed silence, and admonishment is conveyed in these lines: self-effacement is essential in view of the sacred nature of the nest, the 'bird's home of love'. Clare is an admirer, not an intruder.

The setting in which the bird is to be found emphasises the spirit of the poem:

> this very spot
> Just where that old mans beard all wildly trails
> Rude arbours oer the road and stops the way
> And where that child its blue bell flowers hath got
> Laughing and creeping through the mossy rails
> There have I hunted like a very boy

As so often, the perspective of time is stressed; the nightingale exists in a context of the past as well as the present, so that in effect the bird is sanctioned by the extremes of age and youth, both protected and sought after. The natural untamed quality of the setting emphasises the protection, as well as the qualities of the bird: wildness and rudeness are inherent, valuable to Clare because of their connection with freedom and privacy. The child's enthusiasm dispels all fears, as the transition is made from the present to the poet's past, by way

of the bluebells, simply and effectively. It is suddenly Clare
himself who is creeping through the thorns, to find the nest;
the nest seemed 'as hidden as a thought unborn', and hence its
importance. Clare's interest in the search is not simply that of
a naturalist, but the mystery and the secrecy require authen-
ticity :

> And where these crimping* fern leaves rampt† among
> The hazels under boughs – Ive nestled down
> And watched her while she sung

Clare becomes the detached observer and the impassioned par-
ticipant in a sacred ritual, as he alternates between detailed
record and a poetic assimilation of the importance of these
details :

> and her renown
> Hath made me marvel that so famed a bird
> Should have no better dress than russet brown
> Her wings would tremble in her extacy
> And feathers stand on end as twere with joy
> And mouth wide open to release her heart
> Of its out sobbing songs – the happiest part
> Of summers fame she shared – for so to me
> Did happy fancys shapen her employ

Her ecstasy is perfectly compatible with her timidity and
drabness. But it is an extremely delicate ecstasy :

> But if I touched a bush or scarcely stirred
> All in a moment stopt – I watched in vain
> The timid bird had left the hazel bush
> And at a distance hid to sing again
> Lost in a wilderness of listening leaves
> Rich extacy would pour its luscious strain

Clare continues to emphasise the unique combination of cau-
tion and richness, the ecstatic sound emerging from the tiny
frame. Her singing encourages the thrush to join in, as Clare
echoes the conventional theme of the birds' chorus, only to
elaborate on it, pointing a contrast between the thrush, with

---

* Wrinkled.
† Grow richly.

its winter cares, and the nightingale, a summer bird:

> Her joys are evergreen her world is wide ...

At this point Clare reverts to the present, reiterating the opening tone of friendly conspiracy. By exploring his own personal reminiscences, by reaching back into the past, Clare has explained something of the mystery and wonder of the bird, and sanctioned it with reference to his own childhood. The portrait of the bird and its nest, which follows, depends for its full validity on this opening evocation. The conversational tone returns, as the bird's existence is threatened by this intrusion. So Clare decides not to continue with his search, contenting himself with a glimpse of the nest. The place is too sacred to harm. After this confrontation, Clare turns to describing the nest, in all its ordinary mundane detail, with an honesty that distinguishes him from other descriptive poets. With a unique mixture of wonder, excitement, matter-of-factness, admiration and folklore, Clare encompasses the meaning of the nest:

> How curious is the nest no other bird
> Uses such loose materials or weaves
> Their dwellings in such spots – dead oaken leaves
> Are placed without and velvet moss within
> And little scraps of grass – and scant and spare
> Of what seems scarce materials down and hair
> For from mans haunts she seemeth nought to win
> Yet nature is the builder and contrives
> Homes for her childerns comfort even here
> Where solitudes deciples spend their lives
> Unseen save when a wanderer passes near
> That loves such pleasant places – deep adown
> The nest is made an hermits mossy cell
> Snug lie her curious eggs in number five
> Of deadened green or rather olive brown
> And the old prickly thorn bush guards them well
> And here well leave them still unknown to wrong
> As the old woodlands legacy of song

Clare approaches a speech rhythm in this poem, much more so than in any previous poem, apart from occasional sonnets.

The diction is free from awkwardness, and those words and phrases which are more obviously poetical are assimilated into the texture of the verse, contributing to the richness of effect, rather than detracting from the quietly conversational tone. Clare does not achieve the sonority of Coleridge, but he does sustain a tone of discursive serenity not found before.

In spite of the similarity of theme, the nest poems do not repeat each other. In 'The Ravens Nest', for example, which dispenses with rhyme (as in a few sonnets), although there are occasional half-rhymes and assonance ('loss/pass'; 'one/known'; 'top/cock'; 'days/way'),[29] the emphasis is on time and tradition, as exemplified in the old men's tales. But this perspective of the past serves to reinforce the sense of timelessness inherent in the scene. The birds are like the old men, the 'wood's patriarchs', firm and secure, symbols of inviolability. Only once has the nest actually been seen, long ago in the memory of the oldest men :

> and thence acchieved
> A theme that wonder treasured for supprise
> By every cottage hearth the village through

The two 'ancient' birds are still there, and the oak is

> like a landmark in the chronicles
> Of village memorys ...

This conclusion is inherent in the poem's theme. The imaginative importance of the tree and the nest is linked to the apprehension of them as things : the tree's 'massy bulk', its 'mealy trunk' is something to be climbed, and Clare describes in some detail the methods for climbing. At the same time, the birds are mysterious, unvisualised figures, seen only once in the history of the village, and important to the poet precisely because of their hidden quality.

It was a comparatively short step from these poems on birds' nests to the more formal odes on summer and autumn. Clare had been attracted by the long stanzaic poem some time before he wrote his extended odes.[30] As so often, these poems were written and rewritten over a period of years : although 'Autumn' did not appear in print until 1829,[31] it was begun in 1824, and the drafts are often close in the manuscripts to drafts of 'Summer Images', which in its original form was written before 1824. In a sense these poems are uncharacteristic, in that we do not normally associate Clare with the luxuriant rhythms and misty splendours of Collins.

But clearly Clare himself regarded these poems, in particular 'Autumn' and the two versions of 'Summer Images', with particular affection and concern; Mrs Emmerson's praise could hardly prompt this, as she did not see the poems before 1828.[32] Throughout a number of manuscript books and scraps, these two poems are gradually worked out, built up and expanded, with an extremely careful attention to the need for the right word and inflection. As we have seen, Clare was not always given to correction, and when he did alter and revise, it was often none too substantial a variation on the first draft. But with these poems he went to considerable lengths to gain the right effect. This care may reflect some of the difficulty he had with this more complex form. The ready fluency of his couplets, his octosyllabics, and his sonnets, is not to be found in these more formal poems, for he is writing outside his usual self-imposed limits; or rather he has imposed on himself more stringent restrictions, together with a more ambitious idea of what the poet should be doing. It is here that the debt to Collins is so apparent.

Just what the appeal was of Collins to Clare, and why it should be so powerful in the middle and late 1820s is worth some consideration. Clare is explicit on a few points: he was obviously aware of Collins from an early age, since on his first trip to Stamford, as a boy, to get a copy of Thomson's *Seasons*, he met another youth 'who had a book in his hand which I found to be "Collins' Odes and Poems" '.[33] Although there is no record of when he first had a glimpse himself of Collins's poetry, Collins is included in one or two of his book lists.[34] Certainly by 1824 he was a knowledgeable admirer of Collins: this is apparent from several entries in his *Journal*. On 25 September 1824 he had been re-reading some of the odes: what appealed to Clare was the lack of pomp, the integrity of utterance, and the mellifluous verse of Collins: he could see the difference between Collins and a hack versifier.[35] The context in which Clare was reading these poems is itself of some importance. Countering one of his most severe bouts of melancholic depression he turned naturally to poets who present a view of melancholy that is creative and inspiring, instead of merely nullifying. The serenity of Collins was an antidote to his own miserable despair. At about the same time he was reading Milton: aroused to tears by the sublimity of the opening and close of *Paradise Lost*, and by Milton's account of his blindness ('very pathetic'), he treasured especially the descriptive beauty of *Comus*, *L'Allegro*, and *Il Penseroso*; he gave as an instance:

> what time the laboured ox
> In his loose traces from the furrow came
> And the swinkt hedger at his supper sat.[36]

Clare seldom if ever wrote like that: but it is easy to see the connection he made between Milton and Collins, and his own desire to write a formal poem in the manner of Collins (a form based on Milton, in turn based on Horace). It is scarcely surprising that Clare included the 'Ode to Evening' in his list of poems that had particularly appealed to him, in which poets 'went to nature for their images', one of the poems of which he was constantly reminded when in the presence of nature because of its fidelity to the spirit of nature.[37]

Collins was only one of several poets on this list. The tradition of gloom was further represented by Milton, Dyer, Gray and Thomas Warton. I have already referred to this more general tradition and its effects on the early sonnets in particular. Early poems such as 'Holywell' and 'Cowper Green' as well as 'Solitude', in their lilting octosyllabics echoed Dyer's 'Grongar Hill' and 'Country Walk', as well as Thomas Warton's 'First of April', 'Approach of Summer', and 'Pleasures of Melancholy'. Mrs Emmerson noted the resemblances between 'Solitude' and Kirke White. The debt is, however, for the most part, general rather than particular. Clare's predilection for the tradition was strengthened in 1824 by his illness and the persuasions of Mrs Emmerson to read Warton, Blair and Young.[38] It was only natural that Collins should be added to the list. But he was a special case, much more important than the others: his influence resulted in just the right combination of literary allusion and imaginative recreation. Clare's own melancholy found an echo in that of Collins, and at the same time an inspiration and a cause for hope. For there is no doubt that the tone of Clare's poem on 'Autumn' is regenerative. These poems as a whole are positive gestures towards the past, and towards his melancholy. Mrs Emmerson was right when she told Clare that he need not worry about the presence of Collins's 'Ode of Evening' behind his own 'Autumn'; for her, Clare's poem replaced that of Collins, restating its terms.[39]

The achievement necessitated experiment. In the early 1820s Clare wrote the first draft of 'Summer Images', with the stanzaic structure of Collins's 'Ode to Evening': this was the form he later used in 'Autumn', although there he joined two stanzas together, to make an eight-line stanzaic unit. Like Collins, Clare dispensed with rhyme. The most noticeable difference between these poems and *The Shepherd's Calendar* is the abandonment of an objective, detailed approach to nature in favour of something more grandiose: the world of nature becomes stalked by the half-remembered shades of mythology. Clare's attempt to fuse these two elements in the first version of 'Summer Images' fails mainly because he is obviously so much happier when getting back to his old ways. He inherits from Collins a tone of gentle melancholy which makes the poem autumnal rather than summery, and in this self-induced somnolence Clare doesn't see that he has lost the tautness that the sonnet form in particular had given him: there is nothing to hold his delicate perceptions together. His own uncertainties, of mood and mode, show through unmistakably. It is only in the revised version of the poem that he begins to solve this problem, and then only at the cost of introducing a whole host of poeticisms one feels he would be happier without, such as 'embrowned', 'precedence', 'rosey-fingered', 'zephirs wing', 'toiling clowns', 'lightsome step', 'as of wont', 'fain', 'haply'. But here at least the new richness of detail is something the sonnet form had in effect denied him:

> And see the wild flowers in their summer morn
> Of beauty feeding on joys luscious hours
> The gay convolvulus wreathing round the thorn
>   Agape for honey showers
> And slender king cup burnished with the dew
>   Of mornings early hours
>   Like gold yminted new ...

And now the homebound hedger bundles round
His evening faggot and with every stride
His leathern doublet leaves a rusling sound
    Till silly sheep beside
His path start tremolous and once again
    Look back dissatisfied
    And scan the dewy plain ...[40]

There is a mellowness that contrasts sharply with the sparser particularity of the sonnets, an emphasis on the harmony of the landscape :

Rich music breaths in summers every sound
And in her harmony of varied greens
Woods meadows hedgrows cornfields all around
    Much beauty intervenes
Filling with harmony the ear and eye
    While oer the mingling scenes
    Far spreads the laughing sky[41]

'Autumn' confirms this tendency, while at the same time altering the emphasis that we have seen in *The Shepherd's Calendar* between joy and sorrow : here Clare embraces autumn's melancholy only with the inherent possibility of joy. The poem is couched in terms of search, the lonely poet set against the exhilarating, terrifying, lawlessness of nature, in which the brook itself struggles and chokes. These lines show how Clare has shifted his perspective, how the particular Northamptonshire scene has become universalised :

And mark the hedger front with stubborn face
The dank blea wind that whistles thinly bye
    His leathern garb thorn proof
    And cheeks red hot with toil

While o'er the pleachy lands of mellow brown
The mower's stubbling scythe clogs to his foot
    The ever eking whisp
    With sharp and sudden jerk,

Till into formal rows the russet shocks
Crowd the blank field to thatch time-weathered barns,
    And hovels rude repair,
    Stript by disturbing winds.[42]

This was always the possible direction for Clare's poetry to take: in his mature poetry before this he had refused to do so. But now there is a personal reason why he should accept the blandishments of generalities. For the season's melancholy is the poet's too:

> Soon must I mark thee like a pleasant dream
> Droop faintly and so sicken for thine end
>   As sad the winds sink low
>   In dirges for their queen

But contained in this death is the promise of spring, as the lark hints at the coming rejuvenation:

> While in the moment of their weary pause
> To cheer thy bankrupt pomp the willing lark
>   Starts from its shielding clod
>   Sweet snatching scraps of song

Autumn's death is inglorious, muddled and overhasty, as she is buried in silence beneath her own coloured leaves. But this death is an 'ivied trance', from which she will awaken when summer itself has in turn died. The solemn finality of this stanza is mitigated by the hope of the next:

> Thy life is waining now and silence tries
> To mourn but meets no sympathy in sounds
>   As stooping low she bends
>   Forming with leaves thy grave
> To sleep inglorious there mid tangled woods
> Till parch lipped summer pines in drought away
>   Then from thine ivied trance
>   Awake to glories new[43]

The eternity of nature is here stated in terms of the seasonal cycle, and contained within the bounds of the formal ode. Undoubtedly one of Clare's most consciously shaped poems, 'Autumn' shows how deeply he had been influenced by Collins. But it also shows how far Clare had developed since his first fumbling attempts to capture the melancholy spirit of nature.

III

The Shepherd's Calendar had left Clare embittered and bewil-
dered. His illness increased, only occasionally relieved by the
ministrations and potions prescribed by Dr Darling in London.
The correspondence of the years 1825 to 1832 shows the fluctu-
ations of temperament that caused his wife and friends such
anxiety : optimistic one day, the next he is plunged into dreadful, black morbidity, noting the failure of his hopes and the loss
of his friends in the same breath. His poetry takes on an edge
and a clarity all the more moving when seen in the context of
this perpetual, debilitating struggle simply to keep going. In a
series of crabwise movements Clare finds the way towards some
sort of solution to the problems that nag at him – his own
identity as a poet, the value of his work, the relevance of
the past for the present, the need to find again the innocence
lost with Mary and enclosure.

The connection between innocence and nature is forcefully
made in 'The Destroyer'.[44] In the opening lines the luxury of
May is magnificently achieved, with economy and decorum :

> In suns and showers luxuriant May came forth
> And spread her riches as of nothing worth,
> Cowslips and daisies, buttercups and crowds
> Without a name as if they dropt from clouds,
> On green and close and meadow everywhere,
> So thick, the green did almost disappear
> To gold and silver hues, and blooms did vie
> With the rich grass' luxuriant mastery.

The gay abandon of the month, her prodigal scattering of
bounty on the earth is to be offset by what man contributes.
After this grand and assured crescendo comes the crushing
finality of the simple shepherd, who stamps thoughtlessly on
the flowers : the ameliorating 'simple' does not make things
any better, and the qualifying 'early' and 'almost every', together with the lack of fuss in 'crushed a flower', only make
the indictment more telling.

> The simple shepherd in his early hour
> With almost every footstep crushed a flower.

The feeble attempts of the wind to resurrect the flowers are to
no avail: but ironically, those beaten down by the dogs re-
cover, and become as 'happy as the wind': man is the sole
destroyer. From this point the poem moves to its climax:

> And who could think in such a lovely time
> And such a spot, where quiet seemed in prime,
> As ne'er to be disturbed, that strife and fear
> Like crouching tigers had howled havoc here?

This is a poem of surprised and violated innocence, based
on a tangible, sensuous appreciation of life in its richness and
glory; the last four lines express this astonishment that such
a world, at such a time, can be torn apart. The most remarkable point about the poem is that any suggestion that Clare
is making a fuss about nothing becomes irrelevant; a common
everyday occurrence is for Clare, without any suggestion of
sentimentality or portentousness, an event of the utmost significance. The poem is a supreme expression of a most singular
and personal vision, one of great strength and uniqueness:
it says much about the rest of Clare's poetry and his ability
to transform the apparently trivial and commonplace into
a burning statement of personal belief.

The anger that we find in 'The Destroyer' is given full vent
in 'The Mores', one of the most pessimistic poems about the
effects of enclosure on Clare's vision.[45] It picks up the theme
explored in a less successful poem 'Emmonsales Heath', the
connection between the wildness of the heath, in itself an
attraction, and the remote past, of which the heath is a
survival. In fact, if we take these two poems together, we can
see the two lines of development, in terms of argument, open to
Clare. The earlier poem, in celebrating the wildness of the heath,
sets against it the whole absurd paraphernalia of civilisation:

> Stern industry, with stubborn toil
> And wants unsatisfied
> Still leaves untouched thy maiden soil
> In its unsullied pride.
>
> The birds still find their summer shades
> To build their nests agen
> And the poor hare its rushy glade
> To hide from savage men[46]

The point about this heath is its timelessness:

> Things seem the same in such retreats
> As when the world began
>
> Furze ling and brake all mingling free
> And grass forever green
> All seem the same old things to be
> As they have ever been

This leaves the way open for philosophical resignation, for retreat into an idyll, for comforting platitude. The vision of paradise that he glimpses here enables Clare to reconcile the present with the past, and it eventually leads to the poems on the eternity of nature in which hope can, after all, be salvaged. But the trend in the opposite direction is just as strong, as 'The Mores' shows: once wildness has been lost, it is much harder to believe in the revivifying powers of memory.

The structure of 'The Mores' is based on the direct opposition of the past struggling against the present. By a nice irony, the opening lines, forming a paean to freedom, constitute in effect a self-contained sonnet.

> Far spread the moorey ground a level scene
> Bespread with rush and one eternal green
> That never felt the rage of blundering plough
> Though centurys wreathed springs blossoms on its brow
> Still meeting plains that stretched them far away
> In uncheckt shadows of green brown and grey
> Unbounded freedom ruled the wandering scene
> Nor fence of ownership crept in between
> To hide the prospect of the following eye
> Its only bondage was the circling sky
> One mighty flat undwarfed by bush and tree
> Spread its faint shadow of immensity
> And lost itself which seemed to eke* its bounds
> In the blue mist the orisons edge surrounds[47]

The self-perpetuating levelness of the land has become 'eternal green', and paradoxically Clare is betrayed into a false sense

---

* Increase.

of security, relishing the unrestricted view, rooted as he is in Helpstone but seeing out beyond its confines into the distance: but the green is not, either spatially or temporarily, eternal. Then comes the 'blundering plough', disastrously destructive, isolated in the verse between the two accounts of long time and eternity. The rule of nature suggests the freedom that has been lost, 'uncheckt' and 'unbounded'; there was no sense of possession, no 'fence of ownership'. Clare exults in the flatness of the plains; they have their own shadow, much grander than any shade afforded by trees: in this vast immensity, freedom and wildness seem endless. But this is all past:

> Now this sweet vision of my boyish hours
> Free as spring clouds and wild as summer flowers
> Is faded all – a hope that blossomed free
> And hath been once no more shall ever be
> Inclosure came and trampled on the grave
> Of labours rights and left the poor a slave
> And memorys pride ere want to wealth did bow
> Is both the shadow and the substance now

All that survives is memory, and for the rest of the poem Clare plays on the power of memory to recreate the past; gradually the freedom of the opening paragraph is extinguished as the present impinges increasingly on the past. The moors become skybound, the plain is fenced off, personal liberty is eroded. The verse becomes more intense and bitter; and echoes of Crabbe can be heard. Clare makes the word 'little' sound superbly diminishing:

> Each little tyrant with his little sign
> Shows where man claims earth glows no more divine

These lines emphasise a point made earlier:

> Fence now meets fence in owners little bounds
> Of field and meadow large as garden grounds
> In little parcels little minds to please
> With men and flocks imprisoned ill at ease

The security of the 'eternal green' was, after all, illusory. 'These paths' to freedom and fancy 'are stopt'. The disaster for Clare is that enclosure has taken away from the 'mores' their identity :

> And birds and trees and flowers without a name
> All sighed when lawless laws enclosure came

Clare echoes this lamentation, because it spells the end of his own freedom, his own vision of poetry.

There are many poems which confront the familiar theme of lost childhood, but few equal in stature the three poems of 1832, 'Remembrances', 'Decay' and 'The Flitting'. 'Remembrances' is certainly not pretentious any more than, say, 'Boyhood Pleasures',[48] but it is grander in design, and bolder in execution; the emotional temperature is higher, the regret more bitter and more poignant. Clare's poem succeeds where Reynolds's 'Shrewsbury' fails, partly because of Clare's more subtle and haunting use of rhythm; Reynolds's poem never takes flight.[49] The biographical circumstances of Clare's poem are not as relevant as has sometimes been supposed. In May 1832 Clare moved three miles away from Helpstone to a cottage at Northborough. He was apprehensive about the move, dreading the separation from the scenes of his youth. But he looked forward to the chance to start again, to break out of the stultifying melancholy which had consumed him for so long. Although his initial reaction on arriving at Northborough was one of deep depression, this did not last. He undoubtedly felt the wrench when he had to leave Helpstone, but the whole episode has become sentimentalised, partly because of lack of evidence, and partly because of Martin's romanticised account in his *Life*.[50] An added difficulty is that the dating of these poems is far from certain : although 'The Flitting' clearly belongs to the days after the move to Northborough, there is no manuscript evidence to suggest that 'Remembrances' or 'Decay' were written then, while there is considerable internal evidence to suggest that they were written just before the move, and therefore express a deeper malaise than one explicable by his uprooting from the scenes of his childhood. Even before the move, he knew only too well, the scenes of childhood had been swept away. 'Remembrances' is moving in its acceptance of an impossible dilemma, reflected in the temporal imagery and the

structure of each stanza, as the lilting nostalgic metre slides
into the deadened awareness of the present in the last line :

> Summers pleasures they are gone like to visions every one
> And the cloudy days of autumn and of winter cometh on
> I tried to call them back but unbidden they are gone
> Far away from heart and eye and for ever far away
> Dear heart and can it be that such raptures meet decay
> I thought them all eternal when by Langley bush I lay
> I thought them joys eternal when I used to shout and play
> On its banks at clink* and bandy chock* and taw* and
> > ducking stone
> Where silence sitteth now on the wild heath as her own
> Like a ruin of the past all alone[51]

This antithesis is central to the poem, and it works partly because of the significance for Clare of named objects and places :
just as in the asylum he was to write letters consisting of a
string of 'old associations' so here it is enough to name the
places and the employments of youth. Against the particularity of the past is set the anonymity of the present :

> When I used to lye and sing by old eastwells boiling spring
> When I used to tie the willow boughs together for a swing
> And fish with crooked pins and thread and never catch a
> > thing
> With heart just like a feather – now as heavy as a stone
> When beneath old lea close oak I the bottom branches
> > broke
> To make out harvest cart like so many working folk
> And then to cut a straw at the brook to have a soak
> O I never dreamed of parting or that trouble had a sting
> Or that pleasures like a flock of birds would ever take to
> > wing
> Leaving nothing but a little naked spring[52]

Detail has been banished from his world : the world he knew
has gone. The whole premise of Clare's verse up to this point in
his life appears to have been eroded – 'O words are poor re-
ciepts for what time hath stole away'. Everything is reduced to

* Marbles.

an undifferentiated 'nature' that hides her face, like the sun
hidden by a permanent black cloud. Whatever had remained
of the old landscape has been obliterated by enclosure, which
'like a buonaparte let not a thing remain'. The despair and
futility come over with stunning impact in the final stanza,
which is in effect a crystallisation of the poem as a whole:

> O had I known as then joy had left the paths of men
> I had watched her night and day besure and never slept agen
> And when she turned to go O I'd caught her mantle then
> And wooed her like a lover by my lonely side to stay
> Aye knelt and worshiped on as love in beautys bower
> And clung upon her smiles as a bee upon a flower
> And gave her heart my poesys all cropt in a sunny hour
> As keepsakes and pledges all to never fade away
> But love never heeded to treasure up the may
> So it went the common road to decay[53]

Part of the strength of the poem derives from the emotional
tension inherent in this desperate last gasp, eloquent and
pathetic: for Clare is deceiving himself.

'Decay' is very similar stylistically to 'The Flitting', and the
two poems have commonly been taken together. But 'Decay'
refers to a more general despair, whereas 'The Flitting' is more
particular in its concerns, and finds cause for hope where
'Decay' finds none. 'Decay' gives us some idea of what the
loss of poetry meant to Clare: the problem faced here is
similar in some ways to that faced by most of the Romantic
poets, the loss of poetic power; but this has different implications for Clare. He is tackling ideas in a very conscious way,
engaging in a struggle with himself, as he did increasingly in
this period, and there can be no doubt about the intensity
of his dejection here, made more poignant by the connection
between his own personal plight and the wider implications of
a loss of poetic inspiration.

The structural device of the poem, with a repetitive final
couplet at the end of each stanza, and the slight variations
from stanza to stanza recall the incremental repetition of the
ballad, a form to which he turned increasingly, especially in
the asylum. This formal nature of the poem is supplemented by
its universal quality:

> O poesy is on the wane
> For fancys visions all unfitting
> I hardly know her face again
> Nature herself seems on the flitting
> The fields grow old and common things
> The grass the sky the winds a blowing
> And spots where still a beauty clings
> Are sighing 'going all a going'
> O poesy is on the wane
> I hardly know her face again[54]

Decay is seen in terms of the waning of poesy. Poetry has changed out of all recognition, and nature too is 'on the flitting', just as he himself has to move to Northborough. The old haunts are common things, the ultimate realisation of 'Remembrances'. This sense of loss is perfectly consonant with the sentiment of 'Remembrances', and is also reminiscent of what Clare had written to Taylor in October 1831, when he was anxious to leave Helpstone. In his state of depression he believed that poetry itself was in decline; he had been reading Southey's collection of older poets, and thought it poor. All the poets he admired, including Suckling and Herrick, were not to be found in it. He was beginning to find that his taste generally did not agree with that of others and his writing lacked any 'encouraging aspirations'; but 'instead of that',

> I have nothing but drawbacks & disappointments I live in a land overflowing with obscurity & vulgarity far away from taste & books & friends poor Gilchrist was the only man of letters in this neighbourhood & now he has left it a desert – I see things praised that appear to me utterly worthless & read criticism in the periodicals when I do see them that the very puffers of Blacking & Bearsgrease would be really ashamed of – & I lay my intentions aside having no heart to proceed but I am resolved to show them I can judge for myself & whatever remarks I may make on the ryhmes of others they shall be done honestly & with as little vanity as possible[55]

Clare's dejection was such that he had few regrets about the prospect of a move from the 'place of all my hopes & ambitions'. He had been offended by the cutting down of the last elm tree; an old plum tree had blown down, '& all the old associations are going before me'.[56] The same phrase occurs in a letter of January 1832, again to Taylor : apart from the difficulty of leaving his old haunts, 'other associations of friendships I have few or none to regret'. He greatly looked forward to the independence which he hoped his new home would bring ('the best is that when I get fixed in it will be as certain a home as if it was my own').[57] Of course, as 'The Flitting' makes clear, his optimism was ill-founded. But the terms in which he regretted his move were not those of 'Decay'. For here he laments the passing of a vision; his whole idea of what poetry was and should be was beginning to crumble. He was no longer able to appreciate what Helpstone had to offer; and so the second stanza is not regretting having moved to Northborough, but the fact that the move has to be made; he is saying that previously he would have preferred his own surroundings to the neatly trimmed garden of the new cottage; but his vision has faded to such an extent that he no longer really cares. The connective 'But' of the penultimate line now makes some sense :

> The bank with brambles over spread
> And little molehills round about it
> Was more to me then laurel shades
> With paths and gravel finely clouted*
> And streaking here and streaking there
> Through shaven grass and many a border
> With rutty lanes had no compare
> And heaths were in a richer order
> But poesy is in its wane
> I hardly know her face again

Even in the old haunts, the source of all his poesy, he cannot recapture the visionary gleam. He recalls the time when the 'fields did more than edens seem', when 'Love turned water into wine'; but now as the first stanza declares, the fields 'are old and common things'. The increased despair is measured by the change in the refrain from hardly knowing poesy's face to not being able to find her face again. The fourth stanza is crucial, for Clare uses the sun image as a sign of his faded

* Clothed.

vision. The sun, so often an image of life and energy, love and hope, is here impressed with his own sense of complete hopelessness and disorientation. Just as he wanders in a wilderness, so the sun is a naked stranger:

> These heavens are gone – the mountains grey
> Turned mist – the sun a homeless ranger
> Pursues a naked weary way
> Unnoticed like a very stranger
> O poesy is on its wane
> Nor love nor joy is mine again

The poem accumulates its meanings: poesy is now all the love and joy he experienced in the past. Gradually the personal element has begun to predominate, as Clare explores his disillusion and sense of deception. The sun image acquires new relevance as it is connected with all the deceit of love: the irony is that time has undeceived Clare, and forced an awareness of reality onto him. Nature has been normalised, reduced to what she really is. Poetry has gone with the dream, for it depended on the dream, and on the past, just as the past depended upon her:

> The stream it is a naked stream
> Where we on sundays used to ramble
> The sky hangs oer a broken dream
> The brambles dwindled to a bramble
> O poesy is on its wane
> I cannot find her haunts again

(The echo of 'Remembrances' cannot be missed.) Clare's fading vision sees the real bleakness of nature and of Helpstone: the rapture has gone. Even the emotion of fear is no longer possible, as it was not in parts of *The Shepherd's Calendar*. Nonetheless the vision, while it lasted, was valuable precisely because it was a vision: day was preferable to night; love, joy, youth, and poesy were positive things, as this stanza makes clear. The sun has finally set, and he has left the garden of Eden, yet his heart has been rewarded:

> Aye poesy hath passed away
> And fancys visions undecieve us

The night hath taen the place of day
And why should passing shadows grieve us
I thought the flowers upon the hills
Were flowers from Adams open gardens
And I have had my summer thrills
And I have had my hearts rewardings
So poesy is on the wane
I hardly know her face again

But the last stanza provides little comfort: friendship is no more than a deception, and hope is but 'a fancy play'. Joy is 'the art of true believing', and it is this inability to believe in his visions which informs the whole poem. He has not lost his sense of what joy can be; but no longer can he cling to it without question. The final lines express his desperate loss of belief:

For poesy is on the wane
O could I feel her faith again

In the course of these eight stanzas, the poem opens out and comes to terms with itself, facing at the end what it shirks at the start. Poesy grows from a way of expressing to what can no longer be expressed. Although a poem, basically, of defeat, this defeat is not due entirely to a failure of nerve, nor to any poetic constipation. There is a sickness at the heart of the world, larger than Clare's own narrow confines, although it is within these confines that the poem begins and ends.

The move to Northborough had its cathartic effect on Clare. He found again the faith in poesy which he had lost. 'The Flitting' is a more honest appraisal of his situation than, say, 'On Visiting a Favourite Place',[58] and a better poem. According to Frederick Martin, this was written as soon as Clare and his family had arrived in Northborough, on 20 June 1832.[59] The date may be correct (although Martin is not always reliable), but the circumstantial details are suspect. Nonetheless, Clare's attachment to the place of his birth, and his recent removal from such a place, is the relevant biographical fact behind this poem. There are inconsistencies, when we compare the poem with the other two major poems from this period or just before; it is characteristic of Clare to idealise the place he has just left, but it is surely ironic to hear him talk of home 'Where envy's sneer was never seen/Where staring malice never comes' in view of the deceit of friendship he had mentioned so bitterly in 'Decay'. The form of the poem is similar to 'Decay', with a comparable use of primary symbols to express his deprivation. He lists the things he misses, the things mentioned in a letter to Taylor, in which he said that he found it hard to part with these objects, but that Northborough had its compensations. At first in this poem, however, these compensations are not readily apparent. The importance of home is crucial : at this stage the cottage at Northborough is not transformed into the home he had hoped for. Home is still Helpstone, where 'The very crow/Croaked music in my native fields'. Home, like poesy, had the power to transform the ordinary into the magical. He dislikes what is strange and new, the unfamiliar bird music, and remembers the 'sailing puddocks shrill "peelew"/Oer royce wood', characteristically placing the bird in a landscape he knew and could name. What is in the past is described in detail and with attention; the present by comparison is blurred over.

He recalls all that is missing, as he realises that he is 'Far from spots my heart esteems'. Turning to books for comfort, he finds the same overthrow of the past. Their way is lost, like the sun who 'een seems to lose its way/Nor knows the quarter it is in'; they 'follow fashions new/And throw all old esteems away'. Books contain the pomp of the moment, but true sublimity belongs

> to plain and simpler things
> And David underneath a tree
> Sought when a shepherd Salems springs
>
> Where moss did unto cushions spring
> Forming a seat of velvet hue
> A small unnoticed trifling thing
> To all but heavens hailing dew
> And Davids crown hath passed away
> Yet poesy breaths his shepherd-skill
> His palace lost and to this day
> The little moss is blooming still

Here lies the first hint of a solution to the divorce of past and present. Both poesy and the little moss have survived; the past can live on into the present. Clare reverts to the joys he has lost:

> Strange scenes mere shadows are to me
> Vague unpersonifying things
> I love with my old hants to be
> By quiet woods and gravel springs[60]

The sound of water on the pebbles warms his spirits into 'singing moods': a connection is in the process of being made between the past, unseen things, what he has lost, and the power of poetry to live on, as the moss survives. Encouraged, Clare remembers episodes in the past, the sense of tradition when girls 'sung sweet ballads now forgot/Which brought sweet memorys to the mind', the perspective of the past which has momentarily left him, the beauty of nature which inspired him. The precise nature of this beauty is stated in this crucial stanza:

> All tennants of an ancient place
> And heirs of noble heritage
> Coeval they with adams race
> And blest with more substantial age
> For when the world first saw the sun
> These little flowers beheld him too
> And when his love for earth begun
> They were the first his smiles to woo

Clare realises that these flowers still bloom. Rejecting pomp and splendour for the poetry of nature, he turns his attention to the preservation of all living objects, especially the small and simple and unseen. Every weed means something to him; mention of the shepherds-purse reminds him of the same weed that grew in his old home, and enables him to complete his argument:

> and I
> Feel what I never felt before
> This weed an ancient neighbour here
> And though I own the spot no more
> Its every trifle makes it dear

The realisation of this encourages the stoicism of the last two stanzas: parting is inevitable, as is change, but nature 'can make amends', because of the power of memory, related to the eternity of nature. Grandeur is seen to fade, but grass springs eternally. Here lies what hope there is for Clare, as his personal sorrow gives way to a comprehensive philosophy of the value of the poetry of nature.

This might seem too easy a solution. But Clare does make his poem work towards it, even at the expense of concision. Expression is often loose and awkward, the dejection of the opening more convincing than the buoyancy of the close. But, unlike the conclusion of 'On Visiting a Favourite Place', this is sanctioned elsewhere in his poetry. In fact, there is a parallel progression towards a similar conclusion in his poems on the nature of poetry and his own poetic aspirations, and the two aspects of his development illuminate each other.

In 'To the Rural Muse' Clare had wondered about the fate of his poetry, as he had in several of his sonnets of this period, from 1824 onwards. He vowed to serve the muse to the best of his ability, promising if he succeeded to lay his poetry on her altar, more permanent than deeds of graven brass:

> Filling a space in time that shall not fade;
> And if it be not so – avert disdain,
> Till dust shall feel no sting, nor know it toiled in vain.[61]

He dared not hope for success, but nonetheless dedicated himself to the service of poetry. His poetry is an attempt to return to his past:

> Life's grosser fancies did these dreams defile
> Yet not entirely root them from the mind;
> I think I hear them still, and often look behind.[62]

'The Progress of Ryhme', another autobiographical poem, further explains his life of service to the muse, his constant source of hope and comfort.[63] He would try to repeat the songs of nature. Mary became synonymous with the muse, and with nature; but his hopes of gaining her love were confounded:

> But I mistook in early day
> The world – and so our hopes decay

Only poesy remained faithful to him:

> Yet that same cheer in after toils
> Was poesy – and still she smiles
> As sweet as blossoms to the tree,
> And hope love joy are poesy[64]

This important statement of his poetic creed is supplemented by 'Pastoral Poesy', a rather curious amalgamation of ideas culled from his reading of Coleridge and Wordsworth. Not an exciting poem, it states in awkward language too simple for the purpose, something of his belief in the inherent poetry of nature.[65] 'True poesy is not in words', but is part of the language of the fields, 'A language that is evergreen/That feelings unto all impart'. This language is one of silence, related to nature's beauty. The poetry of nature can stir the simplest hearts to 'elevated happiness'. (But if this experience is open to all, not every one can become a poet.) In 'Shadows of Taste' he declares that everyone has his share of joy, all part of the joy of nature: man's life is an attempt

> To follow taste and all her sweets explore
> And Edens make where deserts spread before[66]

Poetry can preserve what is past, and nature is perpetuated:

> A blossom in its witchery of bloom
> There gathered dwells in beauty and perfume
> The singing bird the brook that laughs along
> There ceasless sing and never thirsts for song

The landscape becomes 'heard and felt and seen', a harmony of nature that will last for ever;

> Thus truth to nature as the true sublime
> Stands a mount atlas overpeering time

The relevance of these various gropings towards a comprehensive poetic theory begins to emerge in a sonnet like 'The Shepherd's Tree', where Clare looks for a link between the past and the future, by way of his imagination. As he reflects on the history of the huge elm, he looks beyond the turmoil of 'Life's sordid being':

> The wind of that eternal ditty sings
> Humming of future things, that burn the mind
> To leave some fragment of itself behind.[67]

This was Clare's hope for fame; not a fame of fashion, but one dependent on the worth of his work, and which would at the same time lend meaning to his life, for he would have contributed to posterity. There are several poems which state a similar theme. But two poems in particular achieve an especially rounded expression of his belief, not only in the eternity of poetry, and therefore the possibility of his own poetry surviving, but also the eternity of nature, and the connection between the two. 'The Eternity of Nature' works towards one of the supreme vindications of Clare's lyricism in 'Song's Eternity'. However hackneyed the theme, however flawed the poem is as a unity, it has force and integrity. This opening passage assumes its own logic in a statement as confident in its movement as anything Clare wrote:

> Leaves from eternity are simple things
> To the worlds gaze – whereto a spirit clings
> Sublime and lasting – trampled under foot
> The daisy lives and strikes its little root
> Into the lap of time – centurys may come
> And pass away into the silent tomb
> And still the child hid in the womb of time
> Shall smile and pluck them when this simple ryhme
> Shall be forgotten like a churchyard stone,
> Or lingering lie unnoticed and alone[68]

Clare rises to his theme here, his scornful attitude to the outside world emphasising the importance to him of the essential spirit, and the experiencing of it, however simple in appearance. Indifference to the human world is the essential characteristic of elemental life, and this is caught in the neat juxtaposition of 'Trampled under foot/The daisy lives', providing a positive action in response to a negative one. The earth is 'the lap of time', 'the womb', for the future exists in the present, merely waiting to be born, and the child shall appear when the daisy appears:

> Aye still the child with pleasure in its eye

Shall cry the daisy – a familiar cry
And run to pluck it – in the self same state
As when time found it in his infant date
And like a child himself when all was new
Wonder might smile and make him notice too

Throughout this passage there is a play on the idea of the dead past – the silent tomb, the churchyard stone, neglect, old age – and also on the cocoon of promise, of future hope and continuity. The child becomes a reincarnation of the spirit of creation : however far forward into time we go, into maturity, we are still held onto the beginning of time, just as the daisy symbolically and positively strikes its roots into the ground. This leads naturally to the extension of the metaphor of Adam and Eve, and the exile from the Garden of Eden : again the accent is on death, as the daisy 'smiles on the lap of death', but it is accounted for, and overcome.

– Its little golden bosom frilled with snow
Might win een Eve to stoop adown and show
Her partner Adam in the silky grass
This little gem that smiled where pleasure was
And loving Eve from eden followed ill
And bloomed with sorrow and lives smiling still
As once in eden under heavens breath
So now on blighted earth and on the lap of death
It smiles for ever

A series of examples follows, of aspects of nature that shall survive, when 'kings and empires fade away' : the cowslips, the little brooks, the bee, the robin, the seasonal cycle. Clare writes beautifully here, explaining the inherent impulse of nature, its implicit timelessness, the soul of all its parts, 'to whom all clings/Of fair or beautiful in lasting things'. Clare turns to himself, and tells how he looks for these things in seclusion. We witness the joining of their music with the essential quietness of his spirit, which they cause. He can now hope, as he could not at the start of the poem, that he might have an audience in days to come, just as people will admire the daisy. He hopes to appropriate the eternity of nature to his own song. But more important than any hope for fame, however high-minded, is the joy that arises from this communion, a joy that is silent in its song, eternal and above the crowd ('Birds singing lone flie silent past the crowd'); the poem thus lays the logical foundations for 'Song's Eternity', a much more lyrical, more perfect distillation of his vision of eternal joy. The poem's importance lies in its application of the principle of eternity to various parts of the creation, and to Clare's place as a poet. Throughout the poem runs an awareness of hope and despair, the inevitability of death, but nature's renewal in the face of death. Parallel to this rejuvenation is the birth of hope for his own poetry. There are loose ends in the poem, certainly, but it approaches an authority lacking in some of the theoretical poems of this time.

'Song's Eternity' has a serenity and a transparency not found even in the other poems of 1832.[69] Basically it is a song about the essence of song. The form of the poem indicates Clare's sureness of touch, his hold on his theme. Asking questions, he knows the answers.[70]

> What is song's eternity?
>   Come and see.
> Can it noise and bustle be?
>   Come and see.
> Praises sung or praises said
>   Can it be?
> Wait awhile and these are dead —
>   Sigh, sigh;
> Be they high or lowly bred
>   They die.

Against these negatives comes the affirmative vitality of the second stanza, its springy buoyancy underlining the languorous melancholy of the previous stanza. Song's eternity belongs to the 'melodies of earth and sky', stretching back to the time of Adam, the time of innocence.

> What is song's eternity?
>   Come and see.
> Melodies of earth and sky,
>   Here they be.
> Song once sung to Adam's ears
>   Can it be?

> Ballads of six thousand years
>   Thrive, thrive;
> Songs awakened with the spheres
>   Alive.

Once this is established the poet plays variations on the theme, the third stanza echoing the first, showing what is not involved in 'Mighty songs that miss decay', casting a glance back at his own poem on 'Decay'. The fourth stanza similarly echoes the second, addressing the dreamers who see the truth; the way to the vision of truth is through nature, and thus into the past and lost innocence :

> Dreamers, list the honey-bee;
>   Mark the tree
> Where the bluecap, 'tootle tee',
>   Sings a glee
> Sung to Adam and to Eve –
>   Here they be.
> When floods covered every bough,
>   Noah's ark
> Heard that Ballad singing now;
>   Hark hark.

The fifth stanza combines the two emotional elements of the poem; pride and fame are shadows, but nature and eternity are one. In the final stanza (written separately in another manuscript, so there is no evidence that Clare intended it to conclude the poem : in fact the poem is better without it),[71] Clare enters the poem for the first time. Nature in its eternity symbolises the act of the creator, in perpetuity :

> Songs like the grass are evergreen;
>   The giver
> Said 'Live and be' – and they have been,
>   For ever.

As J. W. and Anne Tibble have pointed out, this is a poem of triumph, and of the same mood as the close of 'The Flitting'.[72] For all its purity and impersonality, it is a poem of such personal conviction as he had not written before that decisive year. It is the supreme statement of what he was implying, more falteringly, not only in 'Eternity of Nature', but in all the visionary poetry of this period. This poem, more than any other, explains Clare's philosophy of poetry; it explains the intensity behind his other work, where such ideas were implicit; it shows how the personal torment of his uprooted life could be resolved in terms of his life as a poet. Clare finds a poet's answer to his private problem.

But it was not an all-embracing answer. The beauty of nature, and the eternity of song, did not prevent Clare's decline into melancholy, and his eventual removal, in 1837, to Dr Matthew Allen's asylum at High Beech, Epping Forest.

5

The Storm and the Calm:
Child Harold

I

For four years Clare was looked after by Dr Allen in Epping Forest. Optimistic reports on his health, together with certificates of his continuing insanity, were sent to John Taylor in London. Visitors came to see him; one, the journalist Cyrus Redding, gave an account of his visit, and printed some poems, in the *English Journal* for May 1841: he emphasised the apparent normality of Clare, his fine features, the attributes of genius; Clare leant on his hoe in the field, smoking his pipe, smiling at his visitors.[1] But on 20 July of that year Clare escaped from this 'Hell of a Madhouse',[2] and began his long tramp home to Northborough, a journey of heartrending futility, for the Mary he went back to find was long since dead.[3]

Before he left High Beech, he began what was to be his longest and, in some ways, most ambitious poem. Absorbed in the works of Byron, and imagining himself to be not only Byron, but Shakespeare, Tom Spring the boxer, and Nelson as well, he produced two works within the year: this extensive poetic and spiritual testament, and a satirically vulgar counterpart, *Don Juan*. Clare is disappointingly uninformative about the poems. There are few letters from the period, and those that exist are often only in draft form. But two draft letters written in his notebook (which contains the first version of *Child Harold* and *Don Juan*), when Clare was in Dr Matthew Allen's asylum, mention the two poems. In one letter he writes to his lost love and imaginary wife Mary:

I have been rather poorly I might say ill for 8 or 9 days

before hay making & to get myself better I went a few evenings on Fern Hill & wrote a new Canto of 'Child Harold' &
now I am better I sat under the Elm trees in old Mathew's
Homestead Leppits Hill where I now am – 2 or 3 evenings
& wrote a new canto of Don Juan – merely to pass the time
away but nothing seemed to shorten it in the least & I fear
I shall not be able to wear it away – nature to me seems
dead & her very pulse seems frozen to an icicle in the
summer sun –[4]

The other letter is to Eliza Phillips, mentioned in *Don Juan* :

I am now writing a New Canto of Don Juan which I have
taken the liberty to dedicate to you in remembrance of
Days gone bye and when I have finished it I would send
you a vol if I knew how in which there is a new Canto of
Child Harold also –[5]

The struggles and anguish of the poetry echo the emotional
complexities of the asylum letters. Clare writes to Mary Joyce,
to Eliza Phillips, and to his wife Patty in separate letters; each
is a love letter (as he says to Eliza, 'I do not much like to
write love letters but this which I am now writing to you is a
true one').[6] He also writes jointly to Mary and Patty, as his two
wives :

My dear wife Mary, I might have said my first wife first
love & first everything – but I shall never forget my second
wife & second love for I loved her once as dearly as yourself & almost do so now so I determined to keep you both
for ever[7]

He longs for home, and yet he says that once free, he will get
himself a third wife, 'for I dont care a damn about coming
home now'. In another letter, to Patty, he says that 'I Would
Sooner Wear The Trouble's of Life Away Single Handed Than
Share Them With Others'.[8] Yet he yearns for his family, for
the fireside; the same letter concludes with this P.S.: 'Give
My Love To The Dear Boy Who Wrote To Me & To Her Who
Is Never Forgotten.' These letters, bitter, tender, desperate,
longing, even hopeful, reflect the paradoxes which give birth
to the poetry of this period. Clare struggles with the problems

of existence, of self identity, love and truth, and the effect of 'imprisonment' upon himself, and the interactions of these abstract concepts. The struggle can be seen in the letters, but it is in the poetry that he tries to find his own solution to the problems that confront him : *Child Harold* is unusually dialectical in tone.

When Cyrus Redding visited Clare at High Beech in the spring of 1841, the two talked at some length about Byron's poetry, and about *Childe Harold*. Clare asked for a copy of Byron's poems, and Redding accordingly sent these, as Clare's note indicates: 'Received from C. Redding while in Prison on Leopards Hill.'[9] However, Byron had always been of particular interest to Clare. The first time he saw Byron's poems was when Edward Drury showed him *The Giaour* in 1818.[10] In 1820 he was borrowing copies of Byron from his friend Octavius Gilchrist : he wrote in January, returning one volume, '& beg the Favour of the other a little longer wishing to read "Child Harold" a Second time'.[11] His critical reactions to the poetry varied considerably. He saw through the glitter on several occasions; but he appreciated the particular virtues of Byron, and realised the difference between Byron and Moore.[12] When he was up in London he was greatly moved by the death and funeral of Byron.[13] It was the common people's appreciation of Byron that won Clare's heart, together with his 'Liberal principles in religion & politics'. Byron achieved the kind of fame which Clare thought was right : 'it is better to be beloved by those low & humble for undisguised honesty than flattered by the great for purchased & pensioned hypocrisies.'[14] His considered opinion of Byron's poetry, while acknowledging his faults, and his excesses, concludes :

> ... his powers are beyond my pen & I shall not venture to praise them – the sun does not want the light of a lamp or a candle to show it glory – he carolled among the immortals & shines as the jewel in the crown of modern literature[15]

What seems to have appealed to Clare was Byron's handling of themes which became 'The universal hopes of all human existences' : certainly Clare seems to have taken over some of his ideas on freedom and love. He does not often imitate Byron before the asylum years, but it is possible to see a connection between the two poets in terms of their preoccupations with love and liberty, hypocrisy and truth. We should not then be surprised at the addition of Byron to the list of *personae* adopted by Clare: with his flouting of convention Byron must have seemed especially attractive to him as he wrestled with the problem of having two wives. Even if he was in some ways closer to Cowper, it was Byron to whom he turned for a parallel and a starting point.

Of the two poems, *Don Juan* is the more blatant attempt at imitation, and it is hardly satisfactory, even though Clare proclaims:

> Though laurel wreaths my brows did ne'er environ
> I think myself as great a bard as Byron[16]

The humour is laboured and bitter: Clare lacks the necessary Byronic elegance. But even if we feel obliged to characterise *Don Juan* as a failure, we can glean from it some important indications of Clare's preoccupations, and the nature of his frustration. For the violence of the satire is in sharp contrast to the melancholy and nostalgia of *Child Harold*. Many of the themes of the other poems are expressed here in more general, less personal terms. Deceit and falsehood are seen in the wider context of politics and society: in this sense *Don Juan* continues the vein of *The Parish*. What the poem is important for is the connection made between private and public concepts of love. For example, Clare's preoccupation with the misuse of love is described, in the first stanza, in terms of fashionable society; but this behaviour is, at the end of the stanza, related to his own position as a husband of two wives:

> 'Poets are born' – and so are whores – the trade is
> Grown universal – in these canting days
> Women of fashion must of course be ladies
> And whoreing is the business – that still pays
> Playhouses Ballrooms – there the masquerade is
> – To do what was of old – and now adays
> Their maids – nay wives so innocent and blooming
> Cuckold their spouses to seem honest women[17]

The flavour of this stanza is characteristic of the whole poem. In a sense it is, superficially, a much more Byronic achievement than *Child Harold* : Clare copies the same tricks of improvisation. He declares :

> I really cant tell what this poem will be
> About – nor yet what trade I am to follow ...[18]

When short for rhymes, he acknowledges it :

> – Bricklayers want lime as I want ryhme for fillups
> – So here's a health to sweet Eliza Phillips[19]

or

> And here I want a ryhme – so write down 'jingle'[20]

As in Byron, this manner designedly conceals the serious purpose behind it. For there are certain themes that recur : and Clare's return to his opening lines emphasises their importance for the plan of the poem as a whole. The connection between poets and whores is made starkly and, apparently, incongruously. But there is some method in his madness here. Clare's belief in the powers of genius have been stressed earlier in this study : he begins *Child Harold* with a similar sentiment :

> Many are poets – though they use no pen
> To show their labours to the shuffling age
> Real poets must be truly honest men
> Tied to no mongrel laws on flatterys page
> No zeal have they for wrong or party rage
> – The life of labour is a rural song
> That hurts no cause – nor warfare tries to wage
> Toil like the brook in music wears along –
> Great little minds claim right to act the wrong[21]

This is one of the few stanzas of *Child Harold* which approach the spirit of *Don Juan* : and the connection is clear. Clare is stating his belief in the essential integrity of poetry, based on the life of rural labour : in this there is no room for party politics, for the niggling restrictions attendant upon the desire for flattery and advancement. The poet has to be uncompromising. Although in *Don Juan* Clare becomes the critic of party, and takes up arms, the contradiction is more apparent than real. For in both poems Clare attacks falsehood and deceit; but in *Don Juan* from a particularly cynical angle. This cynicism comes out in the opening stanza. By taking up arms in this violent fashion, Clare is trying to expose the cynicism he resorts to; he fights on the terms of his enemies. But beneath this brave façade lurks the man who, in *Child Harold*, sighs 'a poet and a lover still'.[22]

To return to the opening stanza of *Don Juan*: Clare begins with the statement of belief in poetry, only to thrust it aside in mockery, equating the poet with the whore. Nothing could sum up more concisely his disillusionment and bitterness. This springs from his utter contempt for the society which has overthrown any sense of values. The part played by religion is important (line 2 originally read 'in religious days').[23] God is necessary, as *Child Harold* shows, but the clergy and their cant are not:

> If I do wickedness to day being sunday
> Can I by hearing prayers or singing psalms
> Clear off all debts twixt god and man on monday
> And lie like an old hull that dotage calms ...[24]

The hypocrisy of the Church is echoed in that of fashionable society. The concept of innocence is debased, and that woman is to blame Clare has little doubt. The connection is again apparent when we compare different versions. Clare wrote, in the second stanza:

> Tell me a worse delusion if you can
> Then woman – and I'll teaze the muse no more ...

This became, in the fair copy:

> Tell me a worse delusion if you can
> For innoscence – and I will sing no more[25]

Loss of innocence is the result of over-exposure. Beauty cannot be preserved if it is allowed too much sun:

> The flower in bud hides from the fading sun
> And keeps the hue of beauty on its cheek
> But when full blown they into riot run
> The hue turns pale and lost each ruddy streak
> So 't is with woman who pretends to shun
> Immodest actions which they inly seek[26]

Clare laments this loss of innocence throughout the poem, but, again, in terms quite different from those of *Child Harold*. This innocence is related to the humbug of marriage.[27] If we are inclined to think that Clare is being too hard on marriage here, and its ruinous effects on a man, we do well to remember the lines at the end of a later song:

> Who ever would love or be tied to a wife
> When it makes a man mad a' the days o' his life?[28]

or:

> A hell incarnate is a woman-mate
> The knot is tied – and then we loose the honey[29]

Love cannot survive in captivity: a distinction has to be made between this enforced captivity, where love withers on attainment, and the desired captivity of ideal love, expressed in *Child Harold*, where Clare yearns to be imprisoned by Mary's love. The difference is between his enforced marriage to Patty, and his own self-willed marriage of the spirit to Mary. His anger is directed at 'married dames' rather than single women: however casually the Song to Eliza Phillips is introduced, it is a moving love song which, if it does not cancel out the prevailing cynicism, certainly counterbalances it. But Clare's wrath is also directed at Mary, and the deceit and betrayal of love in connection with her.[30] Here he seems to be washing his hands of everyone. Women, by disregarding the modesty he deems essential to them, become mere objects of abuse and lust. In his anger and despair he becomes vulgar and obscene. Yet although able to descend to the depths, he can still see the terrible irony of his predicament: his desires and regrets are caught in this stanza, soon after the Song to Eliza Phillips:

> Lord bless me now the day is in the gloaming
> And every evil thought is out of sight
> How I should like to purchase some sweet woman
> Or else creep in with my two wives to night
> Surely that wedding day is on the coming
> Abscence like phisic poisons all delight –
> Mary and Martha both an evil omen
> Though both my own – they still belong to no man[31]

The penultimate stanza reveals more than Clare's cynicism: it shows the complete hopelessness of his position, in which, after such vilification of women and love and marriage, he is still able – in fact he is forced – to turn to the women he has vilified, for the only comfort he is likely to get.

> I have two wives and I should like to see them
> Both by my side before another hour
> If both are honest I should like to be them
> For both are fair and bonny as a flower
> And one o Lord – now do bring in the tea mem
> Were bards pens steamers each of ten horse power
> I could not bring her beautys fair to weather
> So I've towed both in harbour blest together[32]

II

Child Harold is essentially a pathetic poem, one to which it is particularly difficult (and perhaps inapposite) to apply the usual critical responses. Anyone who has handled the small note-book which Clare carried with him on his long trek home, – the notebook crammed full of rough workings, prayers for his family, written wherever he found somewhere to sleep for the night, the diary of that very trek, – can no longer view the poem objectively: the experience out of which it grew is too harrowing. For all its faults and shortcomings (and they are many and indisputable) *Child Harold* is testimony to Clare's resilience, at the very least. But it is more than that; although Clare writes out of desperation, he achieves more than the jottings of a disintegrating mind. He displays a courageous unconcern for posterity:

> Flow on my verse though barren thou mayest be
> Of thought – Yet sing and let thy fancys roll
> In Early days thou sweept a mighty sea
> All calm in troublous deeps and spurned controul
> Thou fire and iceberg to an aching soul
> And still an angel in my gloomy way
> Far better opiate then the draining bowl
> Still sing my muse to drive cares fiends away
> Nor heed what loitering listener hears the lay[33]

Simply by persisting, by going on singing, Clare turns his raw
experience into something moving and memorable. It is, inevitably, an uneven poem : as I hope to show, there is cohesion
of sorts, but as a whole the poem lacks structure and polish.
Several of the songs that intersperse the nine-line stanzas are
trite in sentiment and expression, and the stanzas themselves
are extremely variable in quality. But it is unwise to put biographical considerations on one side. For we get, in *Child
Harold*, perhaps the fullest picture of Clare the suffering man
that we have, apart from his prose and letters. We see him in
all his candid honesty, his frustrated aspirations, his repeated
resolutions not to give in to abject despair, and his acknowledgement of this despair; we witness his moments of absurd
self-deception, and his moments of magnificent, proud vision.
He wanders, disconsolate and alone, across the winter
meadows, carrying with him the numbing awareness of his
own dull, frozen self :

> Brown are the flags and fadeing sedge
> And tanned the meadow plains
> Bright yellow is the osier hedge
> Beside the brimming drains
> The crows sit on the willow tree
> The lake is full below
> But still the dullest thing I see
> Is self that wanders slow[34]

And yet the same man writes this sort of ditty :

> While the winter swells the fountain
> While the spring awakes the bees
> While the chamois loves the mountain
> Thou'lt be ever dear to me[35]

He sets by this, in startling juxtaposition, a song that begins,

> In this cold world without a home
> Disconsolate I go
> The summer looks as cold to me
> As winters frost and snow[36]

We see him waiting patiently, and wonderingly,

O when will autumn bring the news
Now harvest browns the fen
That Mary as my vagrant muse
And I shall meet agen[37]

Much of the poem consists of the repetition of a question to
which there is no answer. It is a pained and paining work,
evoking, in its persistent integrity, wonder, surprise, pity,
indulgence, anguish.

Clare faced enormous difficulties in embarking on this poem.
His longest work before this had been *The Shepherd's Calendar*,
which had exhausted and dissatisfied him; the lengthy poems
on his poetic creed (such as 'Solitude', or 'The Progress of
Ryhme') were not particularly successful, however interesting
as comments on his attitude to himself as a poet. Poems such
as 'Remembrances', 'Decay' and 'The Flitting' show how difficult he found it to sustain a developing argument through the
course of a long poem. It comes as no surprise to find Clare
often floundering in *Child Harold*. In a way, the problem here
is similar to that encountered in his early days – how to
discipline emotions, how to get beyond himself. The difference
lies in the fact that then he was extremely conscious of the
relationship between himself and his potential audience, whereas for *Child Harold* there is no audience.

The most pressing problem was undoubtedly the immediacy
of experience. This may be seen in the two songs written upon
his return to Northborough after the terrible and agonising
walk home from Essex. His note to the poems underlines this
immediacy, pointing to the fact that they were composed
'directly after my return home to Northborough last friday
evening'.[38] The journey took him three days, and ended when
he was picked up in a cart by a woman who 'jumped out &
caught fast hold of my hands & wished me to get into the cart
but I refused & thought her either drunk or mad'.[39] It was
Patty, his wife. Clare ended his account of the journey with
this note:

July 24 – 1841 – Returned home out of Essex & found no
Mary – her & her family are nothing to me now though she
herself was once the dearest of all – & how can I forget[40]

Three days later he wrote to Mary, telling her that he was home and had written an account of his escape –

> I would have told you before now that I got here to North-borough last friday night but not being able to see you or to hear where you was I soon began to feel homeless at home & shall bye & bye feel nearly hopeless but not so lonely as I did in Essex – for here I can see Glinton church & feeling that Mary is safe if not happy & I am gratified though my home is no home to me my hopes are not entirely hopeless while even the memory of Mary lives so near me ...[41]

There is nothing of emotion recollected in tranquillity about these songs. In the first, distinctive for its lack of poetic fire, it is as though Clare realises the impossibility of conveying his confused emotional state, and so resorts to oversimplifications. But beneath the apparently trite phrases there is a restraint and a sadness that is bolstered by the formal properties of the song, as it circles round the desolation of his return :

> I've wandered many a weary mile
> Love in my heart was burning
> To seek a home in Mary[s] smile
> But cold is loves returning
> The cold ground was a feather bed
> Truth never acts contrary
> I had no home above my head
> My home was love and Mary
>
> I had no home in early youth
> When my first love was thwarted
> But if her heart still beats with truth
> We'll never more be parted
> And changing as her love may be
> My own shall never vary
> Nor night nor day I'm never free
> But sigh for abscent Mary
>
> Nor night nor day nor sun nor shade
> Week month nor rolling year
> Repairs the breach wronged love hath made
> There madness – misery here

> Lifes lease was lengthened by her smiles
> – Are truth and love contrary
> No ray of hope my life beguiles
> I've lost love home and Mary[42]

The cyclic movement of the poem (with its origins in the cumulative technique of the ballad) emphasises the emptiness, the bleak rhymes picking each other up (Mary's smile in the first stanza echoed in the third – and linked to 'beguiles'; 'contrary' in the first stanza, as part of a bold statement of fact, reverberating in the third as a painful question of bemused betrayal – further hammered home by the rhyme with 'Mary', a dejected repetition of the proud rhyme of the first stanza). The irony of the poem is implicit in its structure, itself built on antitheses, on irreconcilable contraries. It becomes clear that the journey to Northborough was in effect a journey into the past, the past before Mary's deception: her constancy was a delusion, and Clare begins to accept at the end of the poem what in the first stanza he was refusing to admit.

The second song shows Clare back amid his old haunts, but Mary is no longer there.[43] He begins with the particular:

> Heres where Mary loved to be
> And here are flowers she planted
> Here are books she loved to see
> And here the kiss she granted

As he retreats into the past in his memory, the particularisation fades, and in the fourth stanza there is something symbolic about the flowers planted by Mary:

> The churchyard where she used to play
> My feet could wander hourly
> My school walks there was every day
> Where she made winter flowery

But Mary is not yet a spirit, she is the lost angel. Clare does not as in 'Secret Love' find her in the flowers and trees.[44] She might once have made winter flowery, but she was not absorbed into nature. It is only the outward signs of love, and deceit, which remain, the superficial attractions, the rosy cheeks which were of no real use to him. 'Angel Mary' was no angel.

But where is angel Mary now
Loves secrets none disclose 'em
Her rosey cheeks and broken vow
Live in my aching bosom

Both these songs show Clare trying to face the intractability of the denial of love and hope, what he sees as deceit. They do not ask for claims to be made for them : where they are moving is in their resolute attempts to accept the challenge of conflict. *Child Harold* as a whole is impressive because it rises above the rawness of such experience.

Clare's attempts to give the work some kind of architectural structure emphasise his seriousness of purpose, his reaching beyond private self-confession. A comparison between the original drafts and the fair copy of MS. 6 shows Clare's determination to make sense of his diary. Most of the drafts were contained in the tiny notebook which he carried with him on his long trek from High Beech to Northborough: *Don Juan* and *Child Harold* are written side by side, with little indication of what belongs where; amidst the jumble are Biblical paraphrases, drafts of pathetic letters home, prayers for his family, prose accounts of his journey across England, carefully worked arithmetical calculations, based on the money he had in High Beech in Spring and Summer 1841. MS. 6 is neatly written, with little or no confusion. MS. 8 by itself would make little coherent sense, whereas at least in MS. 6 we have a poem, even though it appears to have been left unfinished in the fair copy when Clare was taken to the asylum at Northampton in December 1841.

Partly because the poem was composed piecemeal over the course of several months, and partly because of the circumstances in which it was composed, there is not the structural unity we might expect in a shorter poem. For if the poem is a diary, it is the diary of a particularly harassed and tormented spirit. This means that unity depends much more on Clare's mind, than on any argument; what poetic argument there is is bound to be loosely structured. Some unity is imposed by a skilful use of patterns of imagery and by the careful deployment of varying stanzaic forms. But the spirit of the poem is largely one of changing moods, of contrasts and oppositions.

The diary-like structure allows for the exploration of particular themes, for repetitions and diversions. Clare is writing about the mainsprings of his emotional life here: he cannot afford to be hurried.

In *Child Harold* Clare deploys a nine-line stanza, usually rhyming ababbcbcc (a variation of the Spenserian stanza, which he had already used in *The Village Minstrel*, and several other early poems); and some form of lyric stanza, usually entitled either 'Ballad' or 'Song'. The nine-line stanzas considerably outnumber the songs (as also in *Don Juan*). The connection between song and stanza has been the subject of controversy, although it is now generally recognised that the songs form an integral part of the poem. Clare is extending Byron's practice in his *Childe Harold* and *Don Juan*. This interaction, structurally and argumentatively important for the poem, also lends the poem great variety. Changes of mood are frequently emphasised by a change from stanza to song. The songs themselves are very varied: for example there is the close argument of the opening Ballad, with its curt lack of adornment, followed by the anapaestic lilt of 'The sun has gone down with a veil on his brow', recalling the Byronic nostalgia of *Hebrew Melodies*, or Tom Moore.

Structural devices are paralleled by the use of imagery. There are several recurrent, basic, images in the poem: sunrise and sunset, light and darkness, storm and calm, seasonal contrasts, prison and freedom. In order to appreciate the range and depth of the poem we have to see the working out of these images, and their interrelationships. For in returning to the same theme of love and its permanence, Clare tends to use the same imagery. As the poem advances each image acquires overtones and associations with other images. This cumulative effect is not peculiar to *Child Harold*, but it receives its fullest justification here. (On a smaller local level, it may be seen in several of the asylum poems.)[45]

The image of the storm and of winter permeates *Child Harold*. Whether or not Clare intended the poem to follow the pattern of the seasonal cycle (as Geoffrey Grigson and J. W. and Anne Tibble suggests, but with different textual results),[46] the alternation between storm and calm is essential to the poem's structure. Much of the asylum verse, in fact, centres on this antithesis. The storm is initially dreaded for its violence: Clare is the storm-tossed sailor. But the storm can also be cathartic and visionary, as Clare leaves the world behind. Out of his despair, out of the wreck of his life, he makes a virtue: the desolation in the middle of 'I am' is answered by the calm of its ending; the bleakness of the beginning of *Child Harold* (where the storm image is especially potent) is balanced by the affirmation of independence and triumph at the end of the song, 'Written in a Thunder storm'.[47] The storm itself blasts him out of his indifference into the paradoxical freedom of self-awareness.

The drift is always towards annihilation, towards the freedom gained by the very loss of his own identity, his merging with nature and Mary. As his pre-asylum verse had tended towards the generalising of nature – because only in such terms could he stave off the despair generated by loss of particularity – so here Mary ceases to be a figure of flesh and blood. The same is true of Clare himself: he yearns for release. He ends the first song in the poem with an optimism based firmly on such generalisation:

> True love is eternal
> For God is the giver
> And love like the soul will
> Endure – and forever[48]

That, both in the context of the song, and of the poem as a whole, seems too desperately achieved, too glib. More satisfactory, because more honest in its implicit statement of the conflict, is the stanza that immediately follows this song:

> And he who studies natures volume through
> And reads it with a pure unselfish mind
> Will find Gods power all round in every view
> As one bright vision of the almighty mind
> His eyes are open though the world is blind
> No ill from him creations works deform
> The high and lofty one is great and kind
> Evil may cause the blight and crushing storm
> His is the sunny glory and the calm

Calm is itself an ambiguous condition. The song 'Written in a

Thunder storm' explores the cathartic effects of the storm on a mind dulled with apathy. It is an undisciplined poem, almost hysterical, looking ahead to the apocalyptic poems that characterise the later MS.110 (such as, especially, 'Song Last Day');[49] but at least the storm might jolt him into feeling that 'nature is my throne', when the cosmic pattern will be revealed, and eternity assume some meaning:

> Roll on ye wrath of thunders – peal on peal
> Till worlds are ruins and myself alone
> Melt heart and soul cased in obdurate steel
> Till I can feel that nature is my throne[50]

Freedom is achieved by moving towards a symbolism that obliterates distinctions:

> I live in love sun of undying light
> And fathom my own heart for ways of good
> In its pure atmosphere day without night
> Smiles on the plains the forest and the flood
>
> Smile on ye elements of earth and sky
> Or frown in thunders as ye frown on me
> Bid earth and its delusions pass away
> But leave the mind as its creator free

Because of the sublimity of this, Clare is able, paradoxically, to move into the calm resignation of the next nine-line stanza:

> This twilight seems a veil of gause and mist
> Trees seem dark hills between the earth and sky
> Winds sob awake and then a gusty hist
> Fanns through the wheat like serpents gliding bye
> I love to stretch my length 'tween earth and sky
> And see the inky foliage oer me wave
> Though shades are still my prison where I lie
> Long use grows nature which I easy brave
> And think how sweet cares rest within the grave[51]

This is a far cry from the defiance and anger bursting out of the stanza preceding the song:

> Cares gather round, I snap their chains in two
> And smile in agony and laugh in tears ...[52]

The paradox of the series of stanzas that follow the song 'Written in a Thunder storm' is that their emphasis on the desirability of death has a conviction, a power to move, that derives from the purging effects of the song:

> Tie all my cares up in thy arms O sleep
> And give my weary spirits peace and rest ...[53]

And from here, the transition to the theme of Mary as the haven of rest is easily made, the connection between death and Mary's love clearly implied. The poet looks back into the past, when 'joy was heaven when I called her wife', as opposed to the present when 'Day seems my night and night seems blackest hell'. The present is his hell, as the song 'Written in a Thunder storm' had declared, and as there the connection was between hell and storm, heaven and calm, so here, in these stanzas, Mary is described as his heaven in days of strife, his harbour. She was his symbol of love and truth:

> The only harbour in my days of strife
> Was Mary when the seas roiled mountains high
> When joy was lost and every sorrow rife
> To her sweet bosom I was wont to flye
> To undecieve by truth lifes treacherous agony[54]

His hell is now more grievous, separated as he is from his love;

> But hell is heaven could I cease to mourn
>
> For her for one whose very name is yet
> My hell or heaven – and will ever be ...

The ambiguity and uncertainty of the situation are clearly observable here, where the distinction between heaven and hell has become blurred, as both become merged in Mary, and his doubts about their love. For his own sanity he has to forget her, but at the same time he knows he cannot. But in doubting, falsehood and deceit creep in, to taint their relationship. The harbour in the storm is no longer to be relied upon. This is no mere passing fit of pique: much later in the poem the same sentiment occurs, less obliquely:

> My Life hath been a wreck – and I've gone far
> For peace and truth – and hope – for home and rest

– Like Edens gates – fate throws a constant bar –
Thoughts may o'ertake the sunset in the west
– Man meets no home within a woman's breast[55]

Clare is fully open to the ambiguity of the images that lie
at the base of the poem : hope and despair jostle each other in
the crowded pages of the notebooks. In the letter to Mary
Joyce, quoted earlier in this chapter, Clare had written 'nature
to me seems dead & her very pulse seems frozen to an icicle in
the summer sun –'.[56] This chilled observation reflects the mood
of the poem :

Love is to me a thought that ever aches
A frost bound thought that freezes life to stone
Mary in truth and nature still my own
That warms the winter of my aching breast[57]

In recalling the days of his childhood, he observes :

Yet still the picture turns my bosom chill
And leaves a void – nor love nor hope may fill[58]

Summer itself is seen in terms of winter :

Summer is winters desert and the spring
Is like a ruined city desolate[59]

Because of this sort of association, Clare cannot meet Mary in
winter :

I can't expect to meet thee now
The winter floods begin
The wind sighs throu the naked bough
Sad as my heart within[60]

In spite of the apparent unanswerableness of this pathetic
fallacy, the following stanza again suggests hope, reminiscent
of the comfort of winter as delineated by Thomson and
Cowper :

Tis winter and the fields are bare and waste ...
Yet comfort now the social bosom warms ...
Bare fields the frozen lake and leafless grove
Are natures grand religion and true love[61]

But the desolate song 'In this cold world' redresses the

balance.[62] Similarly in the ante-penultimate stanza of the poem,

> Friends cold neglects have froze my heart to stone[63]

And in the same way, if the sun can symbolise everlasting love, as here:

> For in that hamlet lives my rising sun
> Whose beams hath cheered me all my lorn life long,[64]

or

> I live in love sun of undying light,[65]

it can also symbolise quite the opposite:

> My sun of love was short — and clouded long[66]

Some of these contradictions illuminate the final stanza of the song, 'The sun has gone down with a veil on his brow/ While I in the forest sit museing alone'. The song ends with the poet in his grave, whilst the memory of Mary, his dis-embodied love, shines above him like the sun:

> Though cares still will gather like clouds in my sky
> Though hopes may grow hopeless and fetters recoil
> While the sun of existance sheds light in my eye
> I'll be free in a prison and cling to the soil
> I'll cling to the spot where my first love was cherished
> Where my heart nay my soul unto Mary I gave
> And when my last hope and existance is perished
> Her memory will shine like a sun on my grave[67]

Clare and Mary are momentarily united: his own loss of identity is accompanied by an increased awareness of Mary. The image of the sun merges with that of Mary, so that he is able to write in the stanza that follows this song,

> Mary thou ace of hearts thou muse of song
> The pole star of my being and decay ...

> Mary thy name loved long still keeps me free
> Till my lost life becomes a part of thee

Mary is in some sense Clare's prison; he wants to shackle him-self to his ideal, to find a freedom that entails his becoming part of her, his identity lost in hers.

The contradictions inherent in the imagery of the poem echo the conflict between flesh and spirit, the real and the ideal. To some extent this struggle between Mary as woman and Mary as spirit characterises the difference between *Don Juan* and *Child Harold*: in *Don Juan* woman is all flesh. Much of the poignancy of *Child Harold*, especially the later sections, derives from the close association between nature and Mary. But there is no neat solution to the dilemma. For example the song 'O Mary dear three springs have been' comes after a stanza of hope which concludes:

> And she the soul of life for whom I sigh
> Like flowers shall cheer me when the storm is bye[68]

The song belies this optimism, as the seasons grind on inexorably, each blossoming in turn, while the only flower that matters, Mary, never appears: she is not even to be found in her natural haunts. Hope is again shattered:

> Tis autumn and the rustling corn,
> Goes loaded on the creaking wain
> I seek her in the early morn
> But cannot meet her face again
> Sweet Mary she is abscent still
> And much I fear she ever will[69]

One answer, courageous and defiant, is, as the song 'Written in a Thunder storm' suggests, to leave the world behind. It is worth quoting one of the most impressive affirmations of this attitude in *Child Harold*:

> No single hour can stand for nought
> No moment hand can move
> But calendars a aching thought
> Of my first lonely love
>
> Where silence doth the loudest call
> My secrets to betray
> As moonlight holds the night in thrall
> As suns reveal the day
>
> I hide it in the silent shades
> Till silence finds a tongue

> I make its grave where time invades
> Till time becomes a song
>
> I bid my foolish heart be still
> But hopes will not be chid
> My heart will beat – and burn – and chill
> First love will not be hid
>
> When summer ceases to be green
> And winter bare and blea –
> Death may forget what I have been
> But I must cease to be
>
> When words refuse before the crowd
> My Marys name to give
> The muse in silence sings aloud
> And there my love will live[70]

The other answer is to look for active solace in nature. The descriptive passages in *Child Harold* have a luminous quality entirely different from anything Clare had written before: they are essentially atmospheric, important above all for their repose. Even the accounts of winter tend to minimise the hardship:

> Even in this winter scene of frost and storms
> Bare fields the frozen lake and leafless grove
> Are natures grand religion and true love.[71]

It is generally in the songs that the bitter personal applications come out; what stability there is in the poem derives very largely from the peculiar harmony that Clare senses in the countryside. What is remarkable is the control, the poise, evinced in so many of these stanzas, a control which seems to vindicate the larger, grander claims he makes for nature: such claims have their validity because of the fullness of the response as stated in stanzas such as this:

> What mellowness these harvest days unfold
> In the strong glances of the midday sun
> The homesteads very grass seems changed to gold
> The light in golden shadows seems to run
> And tinges every spray it rests upon

With that rich harvest hue of sunny joy
Nature lifes sweet companion cheers alone –
The hare starts up before the shepherd boy
And partridge coveys wir on russet wings of joy[72]

The poem appears to feel its way towards acceptance and
solitude, where even Mary can be forgotten; the end of the
poem is heralded by this invocation:

Hail Solitude still Peace and Lonely good
Thou spirit of all joys to be alone
My best of friends these glades and this green wood
Where nature is herself and loves her own ...[73]

The penultimate stanza combines the rich luxuriance of nature
with the rejection of love, as though Clare had found the means
of escape he had yearned for earlier ('Now stagnant grows
my too refined clay/I envy birds their wings to flye away'):[74]

Wrecked of all hopes save one to be alone
Where Solitude becomes my wedded mate
Sweet Forest with rich beauties overgrown
Where solitude is queen and riegns in state
Hid in green trees I hear the clapping gate
And voices calling to the rambling cows
I Laugh at Love and all its idle fate
The present hour is all my lot alows
An age of sorrow springs from lovers vows

When we see that Clare is capable of this, the reservations
we might have about the poem fall into place. It is a rare and
valuable poet who can work from such initial, dreadful despair
towards the simple, grand resignation of the close.

The Asylum Poems

Clare spent five months at Northborough after his flight from High Beech. But on 29 December 1841 he left home for the confines of the Northampton General Lunatic Asylum, where he was to spend the rest of his long life. We know all too little of the circumstances which led to his removal from home. The Reverend Charles Mossop had visited the Clare household and found the situation rather strained: he recommended the asylum at Northampton, if it were decided that Clare should require treatment.[1] Clare was accordingly certified insane by Dr William Page and Dr Fenwick Skrimshire. The question of his insanity is a vexed one, and there does not seem to be sufficient evidence to say categorically what form his illness took; the evidence of visitors, and of the poems, is not conclusive.[2] For the period when he was at home before certification there is considerable evidence of sanity: the neatly copied versions of *Don Juan* and *Child Harold*, Biblical paraphrases, the account of his escape from High Beech. His last surviving letter from this period is characteristically direct, with little hint of the troubled undercurrent.[3] But less than two months later, Clare had seen the last of his home and his wife. Frederick Martin's account of his departure (elaborated no doubt, but effective in its pathos), echoes his account of the removal from Helpstone to Northborough ten years earlier:

> He struggled hard when the keepers came to fetch him, imploring them, with tears in his eyes, to leave him at his little cottage, and seeing all resistance fruitless, declaring his intention to die rather than to go to such another prison as that from which he had escaped.[4]

For the third and last time he is uprooted. From Northampton there is no escape. The conditions of his 'imprisonment' have been stated with admirable clarity by J. W. and Anne Tibble and Geoffrey Grigson: it is a tale of kind attention, visits from friends and inquisitive strangers, freedom (eventually restricted) to go into the town; a tale of isolation, courage, despair, the gradual loss of grip.[5] It is saddeningly inevitable, as the slow years drag themselves out in weariness. For Clare did not die until 20 May 1864.

Cut off from his family, his friends and his home, Clare wrote incessantly, until just before his death: always a prolific writer, he did not allow the confines of the asylum to restrict his fluency. In what he writes in this last desperate quarter of his life (no mere dotage) is to be found some of his best poetry, but also some of his worst; for as poetry becomes verse, the doggerel increases, a therapy for the tedious hours of loneliness. The sheer quantity of bad or mediocre verse from this period (and the sameness of so much of it) should be a warning against too sentimental a view of Clare's asylum years. But there can be no doubt that in a considerable number of poems written between 1841 and 1850 Clare attains a new quality of vision: for the most part he begins to write a new sort of poetry, closer to the poems of the 1830s than to the crackling descriptive verse of the 1820s, but often making use of the sort of starkness he had mastered then.

Clare's lyric genius is nowhere more apparent than in the asylum period. He had always been able to jot down a hasty song, and the manuscripts from all periods testify to his facility. Such ease had undoubtedly militated against the achievement of anything really memorable in the early songs. There are occasional felicities, certainly, as Clare avoids the prettinesses of album verse, but even in the late 1820s such songs are frequently marred by too facile a lilt, too unspecific an emotion, too obvious or conventional a response. In the asylum practically all of his poetry is lyrical in vein, and, after *Child Harold*, there is only one attempt at a long poem ('A Rhapsody'),[6] apart from the repetition of *Child Harold*'s structural device in MS. 110 (1845–6), which itself contains some very remarkable verse, frenetic and impassioned, but occasionally supremely controlled, displaying the acceptance and composure that characterise so much of the poetry of this period.[7]

This quality must be acknowledged. For, on the level of the

conventional love song, it is there throughout this period, and it is not only dependent on a more exalted vision. If there are many poems in the Knight transcripts which scarcely warrant a second look, there are as many which show how successfully Clare approaches the spontaneity and the lyricism of the ballads he had always admired; in a variety of rhythms and stanzaic forms he addresses love poems not only to Mary, but to the numerous other girls who at some time or other had caught his fancy. Few of these poems could be said to approach the finesse of the Elizabethan lyricists who were so important an influence on Clare : but in their relish for the joys of love and their unrestrained directness they resemble such pieces more closely than they do the contrived simplicities of Moore or Byron, not to mention Mrs Hemans or Letitia Landon.

In nearly all of his asylum songs Clare recreates an ideal landscape, in which love thrives amidst congenial surroundings. The texture is usually thin, the poem saved, often, by the lilt of the rhythm, nostalgic and haunting; love does not depend, in these songs, upon the past, for many are addressed to girls of his casual acquaintance (often remembered from his childhood days), and pathetically rooted in an idyllic present or future. Occasionally the song form creates its own success, as in 'Love, meet me in the green glen' :

> Love, meet me in the green glen,
>   Beside the tall elm-tree;
> Where the sweetbriar smells so sweet agen,
>   There come with me,
>   Meet me in the green glen.
>
> Meet me at the sunset
>   Down in the green glen,
> Where we've often met
>   By hawthorn-tree and foxes' den,
>   Meet me in the green glen.
>
> Meet me by the sheep-pen,
>   Where briars smell at e'en,
> Meet me i' the green glen
>   Where white thorn shades are green,
>   Meet me in the green glen.

Meet me in the green glen,
  By sweetbriar bushes there;
Meet me by your own sen,
  Where the wild thyme blossoms fair,
    Meet me in the green glen.

Meet me by the sweetbriar,
  By the mole-hill swelling there,
When the west glows like a fire
  God's crimson bed is there.
    Meet me in the green glen.[8]

But often it is as hard to believe in the beloved as in Clare's professed emotions, as the same clichés return, the rosy cheeks and snow-white bosoms, the spring and the summer, morning and evening. Poems on various aspects of nature are frequently the best, and demonstrate that Clare has not lost his grasp of the realities of the natural world, his sheer love of living things, irrespective of their associations. The sonnet 'The flag top quivers in the breeze',[9] or 'Morning',[10] both show this visual and aural awareness: the latter may end on an apparent note of high fancy, but it is very much the familiar pre-asylum Clare here, with none of his powers diminished:

Hedge-sparrows in the bush cry 'tweet'
O'er nests larks winnow in the wheat
'Till the sun turns gold and gets more high
And paths are clean, and grass gets dry
And longest shadows pass away
And brightness is the blaze of day

In several poems the descriptive element is subservient to the nostalgic melancholy, or to the desire to be alone:

How silent comes this gentle wind
And fans the grass and corn
It leaves a thousand thoughts behind
Of happiness forlorn
The memory of my happier days
When I was hale and young
Where still my boyish fancy strays
Corn fields and woods among[11]

The combination of a rhythmic plangency and a yearning for the past comes out in the 'Stanzas', where Clare's pathetic situation is sufficient to make a moving poem :

> The spring is come forth, but no spring is for me,
> Like the spring of my boyhood, on woodland and lea,
> When flowers brought me heaven, and knew me again
> In the joy of their blooming o'er mountain and plain
> My thoughts are confined, and imprisoned – O when
> Will freedom find me my own vallies again?[12]

As so often, the unanswerable question is asked, the impossibility contained in the form of the question :

> O when shall my manhood my youth's vallies meet,
> The scenes where my children are laughing at Play,
> The scenes where my memory is fading away

This poem is interesting for the hope that is salvaged, on the basis of memory : in this it recalls *Child Harold*, as well as other asylum poems, in which the dream is reality, recollection of the past a substitute for living in the present. This repeated worrying at the theme makes something out of otherwise slight poems, such as 'Where love are you?';[13] but it also strengthens a poem as beautifully controlled as 'Winter' :

> How blasted nature is, the scene is winter
> The Autumn withered every branch
> Leaves drop, and turn to colourless soil
> Ice shoots i' splinters at the river Bridge
> And by and bye all stop –
> White shines the snow upon the far hill top
> Nature's all withered to the root, her printer
> To decay that neer comes back
> Winds burst, then drop
> Flowers, leaves and colours, nothing's left to hint her
> Spring, Summer, Autumn's, withered into winter[41]

'It is the Evening Hour', one of Clare's most astonishing love poems, represents the distillation of this theme :

> It is the evening hour,
>   How silent all doth lie,

The hornèd moon he shows his face
   In the river with the sky.
Just by the path on which we pass,
The flaggy lake lies still as glass.

Spirit of her I love,
   Whispering to me,
Stories of sweet visions, as I rove,
   Here stop, and crop with me
Sweet flowers that in the still hour grew,
We'll take them home, nor shake off the bright dew.

Mary, or sweet spirit of thee,
   As the bright sun shines to-morrow,
Thy dark eyes these flowers shall see,
   Gathered by me in sorrow,
In the still hour when my mind was free
To walk alone – yet wish I walk'd with thee.[15]

Here Clare rises above any commonplaces of nostalgia or sentiment, without in any way straining the lyric form he has
chosen. It is part of Clare's achievement that he is able, in so
many poems, to maintain a fluidity of line that works in
harmony with the formal pressures he applies. In this poem,
the opening stanza creates the necessary sense of atmosphere
and place, unobtrusively and with economy, sketching in the
reflective silence of the evening, obliquely referring to himself
as a figure in this landscape in such a way that each serves to
define the other. It is a characteristically deft stroke for Clare
to have written 'we', not 'I', in the penultimate line of this
stanza : in a similar way in the corresponding line of the central
stanza the tense of the verb 'grew' throws us back into the
past, when Mary was more than spirit. It is a poem of opposites
which do not cancel each other out. The past and present vie
with each other, just as the poet's solitude becomes companionship with the spirit of Mary; Mary is both present spirit, and
remembered being of the past. The bright sun of the final
stanza's 'tomorrow' (and it is a test of the poem's achievement
that this look into the future is so moving) is offset by Mary's
dark eyes, Clare's own sorrow. In the same way that the
moon and the sky are reflected in the silent river, so the shifting

moods of the poem, of the depicted moment, mix and blur, until that last line brings us up against the incontrovertible fact of isolation.

Clare clearly does not restrict himself to expressions of love and nostalgia. Many poems explore the implications of this love: these are the poems of real importance for an estimate of the asylum years.

The temptation to trace a developing philosophy here is obvious: Harold Bloom's discussion of some of Clare's later poems suffers from this insistence on pattern, and the parallel course of Clare's illness, as charted in poems and others' observations, is not quite as self-evident as Geoffrey Grigson suggests.[16] The chief difficulty here is the state of the text: for most of this period we have to rely on the transcripts made by the provident W. F. Knight, employed by the asylum in various capacities until 30 January 1850.[17] Very few of the poems are dated, and Grigson supposes that the order of the transcripts is roughly chronological. But it is very difficult to say how rough Knight's chronology is: the most that can be said is that 1844, or the period just before it, undoubtedly represents some sort of high point in the asylum, for some of the best poems are dated precisely in this year, such as 'Graves of Infants' (June), 'Love's Pains' (13 July), 'O wert thou in the storm' (17 July), 'The sleep of Spring' (some time in 1844), 'A Vision' (2 August). Poems such as 'I Am', or 'An Invite to Eternity' are not so easily placed, but quite probably come from 1844–5.[18] There is no reason to suppose that 'A Vision' represents the culmination of Clare's line of thought. As in *Child Harold*, Clare is capable of supreme vision one moment, and bathos or despair the next. 'A Vision' may be one of his most forceful, concentrated poems: but it is certainly not the last word.

It is therefore begging too many questions to examine the poems in the hope of finding the consistent development of ideas. A more useful approach is to establish the relationship between poems, so that, by charting some kind of pattern behind the poetry, we can provide a framework within which to view individual poems.[19]

The most important concept for Clare is still solitude: the despair needs to be felt before we can appreciate the peculiar elation which emerges from it. The short poem 'Left in the world alone' is, because of the utter desolation it embodies, frightening in its lack of hope.[20]

> Left in the world alone,
> Where nothing seems my own,
> And everything is weariness to me,
> 'Tis a life without an end,
> 'Tis a world without a friend,
> And everything is sorrowful I see.

Clare begins by projecting his own despair and alienation onto what he sees. Carefully choosing relevant imagery, he depicts a world that reflects his own weariness. But if this is merely the pathetic fallacy, it is the bleakness of nature, rather than any sympathy that may be derived from it, which is emphasised:

> There's the crow upon the stack,
> And other birds all black,
> While bleak November's frowning wearily;
> And the black cloud's dropping rain,
> Till the floods hide half the plain,
> And everything is dreariness to me.

This point emerges more fully in the third and final stanza; for here, whereas the sun shines (albeit wan and pale), the wind blows (albeit chill), and the leaves quiver on the trees, Clare (note the important 'While') is left alone, chilled like a stone, and the world frowns over him, recalling the frowns of November, as the pathetic fallacy is turned on its head. Nature herself is aloof and alien.

> The sun shines wan and pale,
> Chill blows the northern gale,
> And odd leaves shake and quiver on the tree,
> While I am left alone,
> Chilled as a mossy stone,
> And all the world is frowning over me.

A slight poem this may be, but its slightness is deceptive. The listlessness of the language echoes Clare's emotional sterility. The progression of thought is of interest, moving from an almost prosaic statement of the position in the first stanza, to the generic images of the second stanza, where Clare's predicament is suggested by nature (the floods conceal the plain, as Clare is obliterated by the world), and then to the more potent, ambiguous imagery of the last stanza. By the end of the poem, Clare's isolation has been set in the wider context of the earth's potential vitality, but also the earth's own despair.

Here the dangers of Clare's lyricism, cramping and confined, are apparent. It is easy for the emotional complexities to be thinned out in these songs, quite often because of the rhythm : whereas the lightest of poems is frequently saved by the lilt, anything more serious and purposeful jars against the form in which it finds itself. Even an unpretentious song can achieve this kind of dignity, when the rhythm is firmly controlled :

> The night is still dead Oak leaves strew
> Dyke bottoms and the green grass too ...[21]

The descriptive pieces are frequently the most successful in this respect :

> Spring comes and it is may – white as are sheets
> Each orchard shines beside its little town
> Childern at every bush a poesy meets
> Bluebells and primroses –[22]

In the poems connected with solitude and loneliness several other themes often impinge upon the central idea, such as purity and innocence, the importance of the world of nature, the alienation of man from society, the necessity for retreat, the value of secrecy, the preference of the ideal to the reality. Related to these recurrent themes is his attitude to the past, which develops from mere nostalgia (often extremely poignant and effective on its own level), to a powerful imaginative apprehension of the past, as an act of memory. In this yearning for the past can be seen the relation to the ideal (and to isolation), for Clare is irrevocably cut off from it. Because of the role of nature in the past, love is important, for it is the chief element in his lost dream, the type of innocence and freedom. As he contemplates the past, he recognises life's transience, which leads him to contemplate eternity, and a freedom that transcends all boundaries of place and time. Many of these problems Clare had faced before, both in 1832, and in 1841. But now it

is all that much more desperate, the prison of the asylum that
much more final and constricting.

The short poem 'How can I forget?' is memorable chiefly
for this final question.[23] The refusal to forget, to lose the gleam
of youth, is no mere self-indulgence, but the prerequisite of
emotional and poetic life for Clare. The dream may be over:

> The passing of a dream
>   Are the thoughts I have to-day;
> Cloud shadows they all seem
>   And pass as soon away;

but the vision has not fled, in the sense that Clare still knows
where his heart lies:

> When shall my mind awake
>   In its own loved scenes again?[24]

How central memory is becomes even more apparent in the
'Stanzas' where Clare's memory of Mary is disastrously obliterated. The apocalyptic tone recalls other poems of the period:

> Black absence hides upon the past
>   I quite forget thy face;
> And memory like the angry blast
>   Will love's last smile erase;[25]

although Clare has asked 'How can I forget?' the actual loss of
remembrance is the final disaster, for then dream and vision
both fade.

The emphasis on the past, in particular on childhood, occurs
throughout Clare's work. But it seldom becomes a mere sentimental attachment: childhood is a period of moral and spiritual strength, a time of innocence. This is the theme of two of
Clare's most beautiful asylum poems, 'Graves of Infants' and
'The Dying Child'. The simplicity that one is tempted to ascribe
to these poems is not one of idea, nor in the case of the first of
these two poems, of utterance; it lies in the concept of the
poem, the imaginative act and the tone that embodies this act.
The complete repose of 'Graves of Infants' depends partly on
Clare's use of the Spenserian stanza, but also on the underlying
conviction. Once again he uses an apparently obvious device,

the pathetic fallacy, and creates a poem completely idiosyncratic:

> Infants' graves are steps of angels, where
> Earth's brightest gems of innocence repose.
> God is their parent, and they need no tear,
> He takes them to his bosom from earth's woes,
> A bud their lifetime and a flower their close.[26]

Nature and children are in perfect harmony, so that when nature mourns their death, it is in a spirit of acceptance, for death is their flowering, their fitting end:

> They bowed and trembled, and they left no sigh,
> And the sun smiled to show their end was well.
> Infants have nought to weep for ere they die;
> All prayers are needless, beads they need not tell,
> White flowers their mourners are, nature their
>   passing-bell.

This celebration of innocence excludes the crude adult world: in death the infants are glorified, for in death they earn the flowers' tears, the dewdrops that symbolise their fragile, but lasting, innocence.

'The Dying Child' transposes this belief into lyric terms.[27] Simplicity here involves diction, and Blake provides an obvious comparison. We have only to remember, for example, the sentimentality of Thomas Hood's 'The Death-Bed', or Clare's earlier poems on children and death, to appreciate the economy and strength of this poem.[28] The most basic of properties – trees, green grass, daisies, violets, winter – become the only possible terms in which to see the child's death.

> He could not die when trees were green,
>   For he loved the time too well.
> His little hands, when flowers were seen,
>   Were held for the bluebell,
>   As he was carried o'er the green.

The transition from this opening affirmation to final acceptance is carefully managed. In spite of the fact of intimacy (he knew the bees, 'those children of the spring') death is not

averted; but it is approached cautiously, with the pained
question of the third stanza left unanswered:

> Infants, the children of the spring!
>   How can an infant die
> When butterflies are on the wing,
>   Green grass, and such a sky?
>   How can they die at spring?

The child takes the flowers to bed; but his eyes never open, and
nature mourns his absence, as the poem closes with the barrenness of winter. But the child is free: his death was inherent in
his actions, the frailty of his hands stretched out in the first
stanza for the bluebell, as he was carried over the green, fore-
shadowing the carrying of his frail body when dead. Although
Clare is initially shocked by such a death, he accepts its inevitability if the innocence of spring is to be preserved. The chill-
ing winter of manhood is avoided.

> When winter came and blasts did sigh,
>   And bare were plain and tree,
> As he for ease in bed did lie
>   His soul seemed with the free,
>   He died so quietly.

Just as childhood represents innocence, nature itself is also
free and innocent, hence the growing desire to be absorbed by
nature. The sonnet 'Poets Love Nature' puts the belief simply:
flowers are God's messengers, announcing nature's essential
freedom, and Clare's own freedom is secured for they represent
the religious purity of the fields:

> Even in prison they can solace me
> For where they bloom God is, and I am free.[29]

His belief is not always so categorical and confident as here;
in 'Love of Nature', for example, his confusion of mind results
in a disturbing honesty which conflicts with the affirmative
boldness of the opening stanzas. The poem begins:

> I love thee, Nature, with a boundless love,
>   The calm of earth, the storm of roaring woods,
> The winds breathe happiness where'er I rove,
>   There's life's own music in the swelling floods.[30]

Freedom here depends upon the absence of women:

> From Eve's posterity I stand quite free
> Nor feel her curses rankle round my heart.

Woman's deceit inevitably leads Clare to set his faith in an ideal love, in love concealed amongst the flowers.[31] In this dispirited poem, however, he does not work himself round to this solution: Nature in these circumstances ('Love is not here', he finally declares) is his mother, Clare just a weary child on her breast.

The disgust that he increasingly felt for women and mortal love is even more tellingly put in some 'Stanzas' in which disillusionment with the physical leads him to a spiritualisation of love in nature. Nature, because eternal, is preferable to the decay of humanity: truth becomes associated with nature, consequently the merely human heart is incapable of real love:

> Love lives with Nature, not with lust,
> Go, find her in the flowers.[32]

These lines contain the essence of Clare's philosophy: few antitheses could be so direct, few injunctions so compelling.

Occasionally, as in 'Love is Life's Spring',[33] Clare seems prepared to accept the dual aspect, the heaven and the hell of love, but more often than not his bitterness forces him to reject the world of human values, to retreat into the natural surroundings where he believed a higher, more permanent form of love could be found. Consequently his love poetry becomes a poetry of secrecy and silence. His absorption into the natural world can sometimes be effected by a progression from simile to metaphor, as in the song in MS.110, 'She's like the daisy on the hill', where an apparently conventional series of similes is transformed into an equation of the beloved with the various aspects of nature:

> The all thats beautifull and sweet
> The all thats good and fair
> Is my true lover when we meet
> Where summers wild flowers are[34]

More forthright and personal is 'Secret Love', where the poem's uncertainties of direction and motive are part of its meaning.[35]

The peculiar state of mind induced by his habit of concealing his love is not one which he often discusses in such clinical terms. It is 'to' his 'despite' that he hides his love : his nerves are on edge, as he suffers the effects of this concealment. Yet he could not bear to look at her, and instead bestowed the memory of her wherever he went. This secrecy has its obvious compensations, as the second stanza shows, where nature is both the beloved, and also the lover, the secret and its finder, the lost and the found, silent and yet singing :

> I met her in the greenest dells
> Where dew drops pearl the wood blue bells
> The lost breeze kissed her bright blue eye
> The bee kissed and went singing bye
> A sun beam found a passage there
> A gold chain round her neck so fair
> As secret as the wild bees song
> She lay there all the summer long

But this equilibrium is shattered in the final stanza, as the tone reverts to that of the first stanza; the silence continues to unnerve him, until it too 'found a tongue/To haunt me all the summer long'.

> I hid my love in field and town
> Till e'en the breeze would knock me down
> The Bees seemed singing ballads o'er
> The flyes buss turned a Lions roar
> And even silence found a tongue
> To haunt me all the summer long
> The riddle nature could not prove
> Was nothing else but secret love

This strange upset of nature, is, as the final line admits, the effect of secret love. Such secrecy is not, then, the ideal solution it might appear, for secrecy in love can be stultifying, in that it makes a mockery of what should be natural and unforced, rather than consciously imposed. The main difficulty, from Clare's point of view, is that, in concealing his beloved in nature, he is losing her : he bids his love goodbye when he sees the wild flowers. Innocence and purity are desirable, but they tend to exclude the poet as would-be lover. It is interesting to note how much better is the central stanza where Clare is virtually absent from the scene: the concentration on himself in the other stanzas might make interesting case-history, but it makes less convincing poetry.[36]

Secrecy, however, was not always regarded with such equivocation. By placing his beloved in nature, he was guaranteeing for himself a love that was both depersonalised, and everlasting. But even then there were two possible outcomes: either he became a visionary in the transport of freedom from the physical world, or he left the world resignedly to seek a life that was colourless and tragic, inevitable and chastening. These moods complement each other, rather than one leading to the other: just as sorrow and joy were related for Clare, different sides of the same coin, like sunshine and shadow, so he hovered between the two emotional positions offered by his doctrine of secrecy and seclusion in love.[37] The two most well-known poems that embrace the visionary aspect are 'Love Lives Beyond the Tomb' and 'A Vision'. In the first Clare states definitively his belief in a love that stretches to eternity; it is one of the supreme expressions of his lyricism.

> Love lives beyond
> The tomb, the earth, which fades like dew –
> I love the fond,
> The faithful, and the true.
>
> Love lies in sleep,
> 'Tis happiness of healthy dreams,
> Eve's dews may weep,
> But love delightful seems.
>
> 'Tis seen in flowers,
> And in the even's pearly dew
> On earth's green hours
> And in the heaven's eternal blue.
>
> 'Tis heard in spring
> When light and sunbeams, warm and kind,
> On angel's wing
> Brings love and music to the wind.
>
> And where's the voice

So young, so beautiful, and sweet
    As nature's choice,
Where spring and lovers meet?

    Love lives beyond
The tomb, the earth, the flowers, and dew,
    I love the fond,
The faithful, young and true.[38]

But in 'A Vision', earthly love is put completely behind, in what is one of Clare's most succinct statements of isolation and freedom, of the inviolability of human individuality: here we can see how solitude and freedom and eternity are intimately related, in that he has to be alone to be free, and it is in this solitude that he finds his true identity. In language that is increasingly powerful and direct, he unites the various strands of his poetic creed – his spurning of earth's lusts, his awareness of a higher kind of love and beauty, and the connection of this recognition with his poetic genius, so that the eternal ray of the sun should live on in his verse, leaving earth and its trivialities behind, while he kept his essential freedom of spirit. This poem has not the reverberant quality of Blake; but it has the clarity of vision and expression so common in the asylum poems, the absolute conviction in his own inspiration. This is the most rounded and complete statement of what Clare had moved towards in the year of his 'flitting' to Northborough:

    I lost the love of heaven above
    I spurned the lust of earth below
    I felt the sweets of fancied love
    And hell itself my only foe

    I lost earth's joys but felt the glow
    Of heaven's flame abound in me
    Till loveliness and I did grow
    The bard of immortality

    I loved but woman fell away
    I hid me from her faded fame
    I snatched the sun's eternal ray
    And wrote till earth was but a name.

    In every language upon earth

On every shore, o'er every sea,
I gave my name immortal birth,
And kept my spirit with the free[39]

This poem sets the seal on his achievement; it makes a nicely
rounded conclusion to his life of poetry, explaining everything
while at the same time requiring for its own explanation the
whole of his other work. It is, no doubt, for this reason that it
has appeared so appropriate to regard it as the highpoint of
his work and life, towards which all else moved. But this is
only partially true. It may help to explain the existence of
much of the asylum verse, the sense that all that matters is the
writing of poetry. But Clare did not stop writing after 'A
Vision': poems such as 'I am', 'An Invite to Eternity', 'Come
Hither Ye Who Thirst' – these are the poems in which Clare
really faces the problem of his own personality imprisoned in
the asylum; if these poems are more confused, they are, perhaps, braver. Clare's unique rejection of the world and its
troubles in 'A Vision' is not something that he can sustain for
long.

'Come Hither Ye Who Thirst' anticipates 'An Invite to
Eternity'. The tone here is masterful, with the sense of assured
comfort offset against the appeal to a weary world; Clare is
the comforter, the hermit who has found peace, and wants the
world to share it. Displaying a saddened, mellow sense of joy,
quietly assertive rather than triumphant, it is a poem addressed,
in Biblical tones, to those sick of the 'naughty world'. Nature is
in command here, for she knows not the sins of the town. A
literary convention becomes a personal *cri de coeur*:

> Come hither, ye who thirst;
> Pure still the brook flows on; ...
>
> Art troubled? then come hither
> And taste of peace for ever.[40]

His supreme confidence is joined to an awareness of what this
entails:

> Disciples of sorrow, come hither,
> For no blasts my joys can wither.

The final stanza explains his assurance in his rejection of the world:

> The world is all lost in commotion,
> The blind lead the blind into strife;
> Come hither, thou wreck of life's ocean,
> Let solitude warm thee to life.
> Be the pilgrim of love and the joy of its sorrow,
> Be anything but the world's man;
> The dark of to-day brings the sun of to-morrow,
> Be proud that your joy here began.
> Poor shipwreck of life, journey hither,
> And we'll taste of life's troubles together.[41]

The supreme tranquillity of the poem depends upon the purity of this sacred Eden where the flowers are 'herbs of grace', where nature and God reciprocate their thanks, where the emphasis is on old age, rather than the 'young shoots', on shade rather than the scorching rays of the sun. In the isolation of despair Clare finds hope and companionship, wherein love and joy can be revived, for love of nature and solitude leads to love of mankind. The poem grows out of personal circumstance, but reaches far beyond it in its defiance of the world.

Similar in tone, but more resigned and less assured, is 'An Invite to Eternity'.[42] This is much more haunted, the atmosphere one of morbid sanity that is barely controlled, inevitable rather than hopeful. The full force of this poem, and 'I am', to which it is clearly related, depends upon Clare's sense of the importance of the self as a separate entity, completely individual: he wrote a short prose piece on the topic of 'Self-Identity' which casts light on his attitude towards himself in these poems:

A very good commonplace counsel is *Self-Identity* to bid our own hearts not to forget our own selves & always to keep self in the first place lest all the world who always keeps us behind it should forget us altogether – forget not thyself & the world will not forget thee – forget thyself & the world will willingly forget thee till thou art nothing but a living-dead man dwelling among shadows & falsehood

> The mother may forget her child
> That dandled on her lap has been
> The bridegroom may forget the bride
> That he was wedded to yestreen

But I cannot forget that I'm a man & it would be dishonest and unmanly in me to do so[43]

In these poems he is clinging on desperately to what is left of his self-awareness. Here, the form of the poem, based on the repetition of a question that grows into a statement of doomed fact as it is asked, suggests and reinforces the cumulative gloom, subverting in the process the tradition of neatness and elegance implied by the opening chiasmus:

> Wilt thou go with me sweet maid
> Say maiden wilt thou go with me
> Through the valley depths of shade
> Of night and dark obscurity
> Where the path hath lost its way
> Where the sun forgets the day
> Where there's nor life nor light to see
> Sweet maiden wilt thou go with me

Clare's invitation is hardly inviting; for this is not the promised land of peace and repose of 'Come Hither', but something less natural, involving the negation of family relationships, where life in its accepted form will cease to exist, where the self is lost in a dreaded 'sad non-identity'. But into this non-world Clare asks the girl to come, into this purgatory, where heaven lies, ambiguously, all around them, not simply above, as in 'I am'.

> Where stones will turn to flooding streams
> Where plains will rise like ocean waves
> Where life will fade like visioned dreams
> And mountains darken into caves
> Say maiden wilt thou go with me
> Through this sad non-identity
> Where parents live and are forgot
> And sisters live and know us not
>
> Say maiden wilt thou go with me
> In this strange death of life to be

To live in death and be the same
Without this life or home or name
At once to be and not to be
That was and is not – yet to see
Things pass like shadows – and the sky
Above, below, around us lie.

There will be no recognition in this world of shadows, an irrational world with reason gone, a jumble of present and past, the dead and the living:

The land of shadows wilt thou trace
And look nor know each others face
The present mixed with reasons gone
And past and present all as one
Say maiden can thy life be led
To join the living with the dead
Then trace thy footsteps on with me
We're wed to one eternity

This eternity is the purgatory of his own creation, and the purgatory created by his circumstances. For Clare is in a strange land, lost and deserted, dwelling on past pleasures till they become present sorrows: it is a world he has to leave, but the choice is saddening, even if inevitable. Love has been drained here of the physical, so that this becomes a love poem of immense sorrow and courage, in which love is mentioned not once.

The connection between this poem and 'I Am' is best shown by a stanza from MS.110 describing this loss of identity:

There is a chasm in the heart of man
That nothing fathoms like a gulph at sea
A depth of darkness lines may never span
A shade unsunned in dark eternity
Thoughts without shadows – that eye can see
Or thought imagine tis unknown to fame ...[44]

Here there is nothing of the hope that lurks behind 'An Invite to Eternity', where virtue is made out of necessity, and the same lack of hope characterises the beginning of 'I Am'. The reaching for the past, for the eternity of silence and love, for

an almost mystical union with a spiritual essence, the spurning
of earthly pleasure and woman's love, the despair born of
deception, the hope born of the rejection of the world – all
these conflicts had been fought many times, and it is characteristic that in 'I Am' there is the usual ambivalence. Solitude
is again the dominant factor, as out of it grows a peace and
serenity, as despair becomes resigned acceptance; the almost
hysterical opening is gradually subdued as Clare affirms and
then searches for his self-identity and meaning to existence.
The quality of his life is at issue in this crisis of consciousness.
His confusion and his lostness are captured in the repeated
hammering at the only fact of which he is sure, his 'I am-ness':

> I am – yet what I am, none cares or knows;
>   My friends forsake me like a memory lost:
> I am the self-consumer of my woes –
>   They rise and vanish in oblivions host,
> Like shadows in love frenzied stifled throes
>   And yet I am, and live – like vapours tost
>
> Into the nothingness of scorn and noise,
>   Into the living sea of waking dreams,
> Where there is neither sense of life or joys,
>   But the vast shipwreck of my life's esteems;
> Even the dearest that I love the best
>   Are strange – nay, rather, stranger than the rest.[45]

But the final stanza reflects the paradox of Clare's fear of
solitude, and yet his desire to be alone. In all its pathetic
simplicity, he yearns for the innocent comfort of an un-
inhabited paradise, away from woman's wiles, and man's in-
humanity. There is a beautiful enactment of his childhood with
God, through the placing of the adverb: the possibility of
recapturing the experience is apparently made more remote by
the removal of 'sweetly' from its expected position, emphasising its pastness; but in the next two lines this wish is in part
realised, because of the present tense 'I lie', and the combination of the vowel sounds. Clare is back in the midst of nature's
serenity.

> I long for scenes where man hath never trod
>   A place where woman never smiled or wept

There to abide with my Creator God,
    And sleep as I in childhood sweetly slept,
Untroubling and untroubled where I lie
    The grass below, above, the vaulted sky.

If this seems too simple a reversal, a corrective is provided
by the sonnet which follows on in the transcripts; for here the
visionary gleam of 'A Vision' is recalled as something no longer
possible. The dream has finally faded. There can be little doubt
that this was written later than 'A Vision'.

I feel I am, I only know I am
And plod upon the earth as dull and void
Earth's prison chilled my body with its dram
Of dullness, and my soaring thoughts destroyed.
I fled to solitudes from passions dream
But strife persued – I only know I am.
I was a being created in the race
Of men disdaining bounds of place and time –
A spirit that could travel o'er the space
Of earth and heaven – like a thought sublime,
Tracing creation, like my maker, free –
A soul unshackled like eternity,
Spurning earth's vain and soul debasing thrall
But now I only know I am – that's all.[46]

As he wrote to the dead Mary in 1848, 'there is no faith here so
I hold my tongue & wait the end out without attention or
intention – I am that I am – & done nothing yet'.[47]

But nor was this the end of Clare's poetic life. He continued
to write, and to recapture what he had momentarily lost. Some
of the most powerful poetry after 1844 is contained in the
curious MS.110, a mixture of sustained lyricism and half-mad
invective. The cathartic storm, the visionary release from
earthly trappings, and the day of judgment, all mingle in the
blast of 'Song Last Day': the defiance of this, in its passionate
way, is equal to the prophetic 'A Vision':

Black as the deadly thunder cloud
The stars shall turn to dun
And heaven by that darkness bowed
Shall make days light be done

> When stars and skys shall all decay
> And earth no more shall be
> When heaven itself shall pass away
> Then thou'lt remember me[48]

The warped prejudices of *Don Juan* appear here in grotesquely dissonant, moving lines:

> Wives from their husbands pare off unrelenting
> And like pined pigeons mope about the land
> Couple's awake go silently and dreaming
> And love and faith and madness are but seeming[49]

The delights of nature in all her variety are captured as vividly as ever: Clare's asylum vision is not confined to spiritual withdrawal and ecstasy. He writes of the 'wild sublimity of windy days', as the winds 'unbind/Their foliage to the heavens wild amaze';[50] one of his most daring experiments occurs in MS.110:[51]

> Pale sun beams gleam
> That nurtur a few flowers
> Pile wort and daisey and a sprig o'green
> On white thorn bushes
> In the leaf strewn hedge ...

> Shadows fall dark
> Like black in the pale sun
> And lye the bleak day long
> Like blackstock under hedges
> And bare wind rocked trees ...

The contradictions of love are acknowledged, even the splendidly brazen desire for

> one real imaginary blessing
> Ideal real blessing blasted through
> With sin;[52]

he reminisces over his wooing of gipsy wenches – and yet he rises to the implicit heights of this stanza:

> All nature has a feeling woods brooks fields
> Are life eternal ...
> ... their decay

> Is the green life of change to pass away
> And come again in blooms revififfied ...[53]

The validity and eternity of love and of nature are reaffirmed here and elsewhere, in tones as serene as those of 1844. The love songs continue to pour forth in profusion; the poems on the past continue to emphasise what is lost, the grim funeral that constitutes the present.[54] But Clare does not lose sight of his cherished values, liberty and the innocence of childhood, and the belief in a love 'of holier birth/Not born to fade and pass away'. So strong is his belief. that nature will not decay,

> Till Earth becomes like heaven above
> The paradise of heaven-like love.[55]

As 'Hesperus' bravely concludes. earth shall be forgiven:

> Hesperus! the day is gone,
> Soft falls the silent dew,
> A tear is now on many a flower
> And heaven lives in you.
>
> Hesperus! the evening mild
> Falls round us soft and sweet,
> 'Tis like the breathings of a child
> When day and evening meet.
>
> Hesperus! the closing flower
> Sleeps on the dewy ground,
> While dews fall in a silent shower
> And heaven breathes around.
>
> Hesperus! thy twinkling ray
> Beams in the blue of heaven,
> And tells the traveller on his way
> That Earth shall be forgiven![56]

The quality of the poetry diminishes after about 1850. But by then Clare had written, in the asylum alone, sufficient to make him a poet of far more than merely psychological interest. Few poets have pursued their search for what they believed really mattered, so unremittingly, and at so consistent a level of achievement, as did John Clare.

Notes

Chapter 1. John Clare: The Man and the Poet

1. Clare was angered by Southey's work: he was not mentioned in it. The poets acknowledged by Southey were John Jones (a servant, whose verse prompted the volume), Taylor the Water-Poet, Duck, James Woodhouse, John Bennet, Ann Yearsley and John Frederick Bryant. For further details of the general interest in peasant poets, see Rayner Unwin, *The Rural Muse* (London, 1954), and W. K. Richmond, *Poetry and the People* (London, 1947).

2. 20 April 1819, NMS. 43 (2).

3. *Prose*, p.19.

4. Drury had seen the manuscript version of this and had not been impressed.

5. *Poems*, i, 133.

6. *Poems*, i, 140.

7. For some of the implications of this fact, see John Barrell, *The Idea of Landscape and the Sense of Place, 1730–1840* (Cambridge, 1972), pp.111-15; p.228.

8. Radstock scribbled in the margin of 'The Peasant Boy' (NMS. 3), 'This is radical slang'.

9. *Poems*, i, 3. Characteristically, Clare admitted the influence with equivocation. In a note to Drury, Clare asked him to compare *The Deserted Village* ('I perhaps may have read a hundred lines') and 'Helpstone': 'and then the difference will be seen my imitations I may be proud of I have never taken a single line or sentence from any but what I owned to' (*Life*, p.108).

10. PMS. B1, p.97; NMS. 5, p.17.

11. Drury to Taylor, 5 May 1819, NMS. 43 (3).

12. PMS. B1, p.97.

13. O Come, blest Spirit! what soe'er thou art,
    Thou kindling warmth that hover'st round my heart,
    Sweet inmate, hail! thou source of sterling joy,
    That Poverty itself cannot destroy,
    Be thou my Muse; and faithful still to me,
    Retrace the paths of wild obscurity.

14. NMS. 5, p.25; PMS. B1, p.93; PMS. A3, p.35.

15. Clare wrote to Taylor on 8 February 1822: 'I wish I livd nearer you at least I wish London woud creep within 20 miles of Helpstone I don't wish Helpstone to shift its station I live here among the ignorant

like a lost man in fact like one whom the rest seems careless of having anything to do with –' (*Letters*, p.132). See also his letter to Allan Cunningham, 1830, *Letters*, p.246; and to Taylor, 2 October 1830, *Letters*, p.248. But on 3 April 1828, Clare wrote to Taylor, 'but thank God I am once more in my old corner & in freedom I am as great as his majesty so a fig for the Babelonians' (*Letters*, p.211). The two worlds of London and Helpstone were necessary for Clare, and a constant source of frustration. Even before the asylum, there is a sense in which Clare is permanently homeless. The disparity between his own aspirations and the position he held in the rural community could not be ignored. For an interesting development of this point, in connection with Clare's descriptive technique, see John Barrell, *The Idea of Landscape*, p.123.

16. *Poems*, i, 34-5.

17. *Sketches*, pp.84-7.

18. Clare wrote to Taylor, 11 April 1826: 'I thought once that Mrs Emmerson was everything but I found that the strongest link that held us together was a sheet of paper therefore when I got into my mellancholy moods & ceasd to write she ceasd likewise & I have never had the mind to take it up again if such friendships are so easily dissolved they are not worth the keeping' (*Letters*, pp.189-90).

19. *Sketches*, p.70.

20. *Prose*, p.100.

21. For more on the impact of enclosure, see below, pp.60-5.

22. Writing to his son Charles from the asylum in February 1848, he looked back over his life and recalled, 'in my boyhood Solitude was the most talkative vision I met with' (*Letters*, p.298).

23. *Poems*, i, 37.

24. *Poems*, i, 84.

25. *Poems*, i, 85.

26. *Poems*, i, 11. Clare's poem is very much an imitation of David Mallett's 'Ballad of Edwin and Emma': see *Life and Poetry*, p.34. There are also verbal reminiscences of Mallett's popular 'William and Margaret'. But in the original drafts of the poem, Clare concluded with a dubious moral, introducing a personal application of the story:

> What harden'd brutes such villains are
> To wrong the artless maid
> To stain the lillies virgin bloom
> And cause the rose to fade
>
> O may the charms of Myra bloom
> Each bosom still to warm
> And curse the villain who would dare
> To do such beauties harm ...
>
> Lov'd Myra if these artless strains
> Should meet your kind regard

Let Amy's fate a warning prove
And I have my reward
(PMS. B1, p.99; PMS. A3, p.34; NMS. 5, p.44)

27. *Poems*, i, 232.

28. *Poems*, i, 214.

29. *Poems*, i, 225.

30. *Poems*, i, 227.

31. *Poems*, i, 191.

32. *Poems*, i, 196.

33. *Prose*, pp.224-5.

34. *Prose*, p.225.

35. *Prose*, pp.44-5; cf. PMS. A48, p.5: 'The feelings all that absence leaves/Of youths & loves esteems/Mans lonely aching breast recieves/ Like beautys seen in dreams/When waking from the extacy/Of faces painted there/We feel the sad reallity/That earth owns nought so fair.' See 'Valentine to Mary', *Selected Poems*, p.36.

36. *Prose*, p.105.

37. *Prose*, p.44.

38. *Prose*, p.44.

39. *Sketches*, p.87.

40. This point is made in the sonnet, 'To Mary', *Poems*, i, 529. See also PMS. B3, p.14: 'Anticipation is one of the most innocent & greatest pleasures of life because it is not reality but ideal shaped to suit the fancy as well as the expectation it is like childerns dreams of heaven.'

41. *Prose*, pp.17-18.

42. The pathos is caught in this couplet, PMS. A50, p.56: 'I look behind & like to Adam find/Too late what Eden was I left behind.' For childhood as heaven, cf. PMS. B3, p.103, in connection with the places of childhood: 'O these are spots of peace the heavens of the world.' For the importance of memory, see *Prose*, p.153: 'Memory though a secondary is the soul of time & life the principal but its shadow.'

43. *LP*, p.40.

44. *Poems of Madness*, p.225. The text here is that quoted in Frederick Martin, *Life of John Clare*, 2nd ed. (London, 1964), p.xxxi.

Chapter 2. Approaches to Nature

1. *Prose*, p.25.

2. See William Gilpin, *Three Essays: on Picturesque Beauty; on Picturesque Travel; and on Sketching Landscape* (London, 1792); Uvedale Price, *An Essay on the Picturesque* (London and Hereford, 1794-8); Robert Aubin, *Topographical Poetry in Eighteenth Century England* (New York, 1936).

3. *Prose*, p.24: 'but I knew nothing of poetry then'; cf. *Prose*, p.32: 'my heart burnt over the pleasures of solitude & the restless revels of

ryhme that was eternally sapping my memorys like the summer sun over the tinkling brook till it one day shoud leave them dry & unconscious of the thrilling joys busy anxietys & restlessness which it had created & the praises & censures which I shall leave behind me I knew nothing of the poets experience then or I shoud have remained a labourer & not livd to envy the ignorance of my old companions & fellow clowns.'

4. See especially Ralph Cohen, *The Art of Discrimination* (London, 1964), but also J. J. van Rennes, *Bowles, Byron and the Pope-Controversy* (Amsterdam, 1927); C. E. de Haas, *Nature and the Country in English Poetry* (Amsterdam, 1928); George G. Williams, 'The Beginnings of Nature Poetry in the Eighteenth Century', *SP*, xxvii (1930), 583-608; C. V. Deane, *Aspects of Eighteenth Century Nature Poetry* (Oxford, 1935); J. E. Congleton, *Theories of Pastoral Poetry in England, 1684–1798* (Florida, 1952).

5. Blair, *Lectures on Rhetoric and Belles Lettres*, with an introductory essay by Thomas Dale (London, 1845), p.479.

6. *Monthly Review*, xii (Oct 1793), 216-17.

7. *Lectures*, p.480.

8. See specially Jean H. Hagstrum, *The Sister Arts* (Chicago, 1958).

9. *An Essay on the Plan and Character of the Poem* (London, 1778), p.vii.

10. Quoted in Joseph Warton, *Essay on the Genius and Writings of Pope* (London, 1751), i, 50.

11. *Lectures on Poetry ... translated from the Latin* (London, 1742), quoted in Cohen, *The Art of Discrimination*, p.131.

12. *Essay on ... the Poem*, p.vi. Nobody reading *The Seasons* could have supposed that descriptive detail was of primary importance. Something of Thomson's own attitude comes out in a letter of 1730: 'Happy he who can comfort himself amidst this general night; and in some rural retirement, by his own intellectual fire and candle as well as natural, may cultivate the muses, inlarge his internal views, harmonize his passions, and let his heart hear the voice of peace and nature' (quoted in Alan D. McKillop, *The Background of Thomson's Seasons* (Minneapolis, 1942), p.26).

13. Aikin quotes Warton in *Essay on the Application of Natural History*, p.5.

14. *Essay on the Application of Natural History*, p.2.

15. *Essay on the Application of Natural History*, p.10.

16. *Essay on the Application of Natural History*, p.11.

17. Wordsworth, 'Essay, Supplementary to the Preface' (1815); Taylor, Introduction, *Poems Descriptive of Rural Life and Scenery* (1820), p.xiv.

18. See Myra Reynolds, *The Treatment of Nature in English Poetry between Pope and Wordsworth* (Chicago, 1896).

19. 'Essay I', p.26.

20. Quoted in Walter J. Bate, *From Classic to Romantic* (Cambridge, Mass., 1946), p.2.

21. *Essay on the Application of Natural History*, p.58.

22. *Essay on the Application of Natural History*, p.154.

23. *Letters to a Young Lady*, p.291 : 'They would resemble the Dutch style of painting, did not the writer's elegance of taste generally lead him to select only such objects as are capable of pleasing or picturesque effect.' For Dyer, see p.154.

24. *Observations on the River Wye*, 5th ed. (London, 1800), p.103.

25. *Calendar of Nature*, 2nd ed. (London, 1785), p.55.

26. 'Pastoral Poetry; Lyric Poetry', *Lectures*, p.460.

27. Varley H. Lang, 'Crabbe and the Eighteenth Century', *ELH*, v (1938), 305-33.

28. Quoted in Lang, 'Crabbe and the Eighteenth Century', p.311.

29. The invocation ends, significantly, with a nod at the painting analogy :

> While I wish'd
> The skill of Claude, or Rubens, or of him
> Whom now on Lavant's banks, in groves that breathe
> Enthusiam sublime, the sister nymphs
> Inspire; that, to the idea fair, my hand
> Might permanence have lent.

30. *Blackwood's Edinburgh Magazine*, v (July 1819), 469; see also Jeffrey's review of *The Borough*, *Edinburgh Review*, xvi (Apr 1810), 30-55.

31. [Robert Grant], *Quarterly Review*, iv (Nov 1810), 281.

32. 'Living Authors – No. V, Crabbe', *London Magazine*, iii, (May 1821), 486. This essay was in 1825 incorporated in a longer piece on Campbell and Crabbe, in *The Spirit of the Age*.

33. See Walter E. Broman, 'Factors in Crabbe's Eminence in the Early Nineteenth Century', *MP*, li (Aug 1953), 42-9.

34. 'Crabbe', *London Magazine*, iii (May 1821), 485.

32. 'Living Authors – No. V, Crabbe', *London Magazine*, iii (May (London and Toronto, 1930-4), v, 10.

36. *Coleridge's Shakespeare Criticism*, ed. T. M. Raysor (Oxford, 1930), ii, 174.

37. Wordsworth to Samuel Rogers, 29 September 1808, *Letters of William and Dorothy Wordsworth*, ed. E. De Selincourt (Oxford, 1937), i, 244.

38. *The Critical Opinions of William Wordsworth*, ed. Markham L. Peacock, Jr (Baltimore, 1950), pp.389-90.

39. *Biographia Literaria*, ed. J. Shawcross (London, 1907), ii, 102-3; the Milton passage was *Paradise Lost*, ix, 1100-9.

40. *Prose*, p.174.

41. *Prose*, p.104.

42. *Prose*, p.117. Elizabeth Kent, Leigh Hunt's sister-in-law, had corresponded with Clare about her book.

43. *Prose*, p.176. An example of Clare's concern for accuracy occurs in PMS. A17, p.4, in a comment on some lines from Peter Pindar, 'Merry companys of blue bells dance/Beneath the under wood': 'false image – they seldom stir but like other tenants of wood are remarkable for stillness.'

44. *Prose*, p.173.

45. *Prose*, p.173.

46. Clare to Rev. Isaiah Holland, 1817, *Letters*, p.25; see also *Letters*, p.160.

47. *Prose*, p.69. Clare was not amused by Hilton's portrait: as he wrote to Taylor, 20 May 1820, 'he has forcd poor J. C. from his flail & spade to strut on canvas in the town of humour & I will take him from his "water nymphs" to lye on the hobs of our dirty cotteges to be read by every greazy thumbed wench & chubby clown' (*Letters*, pp.50-1).

48. Bodleian MS. Don. c. 64, fol. 30; cf. Frederick Martin's description of Clare's hovel in *The Life of John Clare* (London, 1865; 2nd ed. 1964), p.5.

49. Clare to Hessey, 4 July 1820, *Letters*, p.56.

50. *Sketches*, p.57.

51. *Prose*, pp.175-6. PMS. A17 is full of quotations from Chatterton and Peter Pindar, and contains drawings of tombstones, with this sort of inscription: 'To the Memory of Chatterton, Keats and Bloomfield.'

52. *Poems*, i, 69.

53. *Poems*, i, 74; cf. Bloomfield 'Winter', *The Farmer's Boy* (London, 1800), lines 239-60, a passage which ends:

> For yet above these wafted clouds are seen
> (In a remoter sky, still more serene),
> Others, detach'd in ranges through the air,
> Spotless as snow, and countless as they're fair;
> Scatter'd immensely wide from east to west,
> The beauteous 'semblance of a *Flock* at rest.

54. *Poems*, i, 77.

55. 'A Scene', *Poems*, i, 116.

56. W. K. Wimsatt, Jnr, 'The Structure of Romantic Nature Imagery', in *The Age of Johnson*, ed. Frederick W. Hilles (New Haven and London, 1949; reprinted 1964), pp.291-303.

57. *Poems*, i, 30-1.

58. 'Summer', lines 113-30.

59. *Selected Poems*, p.7; *Poems*, i, 56.

60. *The Minstrel*, I, xxxix.

61. See F. W. Bateson, *Wordsworth, a Reinterpretation* (London, 2nd ed. 1956), pp.63-4.

62. *Prose*, p.114. He also wrote three sonnets to Bloomfield, BM. Add. MS. 30,809, fol. 67. The sonnets were published in the *Scientific Receptacle*, i (Oct 1825) 306-7, and in the *Amulet* (1829), pp.318-19. See David Bonnell Green, 'John Clare, John Savage, and "The Scientific Receptacle"', *REL*, vii (Apr 1966), 87-98.

63. Clare to Joseph Weston, 7 March 1825, *Letters*, p.167.

64. 10 August 1824, *Letters*, p.158.

65. Clare to Thomas Pringle, 29 August 1828, *Letters*, p.215.

66. See Rayner Unwin, *The Rural Muse* (London, 1954), p.93; Nathan Drake, *Literary Hours*, 2nd ed. (Sudbury, 1800), ii, 445.

67. Unwin, *The Rural Muse*, p.93.

68. 8 September 1799, BM. Add. MS. 28,268, fol. 20ᵛ; in *Selections from the Correspondence of Robert Bloomfield*, ed. W. H. Hart (London, 1870).

69. *Letters*, p.48.

70. But see *Prose*, p.184: 'every trifle owns the triumph of a lesson to humble the pride of man – every trifle also has a lesson to bespeak the wisdom & forethought of the Deity.'

71. *Poems*, i, 19-20.

72. Mary Russell Mitford, *Our Village* (London, 1824), p.103.

73. *Poems*, i, 53-4.

74. 'An elegy on a Pile of Ruins', *Poems, chiefly Pastoral* (Newcastle, 1766), p.63.

75. *Selected Poems*, p.4; *Poems*, i, 14. The quotation is from John Cunningham, 'Day', stanza xxv; but in PMS. D2, p.10, Clare writes:

'Verges in successive rings' not my own alter the couplet thus

> Forcing from each vaunting spring
> Many a curdling ring* & ring

76. 'Day', *Poems, chiefly Pastoral*, p.1.

77. Geoffrey Tillotson, 'The Methods of Description in 18th and 19th Century Poetry', in *Restoration and Eighteenth Century Literature*, ed. Carroll Camden (Chicago, 1963), pp.235-8.

78. *Poems*, i, 65; cf. Thomson, 'Spring', lines 102-5:

> Oft let me wander o'er the dewy fields,
> Where freshness breathes; and dash the trembling drops
> From the bent bush, as through the verdant maze
> Of sweet-briar hedges I pursue my walk.

and Gray, 'Elegy', lines 98-9:

> Oft have we seen him at the peep of dawn,
> Brushing with hasty steps the dew away.

* or *in* as may suit best.

79. Cf. Milton, 'L'Allegro', lines 63-5:

> While the ploughman near at hand,
> Whistles o'er the furrowed land,
> And the milkmaid singeth blithe ...

80. *Poems*, i, 68; see Milton, *Comus*, line 180, 'this tangled wood'.

81. See Ian Jack, 'Poems of John Clare's Sanity', in *Some British Romantics*, ed. James V. Logan et al. (Columbus, 1966), p.207.

82. 15 December 1826, Eg. 2247, fol. 241.

83. Charlotte Smith, *Elegiac Sonnets* (London, 1784): Anna Seward, *Original Sonnets on Various Subjects* (London, 1799).

84. Raymond D. Havens, *The Influence of Milton on English Poetry* (Cambridge, Mass., 1922; reissued 1961), pp.478-548; Walter J. Bate, *The Stylistic Development of Keats* (London, 1945; reissued 1958), pp.8-12; George Sanderlin, 'The Influence of Milton and Wordsworth on the Early Victorian Sonnet', *ELH*, v (1938), 225-51; see also G. Sanderlin, 'A Bibliography of English Sonnets, 1800–1850', *ELH*, viii (1941), 226-40.

85. 9 May 1820, Eg. 2245, fol. 116.

86. Eg. 2245, fol. 132ᵛ.

87. 8 September 1820, Eg. 2245, fol. 211.

88. Taylor to Clare, 17 August 1820, Eg. 2245, fol. 126.

89. Clare to Taylor, June 1820, *Letters*, p.55.

90. 4 July 1820, *Letters*, p.57; Clare saw the manuscripts at Taylor and Hessey's London firm.

91. 16 July 1820, *Letters*, p.60.

92. Clare to Taylor, 3 October 1820, *Letters*, p.70; *Poems*, i, 263.

93. Eg. 2245, fol. 255.

94. Clare to Taylor, 24 March 1821, *Letters*, p.108; *Poems*, i, 272. It is interesting that Clare should have liked Charles Lloyd's sonnets, in view of what Coleridge thought of them (*Prose*, p.115): see Coleridge's letter to Joseph Cottle, ca. 20 November 1797, *Letters of Coleridge*, ed. Earl L. Griggs (Oxford, 1956), i, 357-8. But Clare was wise to see through most of Coleridge's own sonnets.

95. Clare to Taylor, April 1821, *Letters*, p.109; *Poems*, i, 283. This sense of confinement comes out in another way; several sonnets are more than 14 lines in length, e.g. 'The Flight of Birds', 'Farm Scene II', *Poems*, ii, 239, 364. See also a version of 'Morning' (*Poems*, i, 261) in a letter to Taylor, 20 December 1819, not printed in full in *Letters*, p.28, but quoted in A. J. V. Chapple, 'Some Unpublished Poetical Manuscripts of John Clare', *Yale University Library Gazette*, xxxi (July 1956), 37: 'Tis not a 14 lines son: I cannot often be confined wi'in its narrow bounds Especially when the Jingling fit attacks me most warmly.' There is an attempt to improve this sonnet, probably by Mrs Emmerson, in PMS. B2, p.207a. In another letter to a Captain Sherwill (a very minor writer), 12 July 1820, quoted by Chapple, 'Some Unpublished Manuscripts', pp.47-8, Clare compares Milton's rigid application of the rules

in his sonnets, with Wordsworth, who 'defies all art'.

96. 17 January 1822, Eg. 2246, fol. 5ᵛ.

97. *Poems*, i, 117.

98. *Literary Chronicle*, No. 125 (6 Oct 1821), p.625.

99. *Eclectic Review*, n.s. xvii (Jan 1822), 43.

100. *Four Letters from the Rev. W. Allen, to the Right Hon. Admiral Lord Radstock, On the Poems of John Clare, the Northamptonshire Peasant* (London, 1823), p.21.

101. *Poems*, i, 118.

102. *Poems*, i, 260.

103. *Poems*, i, 271.

104. *Poems*, i, 266.

105. *Poems*, i, 524; cf. 'Sudden Shower', *Poems*, i, 517.

106. cf. *Prose*, p.265, on the wryneck: 'when one approachd the nest the old one made a hissing noise & turned her head in an odd motion from side to side.' See also *Prose*, p.16.

107. *Selected Poems*, p.127; *Poems*, i, 518.

108. cf. PMS. B4, p.63 : 'The sunshine wades in clouds of many hues/ And morning's early feet are shoond with dews.'

109. Written 'sons' in PMS. B4, p.63.

110. cf. Bloomfield, 'Autumn', line 345, where hens 'Fly wantonly abroad'.

Chapter 3. *The Shepherd's Calendar*

1. Clare had written his poem before he received a copy of Beattie's Minstrel (1771–4), sent on 6 May 1821 by a visitor from Cambridge, Chauncey Hare Townsend (Eg. 2245, fol. 109). But since 1815 he had possessed a version of the poem in a collection called *The Wreath* (Robert Protherough, 'A Study of John Clare's Poetry', B.Litt. thesis, Oxford, 1955, p.118). Although he expressed surprise at the existence of Beattie's poem when he received Townsend's presentation copy, it is certainly likely that he had glanced at it before he wrote his own poem. Very sensitive to the charge of plagiarism, he went out of his way to stress the point that he had not copied Beattie. In any case, he said, nature at Helpstone was the same as elsewhere (*Letters*, p.48), which was scarcely true (see above p.36). For the similarity between Clare's poem and John Hamilton Reynolds's 'Romance of Youth', see Ian Jack, 'Poems of John Clare's Sanity', in *Some British Romantics*, p.201.

2. *Poems*, i, 141.

3. *Poems*, i, 155-6.

4. *Poems*, i, 93.

5. *Poems*, i, 259.

6. *Poems*, i, 255.

7. *Poems*, i, 97-8.

8. See *Prose*, p.229; Clare to Taylor, 31 January 1822, *Letters*, p.130.

See also the letter to Taylor, 12 March 1826, *Letters*, p.185, in which he contemplates a tragedy: this seems much more important to him than *The Shepherd's Calendar* with its attendant problems.

9. *Poems*, i, 212.

10. *Prose*, pp.79-100.

11. Clare to Taylor, April 1824 (not August), *Letters*, p.159.

12. 21 January 1820, Eg. 2245, fol. 25.

13. *Letters*, p.99.

14. 24 April 1821, *Letters*, p.113.

15. Clare to Taylor, 20 April 1822; and to Hessey, 11 May 1822, *Letters*, p.137. See also Clare to Taylor, 31 January 1822, *Letters*, p.129.

16. See *Life and Poetry*, pp.127-9.

17. See Winifred Margaret Grainger, 'A Study of the Poetry of John Clare with special reference to his Lyrics, Ballads and Ballad Collecting', M.A. thesis, University of London, 1959. For the implications of this habit for his stylistic development, see below, pp.84-7.

18. *Poems*, i, 399, 404. See below, p.216 (n.50).

19. *Selected Poems*, p.134; *Poems*, ii, 3.

20. *Letters*, p.126.

21. 5 December 1821, Eg. 2245, fol. 387.

22. Eg. 2245, fol. 388.

23. e.g. 'The Vicar', 'The Last of Autumn'.

24. Clare to Taylor, 21 February 1822, *Letters*, p.134.

25. Hessey to Clare, 4 March 1822, Eg. 2246, fol. 32.

26. Clare to Hessey, 2 April 1822, *Letters*, p.136.

27. *Letters*, p.136.

28. 23 August 1822, *Letters*, p.139.

29. *Letters*, p.140.

30. *Letters*, p.140.

31. Eg. 2246, fol. 152.

32. 23 March 1823, Eg. 2246, fol. 168.

33. *Letters*, p.75: where dates of letters differ from those given in *Letters*, see Mark Storey, 'Letters of John Clare, 1821: Revised Datings', *N & Q*, ccxiv (Feb 1969), 58-64.

34. NMS. 4, p.1; PMS. B1, p.8, PMS. C1, pp.10, 7a, PMS. D9, pp.69, 75.

35. NMS. 1, pp.56, 61; NMS. 4, p.100; PMS. C1, p.19a.

36. Mrs Emmerson to Clare, 12 November 1825, Eg. 2247, fol. 102.

37. 12 August 1826, *Letters*, p.192.

38. See Barrell, *The Idea of Landscape*, especially the Appendix.

39. *A Memoir of Thomas Bewick*, written by himself (Newcastle upon Tyne and London, 1862), p.33.

40. J. L. and Barbara Hammond, *The Village Labourer*, paperback edition (London, 1966), p.29.

41. *The Agricultural State of the Kingdom, in February, March, and April, 1816; being the Substance of the Replies to a Circular Letter, sent by the Board of Agriculture to every part of the Kingdom.*

42. *The Case of Labourers in Husbandry* (London, 1795), p.6.

43. Second edition (London, 1793), p.73.

44. See also Sir Frederick Eden, *The State of the Poor*, 3 vols (London, 1797). W. E. Tate, *The English Village Community and the Enclosure Movements* (London, 1967), contains a useful bibliography of recent work on enclosures.

45. But Clare did not wholeheartedly support Cobbett : *Prose*, p.221. Kenneth MacLean, *Agrarian Age, A Background for Wordsworth* (New Haven, 1950), p.46, seems to me to misrepresent Clare's attitude. *The Parish* demonstrates that more was at stake than sentimental nostalgia.

46. Clare to Taylor, ? 6 January 1821, *Letters*, p.75; see also the letter to Allan Cunningham (September 1824), quoted in June Wilson, *Green Shadows* (London, 1951), p.146. For Clare's preference for Wordsworth to Crabbe, see James Hogg, *De Quincey and his Friends* (London, 1895), p.91.

47. Elaine Feinstein, ed., *John Clare, Selected Poems* (London, 1968), p.138. I have followed the text of *The Parish* included in this selection, pp.45-81.

48. Clare to Hessey, April 1823, *Letters*, p.144.

49. Clare to Hessey, 17 May 1823, *Letters*, p.147. J. W. and Anne Tibble (*Letters*, p.343), suggest that this is 'Impulses of Spring'; it is more likely to be 'Spring', PMS. B9, p.1.

50. *Letters*, p.149.

51. 1 August 1823, Eg. 2246, fol. 228.

52. Clare to Hessey, August 1823, *Letters*, p.152.

53. Clare to Hessey, P.M. August 1823, *Letters*, p.154: 'anew' here means 'enough'.

54. 25 August 1823, Eg. 2246, fol. 233; 18 September 1823, Eg. 2246, fol. 240.

55. 13 October 1823, Eg. 2246, fol. 245^v.

56. Eg. 2246, fol. 247^v.

57. 9 November 1823, Eg. 2246, fol. 251; 19 November, Eg. 2246, fol. 255.

58. 28 December 1823, Eg. 2246, fol. 268^v.

59. 3 November 1824, Eg. 2246, foll. 405^v-406.

60. 23 May 1825, Eg. 2247, fol. 30^v.

61. No date (but see *Prose*, p.153), Eg. 2250, fol. 329; for Clare's reply, 19 June 1825, see *Letters*, p.172.

62. 27 January 1826, Eg. 2247, foll. 131, 132^v.

63. 3 August 1827, Eg. 2247, foll. 322-322^v.

64. See Dwight Durling, *Georgic Tradition in English Poetry* (New York, 1935).

65. *Miscellany of Poems*, p.48.

66. See *Letters to William Cowper, 1791–1794*, ed. J. Tattersall (Eastbourne, 1927).

67. *Village Curate*, p.61.

68. *Village Curate*, pp.80-1.

69. See Eleanor Sickels, *The Gloomy Egoist* (New York, 1932), who cites as typical examples Leyden's *Scenes of Infancy* (1803), N. T.

Carrington's *Dartmoor* (1826), and Langhorne's 'To the River Eden' (1759).

70. *Retrospective Review*, i (1820), 69.

71. Aikin's *Calendar of Nature* appeared in 1784, and was enlarged by his son in 1798, with the new title *The Natural History of the Year*. Other prose accounts worth a mention were James Fisher's *Spring Day* (1803) and *Winter Season* (1810); Leigh Hunt's *Months* (1821); William Hewitt's *Book of the Seasons* (1831).

72. 'A Summer Sabbath Walk', lines 1-14. It comes as no surprise, incidentally, to find the poems of Grahame and Crabbe together between two covers in an edition of 1856.

73. *A Descriptive Review*, p.5. The later version read, 'The Changing winds will soon our ships unmoor,/And commerce gladden Britain's happy shore'.

74. *A Descriptive Review*, p.13.

75. *A Descriptive Review*, p.13.

76. *A Descriptive Review*, p.17: the later version was considerably expanded.

77. Preface, pp.v-vi.

78. Preface, pp.viii-ix.

79. *Poems*, i, 453.

80. 9 May 1821, Eg. 2245, fol. 316^v.

81. 1 January 1821, Eg. 2245, foll. 267^v-268.

82. Taylor to Clare, 20 May 1826, Eg. 2247, fol. 176^v.

83. *Poems*, ii, 154. For the simplicity of ballads, see *Prose*, p.120.

84. Clare to Taylor, 24 July 1831, *Letters*, p.255; cf. an undated letter addressed to Mrs Emmerson, NMS. 29, p.11, in which Browne is described as 'the most original in description & truest to nature', 'a sort of Isaac Walton in verse', and his poetry as 'a sort of common place Book' for other poets to follow.

85. *SC*, p.30.

86. Anne Elizabeth Baker, *Glossary of Northamptonshire Words and Phrases* (London, 1854), i, 213-14.

87. *SC*, p.32.

88. *SC*, p.31.

89. *Glossary*, ii, 11.

90. 'Spring', lines 44-7.

91. *SC*, pp.47-8.

92. Not everyone accepted them: the *Literary Chronicle*, No. 125 (6 Oct 1821), p.625, thought Clare improved the further he got away from such things.

93. *Poems Descriptive*, pp.viii-ix.

94. Eg. 2245, foll. 277-277^v.

95. 20 March 1821, *Letters*, p.107. (The exact date, although clearly written, is not given in *Letters*.)

96. 16 February 1821, Eg. 2245, foll. 287-8; no date, Eg. 2245, foll. 295-6.

97. 31 August 1822, Eg. 2246, fol. 99.

98. *Biographia Literaria*, ed. J. Shawcross (London, 1907), ii, 26-68.

99. NMS. 1. For Clare's sensitivity about his debts to Burns, see Protherough, 'A Study of John Clare's Poetry', pp.41-50.

100. For 'homespun', see the letter to Rev. I. Holland [1818], *Letters*, p.26.

101. *Poems*, i, 25, 89.

102. *Letters*, p.67 (October rather than September).

103. *SC*, p.10. For the whole scene, cf. Hurdis, *Favorite Village*, p.74:

> At his foot the cur
> Sleeps on the hearth outstretch'd, and yelping dreams;
> Or lifts his head, astonish'd at the dance
> Of frisking puss, who on the sanded floor
> Gambols excessive.

104. *SC*, pp.27-8.

105. *SC*, pp.30, 31.

106. *SC*, p.32.

107. *SC*, p.33; cf. Cary's translation of Dante, 'Hell', v, 46-8: 'As cranes,/Chanting their dolorous notes, traverse the sky,/Stretched out in long array' (*The Vision of Dante*, Oxford edition (London, 1910)); also Thomson, 'Spring', line 25: 'And sing their wild notes to the list'ning waste.'

108. 'Life of Thomson', *Lives of the Poets*, ed. G. B. Hill (Oxford, 1905), iii, 281.

109. *SC*, p.1; cf. Hurdis, *Favorite Village*, p.110: 'A feathery shower/Of flakes enormous follows, 'lighting soft/As cygnet's down, or egret from the head/Of thistle ravished'; Cowper, *Task*, v, 26: 'And fledg'd with icy feathers, nod superb'.

110. cf. Cowper, *The Task*, i, 357-9; v, 29-51.

111. Thomson, 'Spring', lines 36-7; Bloomfield, 'Spring', line 65; Thomas Warton, 'Pleasures of Melancholy', line 149: 'Fix'd in the unfinished furrow rests the plough', *Pastoral Works*, ed. R. Mant (Oxford, 1802); cf. Virgil, *Georgics*, iii, 517.

112. cf. Bloomfield, 'Winter', lines 37-40:

> Till Giles with pond'rous beetle foremost go
> And scatt'ring splinters fly at every blow;
> When pressing round him, eager for the prize,
> From their mixt breath warm exhalations rise.

113. *SC*, p.5.

114. 'Winter', lines 245-56; a similar passage occurs in Hurdis's *Favorite Village*, p.123.

115. cf. Milton, *Comus*, line 730, 'the wing'd air dark'd with plumes'.

116. cf. Bloomfield, 'Winter', lines 41-6: 'In beaded rows if drops now deck the spray,/While the sun grants a momentary ray,/Let but a cloud's broad shadow intervene,/And stiffen'd into gems the drops are seen;/And down the furrow'd oaks broad southern side/Streams of dissolving rime no longer glide.'

117. Pope, 'Epistle to Mr. Jervas', line 17; 'Epistle to Robert Earl of Oxford', line 15, *Works*, Twickenham edition (London, 1961–7), vi, 156, 238.
118. *SC*, pp.18-19.
119. *SC*, p.50.
120. *SC*, p.115.
121. *SC*, p.123.
122. *SC*, p.63.
123. *SC*, p.65.
124. *SC*, p.66.
125. *SC*, p.68.
126. 'Summer', lines 333-400.
127. *SC*, p.69.
128. *Selected Poems*, p.64.
129. *The Shepherd's Calendar* (1827), pp.144-5.
130. *Poems*, i, 462-3. It is interesting to compare this tale with Crabbe's 'Procrastination'. 'The Memory of Love' seems to echo 'Edward Shore'.

Chapter 4. 'This Visionary Theme': The Rural Muse

1. Mrs Emmerson's suggestion of *The Rural Muse* as the title is contained in a letter to Clare, 3 August 1833, Eg. 2249, fol. 158. On 31 August 1833, she announces her appointment as editor (Eg. 2249, fol. 161ᵛ). Taylor approved of her selection from the manuscripts: Taylor to Clare, 9 January 1835, Eg. 2249, fol. 259ᵛ.
2. Edmund Blunden, ed., *Madrigals and Chronicles* (London, 1924), p.xi; Ian Jack, *English Literature 1815–1832* (Oxford, 1963), p.136.
3. *Eclectic Review*, n.s. ix (Aug 1865), 126, 127; see Mark Storey, 'Edwin Paxton Hood (Not the Reverend Romeo Elton) and John Clare', *N & Q*, ccxvi (Oct 1971), 386-7.
4. Clare to Taylor, 5 January 1824, *Letters*, p.156.
5. Edmund Blunden recognised this value: 'Clare's sense of colour, sound, and locality enabled him to render rich and strange things not in themselves out of the ordinary', 'Manuscripts of John Clare', *London Mercury*, ii (July 1920), 320. John Wilson ('Christopher North') in his review of *The Rural Muse* in *Blackwood's Edinburgh Magazine*, xxxviii (Aug 1835), 231-47, appreciated the quality of the sonnets, thinking them Clare's greatest successes.
6. Clare to Taylor, 21 December 1828, *Letters*, p.220; Darley to Clare, 14 March 1829, Eg. 2248, fol. 130; PMS. A54, p.8. This poem is printed in W. K. Richmond, *Poetry and the People* (London, 1947), pp.230-42.
7. Taylor to Clare, 31 December 1828, Eg. 2248, fol. 99ᵛ.
8. Clare to Taylor, 3 January 1829, *Letters*, p.222.
9. 18 January 1829, Eg. 2248, fol. 105ᵛ.
10. August 1832, *Letters*, p.268. But in PMS. A49, p.6, Clare writes: 'there is an eternity in trifles – ambitions dwell with heavier things –

Time like a feather will keep on the top of the deepest waters of oblivion ... while weightier things sink to the bottom & sleep into the eternity of forgetfulness & are seen no more.'

11. *Poems*, ii, 115.

12. *Poems*, ii, 150.

13. *Poems*, ii, 126.

14. *Poems*, ii, 125.

15. *Poems*, ii, 121.

16. *Poems*, ii, 126.

17. 'The Crab-Tree', *Selected Poems*, p.163 (*Poems*, ii, 132). This is another of Clare's favourite couplets, and appears in various forms throughout the rough drafts, e.g. PMS. A50, p.58, PMS. A18, p.60. PMS. A50, p.28 has the couplet 'Mary thou muse of all my simple themes/ Thou fairey sunshine of youths summer dreams' (also PMS. A31, p.10). The line 'And thought existence but a fairy dream' occurs in Chatterton, 'Elegy', *Poetical Works*, ed. Henry D. Roberts (London, 1906), i, 183.

18. 'The Sycamore', *Poems*, ii, 132.

19. 'Burthorp Oak', *Poems*, ii, 135.

20. *Poems*, ii, 49.

21. cf. Keats, *Endymion*, ii, 73-4, quoted by Clare in a letter to Taylor, 19 April 1820, *Letters*, p.46: 'in buried paths where sleepy twilight dreams/The summertime away.'

22. *Poems*, ii, 316.

23. *Poems*, ii, 370.

24. *Poems*, ii, 360.

25. Clare continued to write sonnets after the publication of *The Rural Muse* in 1835. Sonnets on the fox and the badger are as good as anything he had done earlier, and show his use of the less rigid rhyme-scheme. In *Poems*, ii, 309, the sonnet 'The Music of Nature', taken from the *Athenaeum*, 21 Jan 1832, is attributed to Clare: J. W. Tibble says that the 'style suggests that it is Clare's', in the absence of a manuscript version (*Poems*, ii, 533). This mistake suggests how necessary it is to particularise about Clare's style.

26. *Selected Poems*, p.84 (*Poems*, ii, 17); *Poems*, ii, 15.

27. [No date], late December 1832, Eg. 2249, fol. 119: the last line of her poem 'On Reading Clare's Nightingale's Nest' reads, ' "Clare" and the "Nightingale" are one!'

28. *Selected Poems*, p.73 (*Poems*, ii, 213).

29. *Selected Poems*, p.78.

30. See especially 'The Summer Shower', *Selected Poems*, p.130 (*Poems*, ii, 36). This is carefully worked in the manuscripts and anticipates the rhythmic flexibility of the longer poems.

31. Printed far from reliably as 'Ode to Autumn' in Cunningham's *Anniversary* (1829), p.75. Allan Cunningham, in a letter to Clare, 20 March 1828, Eg. 2247, fol. 422, indicated his admiration.

32. 18 January 1828, Eg. 2247, fol. 393^v.

33. *Sketches*, p.58.

34. eg. NMS. 17, on the cover: this manuscript contains a working

out of 'Autumn'; also PMS. A61, p.16: a list of books, including Collins, Gray and *European Magazine* (Nov 1825).

35. *Prose*, p.108.

36. *Prose*, p.109 (cf. *Prose*, pp.132-3); *Prose*, p.199.

37. *Prose*, p.175.

38. 19 November 1823, Eg. 2246, fol. 255.

39. See *Life*, p.254. For a comparison between Collins and Clare (and Keats), see Edmund Blunden, *Nature in English Literature* (London, 1929), pp.38-59.

40. *Selected Poems*, pp.147 (cf. 'June', SC, p. 63; see *Prose*, p.175, and Chatterton, 'Songe to Aella'), 150.

41. *Selected Poems*, p.149; cf. the first version of this poem, *Poems*, i, 380-2.

42. *Selected Poems*, pp.135-6 (*Poems*, ii, 3).

43. Of the last three stanzas, Mrs Emmerson wrote, 'If *this* is not poesy & pathos & simplicity, and originality, I have no *discrimination*, or *feeling*, or *taste* in the composition of the pastoral Ode!' (Eg. 2247, fol. 394). Clare's prose account of Autumn, written on 6 November 1824, is pertinent: 'Took a walk in the fields the oaks are beginning to turn reddish brown & the winds have stripped some nearly bare the underwood's last leaves are in their gayest yellows thus autumn seems to put on bridal colours for a shroud' (*Prose*, p.120).

44. *Poems*, ii, 283.

45. *Selected Poems*, p.169 (*Poems*, i, 419).

46. *Selected Poems*, p.166 (*Poems*, i, 382).

47. The phrase 'Her universal green' appears in Bloomfield's 'Spring', without any of the implications of this passage. It is interesting to compare 'The Mores' with 'Solitude', quoted above, Ch. 1, p.12.

48. *Poems*, ii, 262; cf. 'The Past', *Selected Poems*, p.14 (*Poems*, ii, 27). For Clare's awareness of the dangers of reminiscence, see PMS. B3, p.14: 'But we must not indulge in "days gone bye" or we shall grow too sentimental & sorrowfull.' This touching honesty may be seen in his reaction, in 1821, to two favourite trees being cut down (quoted by Taylor in his Introduction to *The Village Minstrel*): 'Yet this mourning over trees is all foolishness – they feel no pains – they are but wood – cut up or not. A second thought tells me I am a fool: were people all to feel as I do, the world could not be carried on, – a green would not be ploughed – a tree or bush would not be cut for firing or furniture, & everything they found when boys would remain in that state till they died.'

49. For the appeal of Reynolds's poetry, see the letter to Taylor, June 1821, *Letters*, p.92: 'That sombre sadness of memory ...'

50. *Life of Clare*, p.246. There seems to be no other account of this episode which does not rely upon Martin.

51. *Selected Poems*, p.174 (*Poems*, ii, 257). PMS. B5, p.40: 'O my pleasures': the 4th line began 'Yet far away from trouble far away', but Clare deleted this (cf. PMS. A54, p.320, 'Summer pleasures ...'). In PMS. B5, p.40, the stanza ends, 'I thought them joys eternal when we used

to shout & play/On Cowper green at taw & ducking stone'. In this version, each stanza has only 8 lines, and there is not the plangent rhythm of the later version. In PMS. B8, pp.119-18 (in reverse), Clare transforms the first version, deleting the final lines of most stanzas, and rewriting them, adding 2 more. This MS. is written over nature notes dated 28 March, 4 April, 1832. PMS. B5 contains 6 stanzas corresponding to stanzas 1, 2, 3, 6, 7, 8 in the later version.

52. Not in PMS. B5.

53. In PMS. B5, this stanza is substantially the same as in the later version, including the last 2 lines. But both PMS. B8 and PMS. A54 conclude '... the common road with decay'.

54. *Selected Poems*, p.182 (*Poems*, ii, 80).

55. *Letters*, pp. 256-7. James Montgomery delivered rather a similar jeremiad in *Lectures on Poetry ... in 1830 and 1831* (London, 1833), pp.393-4.

56. *Letters*, p.257; cf. PMS. F5, p.7: 'All my favourite places have met with misfortune.' See also the letter to Taylor, 20 August 1827, *Letters*, p.201: 'for when I think of days gone bye & the hearts that are cold some in the world & some in the dust & every other association connected with them I am often affected even to tears.' But as his letter to Taylor, late September 1830, shows, he still has 'the warmth of their memorys' (*Letters*, p.248).

57. *Letters*, p.258.

58. *Selected Poems*, p.176 (*Poems*, ii, 251); *Poems*, ii, 259. For a demonstration that 'The Flitting', contrary to the opinion of Eric Robinson and Geoffrey Summerfield, is not a great poem, see John Adlard, 'John Clare: The Long Walk Home', *English*, xix (Autumn 1970), 85-9.

59. *Life of John Clare*, p.248.

60. In PMS. B8, p.51, the first 8 stanzas are as in *Selected Poems*. Then, after a double rule, is a new title 'Pastoral Affections' and the stanza 'These scenes mere shadows seem to be/Dull unpersonifying things ...' (*Selected Poems*, lines 89-96), followed by the stanza 'To sit & think agen a tree' (*Selected Poems*, lines 113-20), and so to the end, as in *Selected Poems*. Stanzas corresponding to *Selected Poems*, lines 65-88 are written in the right-hand margin, clearly later but crucial additions, making out of two shorter poems one argumentative whole.

61. *Poems*, i, 453.

62. *Poems*, i, 450.

63. *Selected Poems*, p.116 (*Poems*, i, 433).

64. *Selected Poems*, p.125.

65. *Poems*, ii, 49. For an analysis of this poem, see Harold Bloom, *The Visionary Company*, revised and enlarged edition (Ithaca and London, 1971), pp.444-56. For a harsher judgement, see Howard Mills, ed., *George Crabbe, Tales 1812* (Cambridge, 1967), p.xxxiv, where he refers to it as a monstrosity, an 'incoherent imitation'.

66. *Selected Poems*, p.113 (*Poems*, i, 442).

67. *Poems*, ii, 130; cf. PMS. B4, p.86: 'A thought unceasing mind/A

thirst enduring flame/Burning the soul to leave behind/The memory of a name.'

68. *Selected Poems*, p.109 (*Poems*, ii, 12.)

69. *Poems*, ii, 266.

70. cf. George Darley, 'Come and See!', *Poetical Works*, ed. Ramsay Colles (London, [1908]), p.25.

71. PMS. A57, p.84.

72. *Life*, pp.311-13.

Chapter 5. *The Storm and the Calm*: Child Harold

1. 'Clare, the Poet', *English Journal*, No. 20 (15 May 1841), pp.305-9; No. 22 (29 May 1841), pp.340-3. See also Redding, *Fifty Years' Recollections* (London, 1858), and *Past Celebrities whom I have known* (London, 1866).

2. Clare to Eliza Phillips, 1841, *Letters*, p.291.

3. See Martin, *Life of John Clare*, pp.303-9. Mary Joyce died in 1838.

4. *Letters*, p.290.

5. *Letters*, p.291.

6. *Letters*, p.291.

7. *Letters*, p.289.

8. 17 March 1841, *Letters*, p.292.

9. *Poems of Madness*, pp.8-9.

10. *Prose*, p.61.

11. *Letters*, p.32.

12. Clare to William Hone, 2 August 1825, *Letters*, p.175.

13. *Prose*, p.99.

14. *Prose*, p.100.

15. *Prose*, p.224.

16. *LP*, p.92.

17. *LP*, p.83.

18. *LP*, p.85.

19. *LP*, p.88.

20. *LP*, p.85.

21. *LP*, p.35; cf. Byron, *The Prophecy of Dante*, canto iv.

22. *LP*, p.49.

23. NMS. 8, p.60; *LP*, p.83.

24. *LP*, p.92.

25. *LP*, p.83.

26. *LP*, p.83.

27. We need to remember Clare's equivocal attitude to his own marriage. He wrote to Taylor in March 1821, *Letters*, p.102: 'I have found out by experience which is a good adviser that I posses a more valuable article in her than I at first expected & believe her from my soul an honest woman her calumniators were all of that sort of lyars that wish to make others as disgraceful as the world knows themselves to be ... Patt & myself now begin to know each other & live happily

& I deem it a fortunate era in my life that I met with her.' Earlier, on 4 July 1820, *Letters*, p.58, he wrote to Hessey: 'I forgot to say "Patty" has got to Helpstone & I think will prove a better bargain then I expected.'

28. *LP*, p.247.

29. *LP*, p.84.

30. Clare regarded the loss of Mary as a betrayal of faith, long before the asylum years: e.g. 'Song', *Poems*, i, 258: 'The spring returns the pewet screams', *Selected Poems*, p.37.

31. *LP*, p.89.

32. *LP*, p.92.

33. *LP*, p.76.

34. *LP*, p.163.

35. *LP*, p.66.

36. *LP*, p.67.

37. *LP*, p.48.

38. *LP*, p.39, fn. 2.

39. Martin, *Life of John Clare*, p.309.

40. *Life of John Clare*, p.309.

41. *Life of John Clare*, p.310.

42. *LP*, p.38.

43. *LP*, p.39; cf. the depersonalisation of the song in MS. 110, *LP*, pp.114-15.

44. *LP*, p.198.

45. e.g. 'Song', MS. 110, *LP*, p.100; 'Twilight', MS. 110, *LP*, p.134.

46. *Poems of Madness*, p.16, pp.73-92; J. W. and Anne Tibble, eds., *John Clare, Selected Poems* (London, 1965), pp.239-78.

47. *LP*, p.42.

48. *LP*, p.36.

49. *LP*, p.108.

50. In this and other apocalyptic poems we get the closest reminiscence of early poems such as 'The Dream' and 'The Nightmare'. The vividness of the description suggests the resemblance; but the emphasis on sin, recurrent throughout his work, is also important. This was a predominant theme of 'The Dream', inspired by De Quincey's accounts of dreams in his *Confessions of an English Opium Eater* (*Poems*, i, 408). The Cowperian influence is also strong. There is an interesting prose account of a dream Clare had in October 1832 (*Prose*, pp.231-3). Clare's reaction to *Macbeth* is instructive: 'the thrilling feelings created by the description of Lady Macbeths terror-haunted walkings in her sleep sink deeper than a thousand ghosts – at least in my vision of the terrible she is a ghost herself & feels with spirit & body a double terror' (*Prose*, p.121).

51. *LP*, p.43.

52. *LP*, p.42.

53. *LP*, p.43.

54. *LP*, p.44.

55. *LP*, p.49.

56. *Letters*, p.290.
57. *LP*, p.43; cf. *LP*, p.48.
58. *LP*, p.55.
59. *LP*, p.53.
60. *LP*, p.65.
61. *LP*, p.65.
62. *LP*, p.67.
63. *LP*, p.79.
64. *LP*, p.59.
65. *LP*, p.42.
66. *LP*, p.77.
67. *LP*, p.37; the first line of the song reads in the manuscript 'his', not 'her', brow.
68. *LP*, p.56.
69. *LP*, p.56.
70. *LP*, pp.51-2.
71. *LP*, p.65.
72. *LP*, p.58. For further discussion of the descriptive sections of *Child Harold*, see Thomas R. Frosch, 'The Descriptive Style of John Clare', *Studies in Romanticism*, 10 (1971), 137-49.
73. *LP*, p.79.
74. *LP*, p.40.

Chapter 6. The Asylum Poems

1. Edmund Blunden, *Keats's Publisher* (London, 1936), p.209.
2. See *Life and Poetry*, p.201; *Poems of Madness*, Introduction; Russell Brain, *Some Reflections on Genius* (London, 1960); Eleanor L. Nicholes, 'The Shadowed Mind: A Study of the Change in Style of the Poetry of John Clare Resulting from the Effects of Schizophrenic Process' (Ph.D. dissertation, New York University, 1950).
3. Clare to George Reid, 17 November 1841, *Letters*, p.296.
4. Martin, *Life of John Clare*, p.291.
5. See also I. M. F. Hooker and N. Dermott Hunt, 'John Clare, Some Unpublished Documents of the Asylum Period', *Northamptonshire Past and Present*, iii (1964), 190-8: Clare's freedom of movement was restricted by Dr Thomas Prichard in 1844. For additional accounts, see [J. F. Callister], 'Poet in Bondage, A Picture of John Clare', *TLS*, 27 December 1941, p.657; Eric Robinson and Geoffrey Summerfield, 'John Clare: An Interpretation of Certain Asylum Letters', *RES*, n.s. xiii, (1962), 135-46; David Bonnell Green, 'Three Early American Admirers of John Clare', *Bulletin of the John Rylands Library*, L (Spring 1958), 365-86.
6. *Poems of Madness*, p.211 (*Poems*, ii, 406).
7. *LP*, pp.97-152.
8. *Poems of Madness*, p.209 (*Poems*, ii, 489).
9. *LP*, p.167 (*Poems*, ii, 438).

10. *LP*, pp.167-8 (*Poems*, ii, 416).

11. *LP*, p.184.

12. *LP*, p.169 (*Poems*, ii, 475).

13. *LP*, p.220.

14. *LP*, p.221.

15. *Poems of Madness*, p.128 (*Poems*, ii, 498).

16. Harold Bloom, *The Visionary Company*, revised and enlarged edition (Ithaca and London, 1971), pp.444-56; *Poems of Madness*, pp.28-50.

17. He was appointed House Steward on 30 April 1845: I. M. F. Hooker and N. Dermott Hunt, 'Some Unpublished Documents', p.194.

18. Geoffrey Grigson is misleading here when he suggests that (1) 'Love Lives Beyond the Tomb', (2) 'It is the Evening Hour', and (3) 'I Am', occur in that order in the transcripts, leading up to (4) 'A Vision' (*Poems and Poets* (London, 1969), p.109). In fact, these poems occur as follows: (1) i, 121; ii, 46; (2) i, 20; (3) i, 111; (4) i, 25. There is obviously some logic in the order of the transcripts: 'Graves of Infants' (June), 'Love's Pains' (13 July), 'O wert thou in the Storm' (17 July), 'A Vision' (2 August), occur at the beginning of the first volume, as follows: pp. 1, 2, 7, 15, 25. But 'Mary I love to sing' (13 May) is at i, 95; poems apparently similar in tone and theme are scattered here and there: 'I Am' (i, 111), 'An Invite to Eternity' (i, 68), 'Come Hither Ye Who Thirst' (i, 132). Obviously, Knight is only reliable chronologically up to a point: it is extremely unlikely that the transcriptions follow any close order of composition. If they do, this only makes Grigson's suppositions more dubious.

19. For a discussion of some of the textual problems, see *TLS*, 27 Apr 1956, p.252; *TLS*, 11 May 1956, p.283; *TLS*, 25 May 1956, p.313; *TLS*, 18 Oct 1957, p.625.

20. *Poems*, ii, 522.

21. *LP*, p.222.

22. *LP*, p.157 (*Poems*, ii, 401).

23. *Poems*, ii, 510; see Martin, *Life of John Clare*, p.309.

24. *Poems of Madness*, p.137 (*Poems*, ii, 519).

25. *Poems*, ii, 509; cf. 'Song Last Day', *LP*, p.108 (see Edward Young, *A Poem on the Last Day* (Oxford, 1713)).

26. *Poems of Madness*, p.120 (*Poems*, ii, 466). Cf. 'Death', *Poems of Madness*, p. 148 (*Poems*, ii, 468).

27. *Poems*, ii, 467. See also *Prose*, p.108 (entry for 24 September 1824): 'Tryd to walk out & coud not have read nothing this week my mind almost overweights me with its upbraidings & miseries my children very ill night & morning with a fever makes me disconsolate & yet how happy must be the death of a child it bears its suffering with an innocent patience that maketh man ashamd & with it the future is nothing but returning to sleep with the thoughts no doubt of waking to be with its playthings again.' Another comment comes in PMS. D14, p.10: 'for the nature & goodness instinct in the breast of a child is of a nobler quality then what most men can either inculcate or

conscieve – their is a sincerity in its very simplicity that might put a mans pretensions to shame.'

28. Hood, *Complete Poetical Works*, ed. Walter Jerrold (London, 1906), p.444; cf. 'On an Infant's Grave', *Poems*, i, 78, and 'To an Infant Sister', *Poems*, i, 516.

29. *Selected Poems*, p.198 (*Poems of Madness*, p.125; *Poems*, ii, 516).

30. *Poems of Madness*, p.153 (*Poems*, ii, 514).

31. For an expression of love as promise rather than fulfilment, see 'Love's Pains', *Poems of Madness*, p.123 (*Poems*, ii, 520).

32. *Poems of Madness*, p.126 (*Poems*, ii, 473).

33. *Poems of Madness*, p.118.

34. *LP*, p.101.

35. *Selected Poems*, p.198 (*Poems of Madness*, p.200; *Poems*, ii, 513).

36. cf. *Child Harold*, *LP*, pp.51-2.

37. See 'To Sorrow', *LP*, p.120 (*Poems of Madness*, p.142; *Poems*, ii, 464). Cf. Darley, 'My Bower', *Poetical Works*, p.419: 'For silence or for sorrow/For meditation made,/E'en joy itself must borrow/A sadness from its shade.'

38. *Poems of Madness*, p.126 (*Poems*, ii, 469). Cf. *Selected Poems*, ed. J. W. and Anne Tibble (London, 1965), p.290: their contention that the Peterborough transcriber's version 'Love Lies Beyond' (as opposed to Knight's) 'gives deeper meaning' and is therefore preferable, is open to question. See *TLS*, 18 Oct 1957, p.625; also Grigson, *Poems and Poets*, p.108.

39. *Selected Poems*, p.198 (*Poems of Madness*, p.133; *Poems*, ii, 526).

40. *Poems of Madness*, p.120 (*Poems*, ii, 473).

41. Shipwreck imagery is frequent in Clare: his reading of Cowper and Falconer made a deep impression.

42. *Selected Poems*, p.196 (*Poems of Madness*, p.130; *Poems*, ii, 513).

43. *Prose*, p.239.

44. *LP*, p.100.

45. *Selected Poems*, p.195 (*Poems of Madness*, p.132; *Poems*, ii, 523).

46. *Selected Poems*, p.196 (*Poems of Madness*, p.133; *Poems*, ii, 524).

47. *Life and Poetry*, p.195.

48. *LP*, p.109.

49. *LP*, p.110.

50. *LP*, p.110.

51. *LP*, p.129 (*Poems*, ii, 404).

52. *LP*, p.144.

53. *LP*, p.134 (*Poems*, ii, 475).

54. See *LP*, p.107 (*Poems of Madness*, p.142; *Poems*, ii, 464).

55. *Poems of Madness*, p.151.

56. *Poems of Madness*, p.143.

Select Bibliography

The following is a list of the main manuscript and printed sources for the study of Clare's work.

I. *Manuscripts*
  i. *Bodleian Library MSS.*
    (a) MS. Don. a.8. Poems written in margins of newspapers: *Lincolnshire Chronicle and General Advertiser*, 27 Aug 1841; *Lincoln Rutland and Stamford Mercury*, 3 Sept 1841. Drafts for *Child Harold* and Biblical paraphrases. Letter to Matthew Allen (*Letters*, pp.294-5).
    (b) MS. Don. c. 58. Corrected draft of Martin's *Life*.
    (c) MS. Don. c. 64. Letters to Hessey, 6 Nov 1822; to Rippingille, 14 May 1826; to Martha Clare, 25 Feb, 29 Sept, 1828, 7 Mar 1860 (*Letters*, pp.208-9, 217, 308-9); to Taylor 2 July 1828; to Artis, n.d. Taylor and Hessey's account for 1819-21 (WM 1829). Notebook inscribed 'John Clare 15th Nov. 1839'.
    (d) MS. Don. d.36. Papers relating to Clare, 1819-58. Letters to Taylor from Hessey, Rev. C. Mossop, M. Allen. Draft of memoir of Clare by Drury dated 6 May 1819 (not, as stated in the Catalogue, by Hessey).
  ii. *British Museum MSS.*
    MS. Egerton 2245-50. Six volumes of letters to Clare, from Taylor, Hessey, Lord Radstock, Drury, Mrs Emmerson and others.
  iii. *Northampton MSS.*
    An extensive collection from all periods of Clare's life, including the majority of the letters, the MSS. for *Child Harold* and *Don Juan*, MS. 110, and the Knight Transcripts.
    [Powell, David] *Catalogue of the John Clare Collection in the Northampton Public Library*. Northampton, 1964.
  iv. *Peterborough MSS.*
    The bulk of the pre-asylum poetry and prose, recently re-sorted and re-catalogued by Margaret Grainger.
    Peterborough Natural History, Scientific and Archaeological Society, *Catalogue of the Centenary Exhibition*. Peterborough, 1893.

II. *Printed Books*
  A. i. *Works of John Clare*
        Poems Descriptive of Rural Life and Scenery. London. Printed for Taylor and Hessey, and E. Drury, 1820.

2nd ed. 1820. ('The Country Girl' omitted.)

3rd ed. 1820. (Following poems omitted: 'My Mary', 'Dolly's Mistake'.)

4th ed. 1821. (In addition to the omissions in the 2nd and 3rd eds, a line from 'Dawnings of Genius' – 'That necessary tool of wealth and pride' – and part of 'Helpstone' – 'Accursed Wealth! ... clear a way for thee' – were also removed. 'Friend Lubin' was omitted.)

The Village Minstrel, and Other Poems. London. Printed for Taylor and Hessey, and E. Drury. 2 vols. 1821. Reissue, announced as '2nd ed.', consisting of the 2nd 1000 copies of the first ed., which had not been bound. 1823.

[Lowndes, in *Bibliographer's Manual* (1857–64), attributes *Moments of Forgetfulness*, 1824, to Clare. No mention of this is made by Clare, nor by any of his correspondents; no copy has yet been found. In view of the detailed correspondence that survives from this period, and Clare's involvement in preparations for *The Shepherd's Calendar*, it seems unlikely that the volume is Clare's work. For discussion of the problem, see 'Written by Clare?' *TLS*, 2 Nov 1961, p.793; 10 Nov 1961, p.805; 17 Nov 1961, p.823; 22 Dec 1961, p.913; 2 Feb 1962, p.73.]

The Shepherd's Calendar; with Village Stories, and Other Poems. London. Published for John Taylor, by James Duncan, 1827.

The Rural Muse. Poems by John Clare. London. Whittaker & Co., 1835.

ii. *Editions*

Blunden, Edmund, ed. *Sketches in the Life of John Clare, Written by Himself*, London, 1931.

Robinson, Eric, and Summerfield, Geoffrey, ed. *John Clare, The Shepherd's Calendar.* London, 1964.

Tibble, J. W., ed. *The Poems of John Clare*, 2 vols. London, 1935.

Tibble, J. W. and Anne, ed. *The Letters of John Clare.* London, 1951.

The Prose of John Clare. London, 1951.

B. *Selections*

Blunden, Edmund, ed. *Madrigals and Chronicles.* London, 1924.

Blunden, Edmund, and Porter, Alan, ed. *John Clare: Poems Chiefly from Manuscript.* London, 1920.

Feinstein, Elaine, ed. *John Clare, Selected Poems.* London, 1968.

Gale, Norman, ed. *Poems by John Clare.* Rugby, 1901.

Grigson, Geoffrey, ed. *Poems of John Clare's Madness.* London, 1949.

Selected Poems of John Clare. London, 1950.

Reeves, James, ed. *Selected Poems of John Clare*. London, 1954.

Robinson, Eric, and Summerfield, Geoffrey, ed. *The Later Poems of John Clare*. Manchester, 1964.

Clare, *Selected Poems and Prose*. New Oxford English Series, London, 1966.

Selected Poems and Prose of John Clare. London, 1967.

Tibble, J. W., and Anne, ed. *John Clare, Selected Poems*. London, 1965.

C. *Biographies*

Cherry, J. L. *Life and Remains of John Clare*. London and Northampton, 1873.

Martin, Frederick. *The Life of John Clare*. London and Cambridge, 1865.

The Life of John Clare. 2nd ed., with Introduction and Notes, by Eric Robinson and Geoffrey Summerfield. London, 1964.

Tibble, J. W., and Anne. *John Clare: A Life*. London, 1932; revised ed., 1972.

John Clare: His Life and Poetry. London, 1956.

Wilson, June. *Green Shadows: The Life of John Clare*. London, 1951.

Index

I. GENERAL

II. CLARE: WRITINGS

III. CLARE: TOPICS